GRACE
IN THE ACADEMIC COMMUNITY

FESTSCHRIFT FOR CECIL R. PAUL

*A Collection of Essays to
Honor the Life of Cecil R. Paul*

MAXINE E. WALKER, EDITOR

POINT LOMA PRESS

SAN DIEGO, CALIFORNIA

Grace in the Academic Community: Festschrift for Cecil R. Paul
Copyright ©1996 by Wesleyan Center Books, a division of Point Loma Press,
the publishing extension of Point Loma Nazarene College, San Diego, Calif.

*PLNC's Wesleyan Center for Twenty-First Century Studies has been created
to inspire a new generation of Wesleyan thinking that will influence the
broader church and social worlds of the twenty-first century.*

Please address any comments or questions to:
Wesleyan Center for Twenty-First Century Studies
Point Loma Nazarene College
3900 Lomaland Drive
San Diego CA 92106
or e-mail: wesleyancenter@ptloma.edu

ISBN: 0-9652698-0-9
Printed in the United States of America.
All rights reserved. No part of this book may be reproduced in any form
without prior permission of the publisher, except in the case of brief
quotations embodied in critical articles or reviews.

Editor: Maxine E. Walker
Cover and Book Design: Stella Vandegrift
Cover Photo: Copyright © Jean-Claude Lejeune
Inset Cover Photo: Fine Light Photography by Mike Ryan
Photo Illustrations: Doug Bowman

CONTENTS

Contributors   5
Acknowledgements   9
Foreword   11
   Jerry D. Lambert

SECTION ONE: NAMING THE MISSION

1. The Nazarene College President as Servant Leader   15
   Jim L. Bond
2. The People Called Nazarenes: Getting There   23
   Cecil R. Paul
3. What Makes a Nazarene College "Nazarene"?   29
   Herbert L. Prince
4. The College-Church Partnership: Past   45
   Stephen W. Nease
5. The College-Church Partnership: Present and Future   59
   Tom Barnard
6. Non-Traditional Education and the Nazarene College: Issues of Mission-Fit, Distinctiveness, and Survival   73
   Wayne Dunlop and Steve Pusey
7. The Symbolic Value of Place   83
   Maxine E. Walker

SECTION TWO: CONFRONTING THE CENTRAL QUESTIONS

8. Thinking About Economics and Ethics as a Wesleyan   99
   Samuel M. Powell
9. From "Barely" to "Fully" Personal: On the Therapeutic Action of Prevenient Grace *Within* the Personality   115
   G. Michael Leffel

10. Ecumenism in Nazarene Higher Education *George Lyons*	133
11. The Nazarene Mind: Sunlight and Scandal *Karl Giberson*	147
12. Excellence in Education: Parrot or Learner *Mary E. Conklin*	165

SECTION THREE: LIVING THE VISION

13. Prophet and Priest: Pioneer and Preserver in Partnership *David P. Whitelaw*	179
14. A Trinitarian Paradigm of Theosis: A Context for the Emergence of a Wesleyan Notion of Christ Transfiguring Culture *K. Steve McCormick*	193
15. Gifts from a Visionary: Continuing the Wesleyan Tradition of the Development of All Persons *Jan Simonson Lanham*	207
16. Retracing the Vision: The Imaginative Mind in a Nazarene College *Margaret "Peg" Bowen*	215
17. Education as Reconciliation *Gerard A. Reed*	225
18. Reflections on a Life *Bruce Paul*	235
Bibliography	241

CONTRIBUTORS

Tom Barnard, Ed.D., Oklahoma State University, Professor of Religion, served as Vice-President for Institutional Advancement under Dr. Cecil Paul. Prior to that appointment he served as Vice-President for Student Development at Eastern Nazarene College and in 1994 was appointed as Vice-President for Church Relations. Previously he served as Dean of Student Development at Southern Nazarene University. His publication interests are in Christian education and ministry.

Jim L. Bond, D.Min., Fuller Theological Seminary, President of Point Loma Nazarene College. His early career was in pastoral ministry and missions. He has served on the boards of several state and national higher education organizations and is a frequent speaker on other college campuses.

Margaret "Peg" Bowen, M.A.T.S, Gordon-Conwell Theological Seminary, is Professor of English, Korea Nazarene University. At Eastern Nazarene College under Dr. Paul, Professor Bowen was an Instructor in English and free-lance copy editor for Nazarene Publishing House. Her interests are teaching English as a second language and teaching English as a foreign language.

Mary E. Conklin, Ph.D., The Johns Hopkins University, is a Professor of Sociology at Point Loma Nazarene College. She specializes in the Sociology of Education and has published "Consistency of Parental Educational Encouragement" and "Problems in American Education" in *Christian Perspectives on Social Problems*. Recently she has given lectures for Korean missionary candidates (Korean Evangelical Holiness Church in Seoul, Korea) on culture learning and culture shock. She participates in an intensive English program in Korea.

Wayne Dunlop, M.A., University of Chicago, was LEAD Program Director (Leadership Education for Adults) under Dr. Paul and is currently Associate Academic Dean of Adult and Continuing Education at Eastern Nazarene College. His scholarly interests are in cognitive development and perspectives on transformation in adult learning.

Karl Giberson, Ph.D., Rice University, is Professor of Physics at Eastern Nazarene College and Director of the General Science Program. He has authored *Worlds Apart* and several major articles on perspectives in science and faith. His scholarly interests include cosmology, the philosophy of science, and the history of science. His essay "Imposing Science on the Liberal Arts Student" has been accepted for June 1996 publication in *Perspectives on Science and Christian Faith*.

Jerry D. Lambert, D.D., Southern Nazarene University, is the Education Commissioner for the International Board of Education, Church of the Nazarene. Prior to this appointment, he served as President of Nazarene Bible College in Colorado Springs, Colorado. He has also been the District Superintendent of the Pittsburgh District.

Jan Simonson Lanham, Ph.D., Boston University, was appointed by Cecil Paul to be the first woman in the Church of the Nazarene to serve as Vice-President for Student Development/Dean of Students. She has served full-time at Eastern Nazarene College since 1976. She co-authored *Choices: In Pursuit of Wholeness* (1982) with Cecil Paul; her teaching interests include physiological psychology, developmental psychology, and the integration of psychology and religion.

G. Michael Leffel, Ph.D., University of Illinois Champaign-Urbana, is Associate Professor of Psychology at Point Loma Nazarene College. As a psychotherapist in private practice and researcher in personality and clinical psychology, he has interests in personality psychopathology, psychoanalytic self psychology, and the psychology of spiritual development. As a 1995 Wesleyan Center for 21st Century Studies Fellow, he is working on a manuscript "Transformation of the Tragic Person: Wesleyan Thought in the Culture of Psychotherapeutic Care."

George Lyons, Ph.D., Emory University, is Professor of Biblical Literature at Northwest Nazarene College and previously taught at Olivet Nazarene University. Professor Lyons has published extensively in scholarly journals on Wesleyan theology and has numerous articles in publications of the Church of the Nazarene. He is editor of the "Wesley Digital Library," a digital collection of 141 Wesley sermons from the 1872 edition.

K. Steve McCormick, Ph.D., Drew University, is Professor of Theology at Eastern Nazarene College. He taught theology as a Special-Assignment Missionary at European Nazarene Bible College and as supply pastor on the New York District. His publication interests are Patristics, orthodoxy, and John Wesley.

Stephen W. Nease, Ed.M. Boston University, D.D., Eastern Nazarene College, has been president of Mount Vernon Nazarene College, Southern Nazarene University, Nazarene Theological Seminary, and Eastern Nazarene College. He also served as Education Commissioner for the Church of the Nazarene and is currently President Emeritus/Executive Director of Capital and Endowment Development at Mount Vernon Nazarene College. He has written extensively for various church publications.

Bruce Paul, M.Div., Boston University, is Associate Pastor of the Bethel Church of the Nazarene, Quincy, Massachusetts. His wife, Mary Rearick Paul, is the Senior Pastor, and their ministry blends the vision for women and men that Dr. Paul encouraged. He is the eldest son of Cecil and Judy Paul. His pastoral ministry interests are in coordinating and leading men's Bible studies. He writes frequently for church publications.

Cecil R. Paul, Ph.D., Boston University, was President of Eastern Nazarene College from 1989-1992. His untimely death on August 1, 1992 ended his long service to ENC and to the Church of the Nazarene. The essay included in this *Festschrift* was delivered at the Leadership Conference of the Church of the Nazarene at Houston, Texas, 1989. At that time he was the Director, Division of Communications, for the Church of the Nazarene and was addressing the theme of "The Church—Past, Present, and Future."

Samuel M. Powell, Ph.D., Claremont Graduate School is Professor and Chair of the Philosophy and Religion Department at Point Loma Nazarene College. His teaching and research interests are in German philosophy and theology and in Wesleyan theology.

Steve Pusey, Ph.D. History, Ohio State University, is Vice-President for Academic Affairs at Trevecca Nazarene University. Previously he held administrative posts at Olivet Nazarene University—Chair, Department of History, Dean of the Division of Education and Dean of the School of Graduate and Adult Studies. His interests are American urban history and futurist themes in higher education.

Herbert L. Prince, M.Div., Nazarene Theological Seminary, is Associate Professor of Philosophy and Theology. He contributes significantly to faculty leadership and is currently chair of the Faculty Council. Point Loma Nazarene College honored him with a D.D. His articles have appeared in denominational publications and in several theological dictionaries.

Gerard A. Reed, Ph.D., University of Oklahoma, is Professor of History, Philosophy and Religion, and College Chaplain at Point Loma Nazarene College. His main interests are ancient and medieval church history, ethics, and American Indian history. He has published articles on Indian history and a book, *The Liberating Law*. He has delivered the American Heritage Lectures at MidAmerica Nazarene College and the Gould Lectures on the Holy Spirit at Eastern Nazarene College.

Maxine E. Walker, Ph.D., University of Kansas, was Vice-President of Academic Affairs under Cecil Paul and currently serves as Dean of Graduate Studies/Administration at Point Loma Nazarene College. She also is the Director of Wesleyan Center for 21st Century Studies at PLNC and Point Loma Press. Her teaching interests include Shakespeare, literary criticism, and interdisciplinary studies.

David P. Whitelaw, D.Th., University of South Africa, is Professor of Historical Theology and Director of Graduate Religion at Point Loma Nazarene College. His scholarly interests are Luther and the Reformation, church historiography, South Africa and Latin America, and the patristic roots of Wesleyan theology.

ACKNOWLEDGEMENTS

It is fitting that a collection of essays honor Dr. Cecil R. Paul. The range of Dr. Paul's work and influence is immense, and he could have written well and wisely on each of the topics himself. Dr. Paul was not a passive thinker; his clear vision and intellectual concerns actively shaped his work as a community, college, and church leader. All of us who worked with Dr. Paul have lost an irreplaceable colleague and friend. He endeavored to awaken the spiritual and moral imagination through the evocative power of a community that has learned to love as Christ loves.

I am particularly grateful to Judy Paul who has found grace and peace that passes understanding and who continues to complement her husband's vision for a community that is shaped by grace.

I am grateful to President Jim Bond, Point Loma Nazarene College, who is a strong and generous supporter of the Wesleyan Center for 21st Century Studies and Point Loma Press. His commitment to the mission of Nazarene colleges and his belief in this tribute to his former colleague, Cecil Paul, has made this publication possible. President Kent Hill of Eastern Nazarene College has also encouraged this recognition of his predecessor. Dr. Paul was "ENC" to the core; however, he would have applauded any Nazarene college celebrating a sister institution. I believe this book suggests the cooperation that characterizes our mutual mission in Nazarene higher education.

Church of the Nazarene officials such as Bob Brower, Jerry Lambert, and Mike Estep have supported me in this reflection on Cecil Paul's life and work.

I am grateful for the essayists and tribute writers many of whom are longtime colleagues, if not in years then in kindred spirit. Their willingness to think about the major themes and topics that historically and presently affect our colleges indicates their dedication to the rich possibilities of their calling and their own place of service. All of the essayists currently hold posts at various Nazarene colleges, and in those assignments, they teach students whose lives will judge the vitality and veracity of what we have said.

I am also thankful for the efficient and meticulous work of Sharon Bowles, Editorial Assistant, Karen DeSollar, Production Director, and Stella Vandegrift, Cover and Book Designer, all of whom creatively touched this book. Robin Evans, my secretary, has been particularly helpful in keeping track of the many details that accompany such a project.

I owe an especially large debt to my husband Keith Walker whose 31 years in Nazarene colleges as a physicist has taught him to love the questions and to be surprised by the answers.

M.E.W.

Excerpts from *Servant Leadership* by Robert K. Greenleaf. Copyright © 1977 by Paulist Press. Used by permission.

Excerpt from *Leading from Within* by Parker J. Palmer. Copyright © 1990 by the Indiana Office for Campus Ministries, 1100 W. 42nd Street, Indianapolis, Ind. Used by permission.

Quotation from *The Gambler* by Don Schlitz. Copyright © 1977 Sony Cross Keys Publishing Co., Inc. All rights administered by Sony Music Publishing, 8 Music Square West, Nashville, TN 37203. All rights reserved. Used by permission.

Excerpt from Chap. 3, 41-42, in *Psychotherapy: The Art of Wooing Nature* by Sheldon Roth. Copyright © 1987 and 1990 by Jason Aronson, Inc. Reprinted with the permission of the publisher.

From *The Works of John Wesley* by Albert C. Outler. Copyright © 1985 by Abingdon Press. Reprinted by permission.

From *Choices: In Pursuit of Wholeness* by Cecil Paul and Jan Lanham. Copyright © 1982 Beacon Hill Press. Used by permission.

FOREWORD

On the brink of the new century, the Church of the Nazarene commemorates her own centennial. At this juncture, the intellectual and theological life of the maturing denomination is nourished by the insights and vision of her own daughters and sons.

Shaped by their Wesleyan/Holiness heritage and formed by our system of Nazarene higher education, thoughtful practitioners and scholar-teachers now offer to their church the fruit of their own creative thinking about the things that matter most.

With keen analysis, insightful perception, and fertile imagination they speak about the Church of the Nazarene, her
> nature,
>> history,
>>> beliefs,
>>>> practices,
>>>>> and her emerging new life.

With reverent reflection, genuine appreciation, and prophetic concern they speak to the Church of the Nazarene, to her
> opportunities,
>> vulnerabilities,
>>> mission,
>>>> and to her relevance for the twenty-first century.

The inspired prophet, Joel, penned this word from the Lord God:

"I will pour out my Spirit on all people
Your sons and daughters will dream dreams,
Your young men will see visions.
Even on my servants, both men and women,
I will pour out my Spirit in these days."

(Joel 2:28 NIV).

This divine word seems tailor-made for this era in our denominational life. How aptly it trumpets the themes that echo through this book.

Grace in the Academic Community is a significant collection of essays and scholarly papers offering a feast of ideas by Nazarene educators. It is a *Festschrift* in honor of Dr. Cecil R. Paul, also a scholar-teacher and thoughtful practitioner. He influenced for good those who studied with him, counseled with him, and those who walked alongside him in the life of the academy, the community, and the church.

I first met Cecil Paul in the late 1950s while he was a student at Nazarene Theological Seminary, Kansas City. We met in the home of mutual Canadian friends. Even then he was a serious thinker, speaking about the nature of the church.

In the 1980s, we served together in planning a leaders' conference for the denomination for which he wrote and delivered a paper "The People Called Nazarenes: Getting There" (Chapter 2 in this collection). With transparency and authenticity, he expressed his hopes, fears, and dreams for the church which reached and educated him in preparation for his life of service.

Shortly before Cecil's death on August 1, 1992, we planned a cooperative educational project for multi-cultural ministerial students. The project was to be sponsored by the two schools we served, Eastern Nazarene College and Nazarene Bible College.

As we move toward the year 2000, I am reflecting on my relationship with Cecil Paul. Certain things about him have had an impact on me that I shall never live long enough to forget. First, his depth of life commitment to Christ and the church quickly became a test of my own. Second, his life was governed by principles rather than self-interest. Last, his decisions were made under grace rather than law whether they affected clients in counseling, students in the classroom, or faculty on the campus. He truly modeled *Grace in the Academic Community*.

How appropriate that a life that spoke so clearly to the church he loved should inspire his colleagues in the academy themselves to speak to the church we love.

Jerry D. Lambert
Commissioner of Education

SECTION ONE

NAMING THE MISSION

As Wesley once said, 'He who governed the world before I was born shall take care of it likewise when I am dead. My part is to improve the present moment.' And together, with God's blessing, we can.

Cecil Paul, from *A New President's View*

CHAPTER ONE

THE NAZARENE COLLEGE PRESIDENT AS SERVANT LEADER

Jim L. Bond

The plethora of challenges facing Nazarene higher education at century's end is daunting. This is neither new nor unexpected. Onerous situations have pounded like the incessant surf on our educational institutions throughout their brief histories. The schools have proven to be amazingly resilient. It is a truly remarkable story of not just survival but substantial growth in every respect. The Nazarene higher education system has become the envy of many denominations throughout our nation.

Regardless of the storied history and the current posture of considerable strength, new challenges—numerous, complex, and ominous—loom on the horizon. These could potentially threaten, minimally, the quality of our educational offerings and, at worst, the continued existence of some of our institutions.

Crucial to a flourishing Nazarene higher educational system in the twenty-first century is, as always, its leadership. Strategic thinking and prudent decision-making are critical in the next five to ten years. Trustees, faculty, administrators, and particularly presidents, will play a vital role in charting the course. It is fair to state that presidents are the key players in this process.

Harold Stoke has defined the president's major function as clarifying the institution's purposes and selecting the appropriate means of achieving them. He states: "One thing is clear: colleges must have presidents and it makes a great difference who they are" (20). As important as who they are is their understanding of leadership and the role of the president in it.

Secular Leadership Styles

In 1981 the American Council on Education published the findings of the Presidency Project that was designed to explore the human dynamics of the college presidency. The book, *Style and Substance: Leadership and the College Presidency*, became a definitive statement of the beliefs and actions of presidents during the late 70s and early 80s. Research was conducted among twenty-five U.S. colleges and universities representing the various segments of the academy. The findings revealed six categories of presidential leadership styles:

The Take-Charge President - This is the hard charger who presides with authority and is the institution's decision maker. This leader is very autocratic.

The Standard-Bearer President - The challenge to this leader is to ensure the continued status of an institution that has "arrived" as one of the elite schools in the nation. The style may be seen then as essentially laissez-faire.

The Organization President - This leader is preoccupied with turning the gears of the complex machinery with as little friction as possible in advancing the institution.

The Moderator President - This type employs a reasonably democratic process in which the leader becomes skillful in capturing and organizing community thought.

The Explorer President - This term identifies the person whose goal is to push the institution to the forefront of innovation. It involves being visionary, a willingness to take risks and a commitment to bring change.

The Founding President - This style is characterized by those individuals who conceptualize and bring into existence an institution designed to meet a perceived need (Benezet 39-71).

Obviously, this is a representative though not an exhaustive list of presidential leadership styles.

Which is the most appropriate style for a Nazarene college or university president in leading our institutions into the twenty-first century? The question has neither a right nor a wrong answer.

Paul Hersey, dealing with leadership in a broad context, proposes a concept called "situational leadership." This approach is predicated on the assumption that no one specific style is always right for every occasion. The leader will carefully collect all the data necessary to make an informed decision and then engage the particular form of leadership which is appropriate for the moment. One may be autocratic, participative, or even laissez-faire in a specific situation—and be right. Success turns on how well one tailors the style for the occasion. Hersey defines this as "organized common sense" (70). Thus a Nazarene college or university president may generally function as, for example, the "Moderator President" though certain circumstances may warrant a "Take-Charge President" or an "Explorer President." It is plausible that more of the latter styles may be necessary as our schools transition into the next millennium.

Integration of Secular and Christian Leadership Styles

A question of some controversy is whether there is anything unique regarding the Christian's approach to leadership. It is true that most leaders and managers in Christian organizations have received their training either from the secular and business world or from a Christian college and/or seminary. If one's training has come from the former, then there may be a lack of understanding regarding Christian leadership principles. If their training came from the latter, then they were probably schooled in Greek and Hebrew, ecclesiology and eschatology, exegesis and homiletics, but received little if any equipping for leadership and management of a Christian organization (other than a pastorate). The end result is that regardless of one's background, there does not exist a thoughtfully designed educational model for preparing a person to lead a Christian enterprise like a college or university. Many Christian college presidents have been extruded into assignments where on-the-job training was their only recourse.

Obviously, one can accept secular leadership principles as being valid even for the Christian organization. It is being practiced widely today. Many Christians lead with theories taken right out of the secular textbooks. It is rationalized that leadership principles are leadership principles and have application in any and all situations. Calling them "secular" or "Christian" is irrelevant.

At the other pole of this debate is the extremist position which holds that there are distinctively Christian leadership principles and employing secular methodologies is totally inappropriate for Christians. Believers must practice only those leadership theories that have a biblical base; all else is rejected. Such hard lines should not be drawn for logic is not on the side of such narrowness.

The most sensible way to address this matter is Carl Mulder's "integrationist" approach. Here, an understanding of both biblical and secular leadership is sought. The integrationist then attempts to "develop a theory which integrates or applies these understandings from secular leadership that are in agreement with or help implement their biblical principles" (80).David McKenna believes this approach has merit because it incorporates the sound theory of the secular world with solid, biblical theology. He does issue a note of warning regarding the starting point:

> By beginning with the premises of secular leadership theory, the assumptions underlying the theory are also accepted. Without a critique of these assumptions which invariably influence the motive and mission of leadership, conflicts will arise when biblical and secular assumptions clash in practice. (14-15)

The integrationist approach has merit. It seems prudent to garner the best from secular theory while not being reluctant to reject anything which violates Christian principles. A Nazarene college or university president must seek to hone leadership skills wherever help can be found, albeit from a secular source or sacred scripture.

A Christian Leadership Distinctive

Some insight into the distinctiveness of the Christian's perspective of leadership is found in Jesus' words to his disciples (Matt. 20:25-28):

> You know that the rulers of the Gentiles lord it over them, and their high officials exercise authority over them. Not so with you. Instead, whoever wants to become great among you must be your servant, and whoever wants to be first must be your slave—just as the Son of Man did not come to be served but to serve, and to give his life as a ransom for many.

What Jesus accomplished by "giving his life as a ransom for many" was unique. He achieved something that no mere mortal could have—he opened the doors of eternal salvation for every person. Not to be overlooked, however, is that in laying down his life, Jesus also established a leadership principle and pattern that is timeless. It is the principle of *diakonia*, a principle which was carried to its limits at Calvary.

The principle of *diakonia* is self-offering rather than self-asserting, self-renunciation in favor of self-seeking, and investing one's life in others rather than exploiting them for personal gain. This principle is reflected in the use of several different words in scripture such as "servant," "service," "serve," "minister," and "ministry." We use these terms almost as though they are synonymous in meaning. While they share the basic root meaning, there are definite shades of difference that distinguish the words. For example, "servant" and "service" are closely allied yet each word has a very distinct meaning, particularly in the Christian context.

Serving others or rendering service to others is not unique to the Christian. Most people, even the most egocentric, are capable of giving some degree of service. They may have their occasional moments when they act benevolently and reach out to address community or individual needs. Thus, anyone is capable of performing humanitarian deeds of service to other human beings.

The Christian has a different perspective of this matter. For the believer, service to others is the natural outflow of one who is living under the authority of Jesus Christ. Thomas Torrance states it well: "Christian service is commanded of us. It is to be referred back to the Lordship of Christ and is to be understood as the pure service rendered to the Lord by those who are His servants" (715).

Herein lies the Christian distinctive: one can render service to others without being a servant, but one cannot be a servant of God without rendering service to others. The Christian has appropriated God's grace in Jesus Christ to willfully denounce self-rule and submit to the authority of God, becoming his servant. Believers are no longer their own masters for they now belong to *Another*. As God's servants, they are consumed by the desire to live in obedience to their Master. Thus they do what they are told and serve others in the interest of bringing honor to their Lord. Torrance adds: "Christian service is not something that is accidental to the Christian, but essential to him, for it is rooted in his basic structure of existence as a slave of Jesus Christ" (715).

The Nazarene College President As Servant Leader

And what are the ramifications of this servant/service concept for a Nazarene college or university president? The office must not be viewed as an exalted position where the president is the recipient of the ministry and service of those within the campus community. In actuality the president is uniquely positioned for significant ministry to others, particularly those employed by the institution. There is theological mandate for the president to minister to the very ones who serve the college at the president's initiation. This is classically illustrated in Jesus' stooping low to wash the feet of his disciples, then saying, "I have set you an example that you should do as I have done for you. I tell you the truth, no servant is greater than his master . . . " (John 13:15,16).

In the context of the great *kenosis* passage, Paul admonishes: "Do nothing out of selfish ambition or vain conceit, but in humility consider others better than yourselves. Each of you should look not only to your own interests but also to the interest of others" (Phil. 2:3,4). This principle, when actualized by a president, will affect the way she or he views and treats every person on campus. Robert Greenleaf thinks that the servant leader will "make sure that other people's priority needs are being served. The best test, and difficult to administer, is: Do those served grow as persons? Do they, while being served, become healthier, wiser, freer, more autonomous, more likely themselves to become servants?" (13,14)

A servant-leader president who desires to serve others on campus will then value each individual on campus—staff, faculty, students, and administrators. The president will endeavor to make working conditions for all campus employees as pleasant and fulfilling as possible. This involves such mundane things as providing the resources necessary for quality job performance, maximizing salaries, and providing opportunities for advancement and promotion.

The president sets a positive and Christian tone to the campus when rendering service to others in the name of Jesus Christ. Hardly anything can contribute more substantively in the building of authentic Christian community than for the chief executive officer of the corporation *to wash the feet of another*. This should not be an exceptional thing on a Nazarene college campus. If our schools are to be Christocentric communities, it must be evidenced by a president who is personally yielding to the authority of Christ, living as His servant, and gladly rendering service to others. Anything less from the president may ultimately negate all the verbiage regarding Christ's Lordship over the school.

I am quick to point out, especially from poignant awareness of personal deficiencies when it comes to servanthood and service, that no person can live out perfectly the servant mind. E. P. Weber points out that "Christ's people are called to a lifestyle of servanthood, but no one lives up even to his own expectations, to say nothing of God's" (44). Regardless, the responsibilities of servanthood cannot be evaded. A servant of Christ is always being called to faithfully render service to others.

Conclusion

Can a person be both servant and leader? Can both roles be fused in one human being? Few have written so forcefully about servant leadership as Robert Greenleaf. His initial interest in the subject came out of reading Herman Hesse's *Journey To The East*:

> In this story we see a band of men on a mythical journey. . . . The central figure of the story is Leo who accompanies the party as the servant who does their menial chores, but who also sustains them with his spirit and his song. He is a person of extraordinary presence. All goes well until Leo disappears. Then the group falls into disarray and the journey is abandoned. They cannot make it without the servant Leo. The narrator, one of the party, after some years of wandering finds Leo and is taken into the Order that had sponsored the journey. There he discovers that Leo, whom he had known first as servant, was in fact the titular head of the Order, its guiding spirit, a great and noble leader. (7)

Greenleaf deduces from the story that "the great leader is seen as servant first" (7). Can a person be both servant and leader? *Yes!* There was One who "being in very nature God . . . made himself nothing, taking the very nature of a servant" (Phil 2:6,7). As in all things, Jesus is our model. Paul admonishes, "Your attitude should be the same as that of Christ Jesus" (Phil 2:5).

Occasionally there walks among us a great leader of people who reflects the servant-mind of Jesus. Such a person was Cecil Paul. This intelligent, compassionate, and multi-gifted man was the consummate Nazarene college president. Along with the other presidents who, like me, were privileged to serve alongside him, we celebrate Cecil Paul, the servant-leader. He was what all of us aspire to be. This *Festschrift* is a fitting tribute to our esteemed colleague.

A word from the always thoughtful Parker Palmer is an appropriate conclusion to this subject of leadership at Nazarene colleges and universities:

> A leader is a person who has an unusual degree of power to project on other people her or his shadow, or her or his light. A leader is a person who has an unusual degree of power to create the conditions under which other people must live and move and have their being—conditions that can either be as illuminating as heaven or as shadowy as hell. A leader is a person who must take special responsibility for what is going on inside her or him self, inside her or his consciousness, lest the act of leadership create more harm than good. (5)

TRIBUTE

Although I never had the privilege of meeting Cecil Paul face to face, I have come to know and respect him. I have encountered his positive influence in the eyes and smiles of countless students, faculty, staff, and community people here at ENC and in Quincy. The legacy Cecil most often left in the lives he touched was compassion and concern. For Cecil Paul, the Presidency was an opportunity to serve—to spend himself entirely "to improve the present moment." This good man not only quoted Wesley, but also transformed words into deeds.

President Kent Hill
Eastern Nazarene College

TRIBUTE

One of the greatest tributes of Dr. Cecil Paul was his ability to affirm people regardless of where in life they found themselves. He served as a role model for each of us in this way. I only wish that I could have had a long time with him to perfect this quality.

Jack McInturff
Vice-President for Financial Affairs (retired)
Eastern Nazarene College

CHAPTER TWO

THE PEOPLE CALLED NAZARENES: GETTING THERE

*Presentation: Nazarene Leadership Conference
February 21-22, 1989*

Cecil R. Paul

Jesus helps us address the question of getting there with some words of caution.

> Nobody sews a patch of unshrunken cloth onto an old coat, for the patch will pull away from the coat and the hole will be worse than ever. Nor do people put new wine into old wineskins—otherwise the skins burst, the wine is spilled and the skins are ruined. But they put new wine into new skins and both are preserved. (Matthew 9:17 N.E.B)

Matters of Mission and Messages vs. Methods and Systems

We stand at a critical time in the history of our church. In the presence of rapidly changing cultures and the growth of the global multi-ethnic and multi-language church we face new challenges with risks and wonderful new opportunities.

Will we sew unshrunken cloth on old coats? If so, there will be some holes.

Will we put new wine into old wineskins? If so, the skins will be broken and the new wine will be wasted.

Samuel Huntington (Harvard University) in discussing the decline of nations notes that the real cause of the decline is not the now fashionable notion of "imperial overstretch," but the phenomenon of creeping inflexibility, what might be called industrial (institutional) sclerosis—precisely the loss of that ability to change and adapt.

A good definition of "sclerosis" is "a pathological hardening of tissues produced by overgrowth—hardening of cell walls."

Are we suffering from institutional sclerosis? Have we lost the ability to change and adapt and confront the risks and the challenges of our day? Have the cells become hardened and inflexible? Is the vitality of the tissue being lost? Are we caught in systems that drive us into indecisiveness and controlling behavior?

Joseph Schumpter identifies creative destruction as a process in which leaders of institutions are *willing* to go through the painful process of destroying old structures and techniques and then renewing them. It is through this process that newness of life, vitality and creative adaptability are born. This is particularly so if we keep the focus on mission and the quality of shared tasks.

The country song says it well. I must preface this quote by noting that the songwriter's comment was brought to mind by a Rook game.

You've got to know when to hold 'em,
Know when to fold 'em
Know when to walk away, know when to run. (Don Schlitz lyrics and tune)

We need to know what to hold on to. What are the cardinal beliefs, the ultimates, the untouchables? *Getting there* is dependent on this.

We need to know when to fold 'em. When structures and systems no longer help us to do mission we need to consider this question: Whether at headquarters or at the district and local church level do we suffer from institutional sclerosis?

Do we have —old garments needing too much mending?
—old wineskins that can no longer hold new wine?

We need to know when to walk or run away from some things. We need to question the quantifying of the tangibles as the top priority. Is our effectiveness measured in corporate language and methods? The tension between mission/message, effectiveness and methods cost effectiveness will always be with us, but the heart of what we are and who we are and what we do in ministry is not easily quantified.

Are we at a point in our history when we need to question the layers of bureaucracy that are so often the result of focusing more on method-and-position than on mission and message? Are we in tension with one another because in subtle ways we have become special interest groups vying for that which will secure the survival of old wineskins and garments because we own them or have a special interest in them? We don't own them, and if we hold on to them, we and the generations to follow us will lose them. As John Wesley once said: "He who governed the world before I was born shall take care of it likewise when I am dead. My part is to improve the present moment." Our task is to improve the present moment. Institutional sclerosis paralyzes us and we are unable to seize the moment.

When policies and operational procedures emerge as the dominant focal point and preoccupation, we are at risk of losing our mission and our vision. The extensive investment of time and energy in these matters signals structural and political defects.

Do we find ourselves taking a decentralist position on secular government while centralizing our own structures and authority?

Do we tend to hold on to some things that may not be cardinal to our mission or message?

Do we tend to find greater security in old methods and systems because we do not want to go through the pain of change or risk adaptation? I have a sense that most of us see the need for change and share a common concern that our systemic condition demands attention. Perhaps we are afraid of the risks. Perhaps we are unsure what to change. Perhaps we do not know our priorities or understand how to go about the process. Perhaps we are too tired! Perhaps we have run the maze so long that we have accepted it in resignation and cynicism. It will take great wisdom for us to know what to change and what to confirm. But we get there (mission) by daring to confront these systemic concerns.

Confronting Central Questions

We cannot get there without confronting the central questions and making critical choices.

The question of *identity* commands our attention. What distinguishes us? If our people are indistinguishable from other organizations, what is our purpose? Are our people becoming increasingly reformed fundamentalists in their world and religious views? Do our people identify with or even understand the Wesleyan-holiness mission and message. Mobilization for ministry begins with a clear understanding and radical commitment to our distinguishing identity and message.

The question of *intimacy* challenges us. What is our heritage? What covenants are sacred? Who are we and who will be my people? Are we the U.S.A. Church of the Nazarene and primarily Anglo? What do our structures, systems, and symbols tell us? The challenge is to be faithful to our heritage and relevant to our day. Ours is the day of the global church with an enlarged understanding of identity and mission.

The question of *values* next confronts us. What are the core, cardinal, moral and ethical values and standards that are solidly based on scripture, reason, experience and tradition? We have something to say to this age that is not easily accomplished within the narrow parameters of fundamentalism.

Related to identity, intimacy and values are questions related to what our people are reading, viewing, and experiencing. Are we more shaped by our society and its media or are we the movers, shakers, and shapers?

Are we prepared to get there through an enlarged understanding of and commitment to a great body of biblical holiness literature?

The question of *vision* confronts us. It is one of the tests for institutional sclerosis. What do we do with visionaries, young men and women who dream dreams of an ever enlarging mission and ministry? Do we give them a place within the fellowship and ministries of the church?

Without their vision we become self-absorbed and stagnate like dead water having no inlets or outlets. Visionless people become frustrated and ingrown and cynical. Visionless people lose their creative energy and become preoccupied with security and survival. Our vision cannot be for the institution, it is for our mission and message. It is profoundly biblical/theological not corporate/political.

Christ and Culture and the Church

Kenneth Kenniston of Harvard University identifies one of the major tasks of the early adult years is negotiating a relationship between oneself and the surrounding culture—of working out some basis for responding and dealing with the institutions of the culture. This is true for a community of believers as well. It is the task identified by Jesus as a major potential crisis. He prayed that we would be in the world but not of the world. Kenniston talks about three ways in which we can negotiate a relationship with the culture and its institutions.

Getting there on the basis of a *revolution solution* proceeds on the assumption that something is terribly wrong with the culture and its institutions. Something needs to be done to change it in radical ways. There certainly is a revolutionary element in the life and teachings of Jesus. This is expressed by many of our people who in prophetic language and compassion are speaking out against injustices while delivering care to the victims of social evil.

Getting there on the basis of the *separation solution* proceeds on the assumption you cannot change the social order, and that it is such a threat to you and your children you isolate from it within the "safety" of a religious ghetto. This is the danger of failing to be in the world as called upon by Jesus.

Getting there on the basis of the *adaptation solution* involves conforming to the culture and its values. While we might assume that we do not adapt since we set up moral standards that contrast with the mores of the world, we do conform in multiplied areas of performance, style, and prestige preoccupation.

Now Kenniston stops with these three approaches to resolving the tension and has missed the Christian answer. Jesus modeled this for us, and it guides us and governs our goals, our motivations and our relationships. H. Reinold Niebuhr sees Christ is against culture (revolutionary), in culture (adaptation), and above culture (separate from). Ultimately, He radically transforms culture and our lives.

The final answer is in the *servant solution*. Here is how we get there. This enables us to keep the focus on message and mission, and on the great commission of the Master Servant.

The Communication of Christian Compassion

We get there by the communication of Christian compassion— through recapturing and expressing it in healing, sustaining, guiding and reconciling ministries of compassion. We cannot get there without serving one another. We are thereby enabled to serve others as we collaborate, cooperate and communicate on our shared mission.

Healing ministry - We get there by establishing relationships that bring hope of healing, health and wholeness to hurting and broken humanity.

Sustaining ministry - We get to our mission by sustaining ministries, that involve standing with people, and just plain being there in the trenches (in the very presence of sin, abuse, neglect and violence). We choose to be where people are so broken there is little hope for the ultimate healing of the spirit.

Guiding ministry - We get there through nurturing, modeling and mentoring ministries, that provide discipline, direction, purpose, vision for life. To a generation looking for heroes in the remoteness and synthetic quality of secular media figures, we offer the servant model and ministries of encouragement. We cannot get there without strong colleges, universities and the seminary, training men and women for every facet of ministry. Guidance works both ways. They are pointing the way for us.

Reconciling ministry - The ultimate getting there is through reconciling ministries. We seek to bring humanity into reconciliation within, between and among its members and most importantly with God. All our methods and programs point beyond the penultimate to the ultimate hope of reconciliation with God.

There are two passages of Scripture that should shock us out of our complacency and inspire us to mission effectiveness. They are near the beginning and end of the Gospels. Jesus points the way! Here is how we finally get there.

In Luke 4:18-19, Jesus has returned in the power of the Spirit and declares:

> The Spirit of the Lord is upon me, because he has anointed me to preach good news to the poor. He has sent me to proclaim release to the captives and recovering sight to the blind, to set at liberty those who are oppressed, to proclaim the acceptable year of the Lord.

We too have been to the mountaintop and viewed the promised land. What a wonderful vision, not without its risks! Those concerned with structures and the law sought to throw him over the city wall. But Jesus had a dream, a Holy Dream and he has passed it on to us.

Matthew 25:36 tells us how to get there as well as points out how we may fail. The sheep and goats are separated and again the basis of judgment is Holy Loving compassion. It is very simple. Personal piety must have a public witness. We show our love and holiness by touching the untouchable, loving the unlovable. We demonstrate the heart of holiness by loving others in all manner of need and conditions of sin. The complete range of human hungers, thirsts, nakedness and imprisonment become our mission, and we get it done by being there in His power and presence. There is no heart holiness without its expression in the holy love of social concern and compassion.

"For God hath not given us the spirit of fear; but of power and of love and of a sound mind." We may feel weak but we are not the children of an inferior God. Our weakness does not come from His inadequacy; it stems from our own failure to tap the resources of His power. After the Holy Spirit is come upon you, you shall be witnesses to the whole world. "You dear children, are from God and have overcome them, because the one who is in you is greater than the one in the world" (I John 4:4).

> God grant us the serenity to accept the things we cannot change. The courage to change the things we can! And the wisdom to know the difference!

CHAPTER THREE

WHAT MAKES A NAZARENE COLLEGE "NAZARENE"?

Herbert L. Prince

If we know what a thing is, we can surely say what it is.
—Plato

We are here to be better off, but to be sure also that we are better.
—P. F. Bresee

Obviously, a college sponsored, staffed and supported by members of the Church of the Nazarene[1] is a "Nazarene" college.[2] Individuals are nominated by Nazarene district assemblies for election as college trustees; presidents are selected because they are Nazarene; a percentage of educational budgets are paid by local Nazarene churches; members of the church, other qualifications being equal, are preferred for faculty positions; students are encouraged to attend Nazarene institutions of higher learning by Nazarene ministers and associates. Could any institution be more "Nazarene"!

The assigned topic allows for an obvious response; however, the obvious is hardly the definitive word for the assigned topic or in a *Festschrift* honoring Dr. Cecil Paul. Nurtured in the intricacies of psychology and the Christian faith, Cecil Paul would recognize the wisdom of Whitehead's counsel, to seek exactness and mistrust it (*Science* 104). A century of Freudian psychology (among others) has sponsored a hermeneutic of suspicion[3], a recognition that existence is often more complex than the apparent as a psychotherapist would readily know. Is there more to "Nazarene" than the personal, vocational, financial and ecclesiological aspects noted earlier? Can an educational institution formally and legally recognized as Nazarene not be "Nazarene"? Is the matter simply a matter of definition, perhaps even a play on a word, or is there something more that must be said?

The present essay addresses the topic heuristically and might best be described as an impressionistic piece.[4] The topic, developed within certain space constraints, uses concepts and terms drawn from theological and philosophical discourse within the milieu of a late twentieth-century environment. Attention is given to the development of western thought with some assessment made about the current bearing of that thought. To that end, Part 1 questions a traditional approach on how the topic is to be defined, and Part 2 suggests a complementary and more personal, relational posture. This personal addition, establishes a measure of identification with *the* Nazarene, Jesus of Nazareth and follows the Wesleyan theological heritage and the Church of the Nazarene.[5]

1

Historically, one avenue for exploring an issue is through the use of interrogative pronouns. Journalists are taught to approach topics in terms of what, when, who, where, why and how. Teachers, psychologists, lawyers, welders, technicians, adults, youth, the learned and the unlearned, all commonly do the same. To find then the interrogative pronoun "what" in the assigned title of the paper is not surprising. This particular interrogative has long been favored in western reflective thought, from ancient Greece to the modern era. Socrates originated what has become known as the What-is-X? question; X stands for something sought after (e.g., courage, temperance, justice)[6] Subsequent philosophers and even theologians exhibit a propensity for the "what." Aristotle, for instance, says that substance can be discussed in terms of "what" something is or "that" something is with the former preferred. "What" is especially interesting since it at times has been taken to suggest a metaphysical or substantial[7] approach to a given topic. That is, the inquirer looks for some essence, substance or nature that gives a person, artifact or institution its identity. However this favoring of "what" was attacked during the Enlightenment period. From John Locke to David Hume substantial thinking became problematical.[8] The past could not be abandoned. Fichte (d. 1814) reportedly said: "The metaphysical only, and not the historical, can give us blessedness"(qtd. in Heron 20). Within a generation it was obvious that just the opposite had occurred. The modern understanding of history had been born and then to reign.[9] Modern historiography has, as Dilthey put it, burst the dam of tradition (Moltmann 230) and appeals to substance remain problematical down to the present for the most part.[10]

The fact that this substantial approach (for want of a better term) has become so imbedded in western culture is apparent everywhere, from the attempt to define what is distinctive in denominations to naming what is unique concerning human existence to designating the essence of a college. Habits are difficult to break. Common sense itself seems to favor such thinking. As one writer recently put it: "In times of shifting identities and disposable values, it is more important than ever to remind ourselves of what makes us, the people called Nazarenes, distinctly us" (Laird 11). Or, in a different context, the question becomes: "Will the Nazarene Colleges maintain their distinctive character" (Metz 68). Both statements imply there is something that makes Nazarenes or Nazarene education distinctive, leading to attempts to name whatever "it" is. Can an institution, even one with a history and established traditions, be given the Nazarene label without having to die "the death of a thousand qualifications" (Flew 97)?

The present paper recognizes the apparent inevitability of the substantial approach, at least in language. The intent is admirable. Institutions without identity, without distinctiveness are institutions in danger for they have no ability to "inform," as Elton Trueblood once said. To inform is to provide structure and direction, to inform is to shape lives with specific purposes and values in mind. Quality educational institutions are forming and informing institutions, just ask any Princeton University graduate. Robert Wuthnow tells of his first teaching day at Princeton. After each name on the attendance sheet, he noticed the student voluntarily put "a curious two-digit number by an apostrophe." It dawned on him later that this "was the students' expected year of graduation: class of '76, class of '77, and so on." For over 200 years, this has been a Princeton tradition. It becomes a part of each student's identity whether they graduate or not, giving each student a place in Princeton history (183-84). To attempt to name the essence or nature or very substance of a Nazarene college remains a formidable and necessary task. For whatever the substantial approach may carry in terms of difficulty, the approach *is* attempting to provide clear identity and continuity of purpose for what takes place within its purview. A Lutheran college is not meant to be a Presbyterian college, nor is a Calvinistic institution meant to be a Nazarene institution. In that regard, Nazarene educators and ecclesiastical leaders are one with Christians from other denominations. Each attempts to define in order to fulfill institutional and God-given responsibilities to educate and train those within the respective sphere of influence. In each case, axiological judgments enter into the picture. This is in keeping with what Whitehead terms a "sense of importance."

For Whitehead, two ideas underlie human experience: One is the notion of importance, and the other is the notion of matter-of-fact (*Modes* ch. 1). Together, he says, they are antithetical, and yet they depend on each other. The former is the product of concentration while the latter provides the necessary details and specifics constitutive of experience itself. A sense of importance allows one to take from the wealth of human experience and see other aspects in its light. Importance shapes experience by selecting what in experience is worthy of immediate attention, while pushing other aspects of experience to the background. In so doing, decisions can be made and actions taken. Matter-of-fact represents the obvious, the routine, the mundane, the overlooked at times due to familiarity and unconcern.

One traditional means for naming the essence or "sense of importance" of a group lies in theological affirmation. This names what the group deems vital for the very existence of the group. Every church body needs some defining aspects to justify its existence. Lutherans are known for justification by grace through faith, Calvinists stress the sovereignty of God, the Society of Friends (Quakers) emphasizes the inner light, Nazarenes are identified with entire sanctification. In each instance, the focus leads to other affirmations continuous with the respective sense of importance. Some churches, for example, reinforce their sense of importance through a confession or creed which is recited whenever the church meets for worship. A distinguished history of just such intentional efforts exists.[11] A church's confession sets parameters and provides a sense of community with a variety of supporting means for nurturing parishioners in the values and perspectives of the particular church group (e.g., through Sunday school classes, Bible studies, a catechism).

A Christian college's mission statement does much of the same; it defines and in the process institutional goals are established to direct campus policies and programs deemed necessary for the institution's continued existence. Trustees, administrators, faculty, staff are all enjoined to fulfill institutional purpose. The values of the sponsoring denomination are preserved and developed further through the educational process. Lines of accountability are drawn and expectations are developed in line with mission. In brief, the college is founded, evolves, fulfills the agreed upon "sense of importance."

Creeds and college-mission statements exemplify distinctiveness by focusing on what this essay has termed the "substantial" approach. Within churches, doctrines and creedal formulations serve this purpose.[12] Within college-mission statements, the matter is more difficult and ambiguous. For not only are church-related colleges meant to be supporters of the sponsoring denomination and its teachings, but also colleges are venues for the exploration and research of ideas and practices that may be in tension with (or even contradictory to) the supporting denomination. This is especially true of liberal arts colleges. By definition such colleges deliberately develop courses to research the past, both Christian and other-than-Christian, with the express purpose of producing critically-aware students who are at home in the various arts, natural sciences and humanities. To accomplish instructional and research interests, objectives in keeping with institutional mission are set forth. These objectives describe what a particular Christian College "is," as any college brochure readily reveals. Somewhere in the objectives will appear exposure to and understanding of the distinctive nature of the sponsoring denomination and its sense of importance. Sometimes this is expressed by adding the church's essential doctrines to the college catalog; at other times it may be simply done by insuring that the essential doctrines are clearly in mind when developing the institution's philosophy of education.

In Wesleyan educational circles, the soteriological[13] doctrines associated with John Wesley serve as benchmarks for thinking "Wesleyan."[14] To paraphrase the philosopher Fichte: What sort of theology one chooses may depend on what sort of person one is; for a theological system is not a dead piece of furniture to be rejected or accepted as one wishes; it is animated by the soul of the person who holds it.[15] At best, theological affirmations are second-order confessions of faith. They serve by giving witness and by declaring at times with boldness "what" it is that is affirmed. This fits well with one side of the classic definition of faith: *fides quae creditur*.[16] A person speaks "about the truth," of having been "taught the truth," or of having "heard the truth." In each case, truth functions in terms of content, in terms of "what." This is also the side of faith that makes possible the pursuit and proclamation of truth on a Christian college campus, and justifies the affirmations of a denomination's confessional document. At their worst, theological affirmations can become sledge-hammers.[17] When taken alone *fides quae creditur* may create a distorted view of institutional identity and, therefore, purpose. For John Wesley the people called Methodists should not be content to be people just of doctrine:

> I am not afraid that the people called Methodists should ever cease to exist either in Europe or America. But I am afraid, lest they should only exist as a dead sect, having the form of religion without the power. And this undoubtedly will be the case, unless they hold fast both the doctrine, spirit, and discipline with which they first set out (258).

2

Doctrine, spirit, discipline—to hold fast aspects as these requires of *fides qua creditur*. This, suggests an ethos that is broader, perhaps even deeper by implication, than simply a view of the world (i.e., a world view).[18] Any broadly based philosophy or theology has an outlook on the world that provides structure, ideas, and categories for dealing with the human and the divine.[19] Assumptions and interests come into play, influencing what or how something can be said to be and described. "Handles," as it were, are provided for putting God, human existence and the world into a coherent frame of discussion and analysis. A scheme of ideas can even be said to have a certain ethos.

Intriguing is the thought that world view and ethos are not necessarily one and the same.[20] Ethos allows a role or empathy for the affective alongside the rational and is in keeping with the historic speculative-affective dimensions that are said to comprise the Anglican heritage. According to Martin Thornton, the English school of spirituality shows

> an extraordinary consistency in maintaining speculative-affective synthesis; the theological and the emotional, doctrine and devotion, fact and feeling. This ... is the deepest meaning of the Anglican *via media*; it is the insistence that prayer, worship, and life itself are grounded upon dogmatic fact, that in everyday religious experience head and heart are wedded. (48-49)

As history shows, synthesis is easy to say but more difficult to live and understand. The Anglican *via media* finds its best expression through "a unity of practice,"[21] not in explanation. Can it be that one of the points of tension between the head and the heart, doctrine and devotion, concerns the extent to which continuity or discontinuity is addressed? Ethos may well recognize "distance," "difference," "discontinuity" in which the integrity of head and heart are respected without collapsing one into the other, as the term "synthesis" implies. World view within a Reformed perspective leads to a focus on the "integration of faith and learning," thereby suggesting "identity," "oneness," "continuity." This line of thinking also leads to the affirmation that truth is one, that all truth is God's truth. For God truth may indeed be one, for God's essence and existence are identical. God sees things holistically. For the human, however, the impact of sin remains. One does see but through a glass darkly, as the Scripture puts it. Might it not be the case that Wesleyan thinking is conjunctive in character, more willing to acknowledge and even accept a measure of tension between head and heart.[22] To believe that life is more than logic is hardly a new thought.

Ethos can also be said to be directive, in the sense that lines of inquiry or identity are suggested. In the words of Enrique Dussel, ethos is "what a group recognizes as a *we*" (23). One's vocabulary, attitude, stance can be affected by not only what is said but also how it is said.[23] Ethos captures something of the mystery, of the ambiguity of life itself without being reductionistic. Symbols, doctrines, even physical structures as buildings can embody ethos for they reflect modes of being within which a group (like a college) thinks and acts in certain ways.[24] Ethos can even be said to produce a "lifestyle." It is a means of self-expression, a form of teaching and of being taught, of learning formally and informally, of "being" and "doing."

World-view thinking can be tied to creation.[25] The issue for a Nazarene educator is that creation is not a Wesleyan starting point. For Wesleyans, God the Creator and Sustainer is primarily and definitively known in and through the person of Jesus Christ. The latter becomes the point of reference. To begin with creation is to succumb to philosophical and methodological as about to the world and how God is known.[26] Those issues in themselves are not only appropriate but also necessary for Christians to consider. However, to put the matter crudely, beginning with creation takes a while to get to Jesus Christ.[27] For an evangelist like John Wesley there was no time to spare. He preached in the fields to people on their way to work. The Good News was set forth, for "today is the day of salvation." Classic themes of sin, of salvation, of what Christ wrought on behalf of all set the context for thinking. To have begun with creation would have put Wesley into a camp he sharply opposed: the deists and pivotal figures within the Church of England with their rational approach to divinity.[28] Thus, it is no small matter that philosophical issues weigh heavily in Reformed higher education circles. From their standpoint, they should. For those who would be faithful to the Wesleyan-Holiness tradition, thinking and education have historically been placed in the context of soteriology.[29]

In a case study on Methodism, Russell C. Ritchey observes that the Methodist *Discipline*, from its earliest editions to the most recent begins with a history of the movement. Ritchey writes: "The first word that Methodists have wanted to say about themselves was an historical one" (481). The *Manual* of the Church of the Nazarene is no different, giving attention to history before addressing other areas.[30] The year 1895 is significant for in that year the Church of the Nazarene began in Los Angeles, California. The name "Nazarene" was suggested for the new church by Dr. C.P. Widney. For him, Nazarene symbolized "the toiling, lowly mission of Christ."[31] Phineas F. Bresee, a close friend of Widney, was the pastor. On the first piece of literature published by the new church, a promotional flyer carried the words of Jesus, "Come unto me, all ye that labor and are heavy laden." The announcement on the flyer continued:

> The Church of the Nazarene is a simple, primitive church, a church of the people and for the people. It has no new doctrines. . . . It seeks to discard all superfluous forms and ecclesiasticism and go back to the plain simple words of Christ. It is not a mission., but a church with a mission. It is a banding together of hearts that have found the peace of God, and which now in their gladness, go out to carry the message of the unsearchable riches of the gospel of Christ to other suffering, discouraged, sin-sick souls. (Smith 111)

For Widney and Bresee, the term "Nazarene" was drawn from the pages of the New Testament. In the Gospel of Matthew, Jesus is called a "Nazarene." "Nazarene" is understood as being derived from the city called Nazareth. Jesus is called Nazarene because he is from Nazareth. His identity is partly formed from his hometown. This sets up what has been termed "the scandal of particularity"; Jesus is a particular person from a particular family in a particular village in a particular time in a particular part of the world.[32]

The selection of the term "Nazarene" by Widney and its acceptance by Bresee is the first clue toward a definition.[33] The Church of the Nazarene derives its name from an historical figure, not simply an impersonal "what."[34] It was a common phenomenon in the nineteenth century to identify with the so-called "historical Jesus" of the Gospels.[35] The most prominent writings of the period depicted Jesus as going about doing good while teaching (in the language of the time) "the Fatherhood of God and the brotherhood of man." Jesus was a revelation of God sent forth to redeem the world (John 3:16). This suggests that the approach to what is distinctively Nazarene should be couched in terms of a personal pronoun rather than the abstract "what." The question becomes: "Who is a Nazarene?" and not "What is a Nazarene?" This frame of thinking "fits" or is at least compatible with the personalistic emphases of the twentieth century, without necessarily becoming philosophical personalism[36] or philosophical existentialism.[37] Who is a Nazarene can be answered on one level as anyone who has faith in the Lord Jesus Christ. Is this definition enough?

According to the current *Manual* of the Church of the Nazarene, this church is composed of those persons who have voluntarily associated themselves together according to the doctrines and polity of said church, and who seek holy Christian fellowship, the conversion of sinners, the entire sanctification of believers, their upbuilding in holiness, and the simplicity and spiritual power manifest in the primitive New Testament Church, together with the preaching of the gospel to every creature. (Par. 25)

By extension, one could say that the definition of the church is also an implicit answer to the question of "Who is a Nazarene?" According to the above, a Nazarene is one who has voluntarily associated with others of like-mind and heart, who seeks to fulfill the various descriptors that accompany the main verbs in the paragraph. In effect, this entire paragraph constitutes a claim as to the identity of a Nazarene. Insofar as these descriptors are embodied, they constitute *what it means to be "Nazarene."* An ontological claim is made, a reality is affirmed. And yet, this is still the "what." It would seem that the paper is right back where it started, caught in the vise of the intractable "what" approach. One may yearn for more. Suggestive is that portion of the line in the *Manual* that reads: "those persons who have voluntarily associated themselves together . . ." This echoes the 1895 flyer: ". . . a banding together of hearts that have found the peace of God." Certain implications would seem to follow:

1. Being Nazarene is not imposed from without but flows from a personal decision made within,

2. Being Nazarene is coming together with certain purposes in mind,

3. Being Nazarene is choosing to embody the descriptors, and

4. Being Nazarene is pursuing the purposes or descriptors completing the paragraph. In all four instances *being* precedes *doing*. Who the person is precedes *what* the person does or attempts to do.

In brief, as the first Nazarene *Manual* (1895) states, a Nazarene is one who loves "the Lord our God with all the heart, soul, mind and strength, and our neighbor as ourselves—Matt.22:37-39" (qtd. in Bangs 217-218). This is both *fides qua creditur* (faith by which one believes) and *fides quae creditur* (faith that is believed) in that order. Faith is first existential and personal trust in the Savior Jesus Christ and then belief that what God has promised he will do with regard to all sin. Can it be?

Long my imprisoned spirit lay,
Fast bound in sin and nature's night;
Thine eye diffused a quickening ray;
I woke, the dungeon flamed with light;
My chains fell off, my heart was free,
I rose, went forth, and followed thee.
                    (Wesley 225-26)

Who makes a Nazarene college "Nazarene"? Nazarenes make a Nazarene college "Nazarene"! Who is a Nazarene? Nazarenes are those who are faithful in devotion to *the Nazarene*, Jesus of Nazareth. Nazarenes are those who love the Lord with heart, soul, mind and strength and one's neighbor as one's self. Nazarenes are those in harmony with the *Manual* paragraph 25. Who are "those," in the preceding sentences? They are the supporters of Nazarene higher education. Their names are responsible educator, dutiful administrator, supportive staff worker, dedicated trustee, inquisitive student, sacrificial pastor, caring associate, energetic youth leader, faithful evangelist, able district superintendent, wise general superintendent, concerned alumnus, devoted missionary, loyal layperson, generous donor, and, yes, to a degree, even the young child who already has it in one's heart to attend a Nazarene college.

What you have as heritage,
Take now as task;
For thus you will make it your own
                    —Goethe

NOTES

1. The English term "Nazarene" normally functions as a noun. Dictionaries list the term as also being an adjective (but historically rare) with the earliest adjectival form appearing around 1275 C.E. See *The Compact Edition of the Oxford English Dictionary* (Oxford UP, 1971): s.v. Some language-conscious Nazarenes prefer that the term appear only in the noun form, as in the denomination's official name. In the present essay the term will be used as a noun and as an adjective, following recent practice.

2. See the relationship between the Church of the Nazarene and the Nazarene college as stated in the current *Manual* 156-57. "The church col-

lege/university, while not a local congregation, is an integral part of the church; it is an expression of the church" (156).

3. Paul Ricoeur, David Tracy and others, have made "the hermeneutic of suspicion" claim popular. See David Tracy, *Blessed Rage for Order: The New Pluralism in Theology* (NY: Seabury, 1975).

4. The present essay emerges from my own college-related experiences and association with other Nazarenes on the Southwest Educational Region. Christian higher education in the Wesleyan-Holiness tradition as found in the Church of the Nazarene deserves corporate participation and cooperative thinking.

5. The Wesleyan theological tradition is identified with the life and work of John and Charles Wesley, especially the former. Regarding John Wesley, see esp. Henry D. Rack, *Reasonable Enthusiast: John Wesley and the Rise of Methodism*, 2nd ed. (Nashville: Abingdon, 1992). The Holiness Movement "consists of those who hold and proclaim what they believe to be a Wesleyan doctrine of entire sanctification," as noted by Paul Bassett in "The Theological Identity of the North American Holiness Movement: Its Understanding of the Nature and Role of the Bible," in *The Variety of American Evangelicalism*, eds. Donald W. Dayton and Robert K. Johnston (Downers Grove, InterVarsity, 1991) 73.

6. See Richard Robinson, *Plato's Earlier Dialectic* 2nd ed. (NY: Oxford UP, 1964), especially chapter 5. Robinson notes that Socrates makes four assumptions with the "what-is-X" question: (1) The word X has one meaning, so it is univocal, (2) The thing sought after has an essence, (3) Some realist assumption of the essence's reality must be made, and (4) The indicated "essence" has a structure that can be understood (58).

7. By substantial is meant the western attempt to define by naming what is foundational as "a substance." As Aristotle could put it: "There are several senses in which a thing may be said to 'be' . . . for in one sense the 'being' meant is 'what a thing is'. . . . And in another sense it means a quality or quantity. . . . While 'being' has all these senses, obviously that which 'is' primarily is the 'what', which indicates the substance of the thing." Aristotle, *Metaphysics*, 1028a10-15.

8. Locke wrote: "we know not what [substance] it is," in *An Essay Concerning Human Understanding*, ed. by Peter H. Nidditch (Oxford: Clarendon, 1975) 297.

9. R. Collingwood, *The Idea of History* (Oxford: Clarendon Press, 1946). While nominalism undermined substance through the British empiricists, nominalism made possible in part the emergence of modern history with its attention on the particularity and uniqueness of historical events.

10. The statement recognizes that some metaphysical interest remains even into the twentieth century, the process philosophy of Alfred North Whitehead being a case in point. However even Whitehead notes the difficulty of resurrecting substance so he uses "actual entity" as an alternative. In the words of Ivor Leclerc: "Whitehead has coined . . . [actual entity] because the traditional term 'substance' . . . is so extremely unsatisfactory and misleading." See Leclerc's *Whitehead's Metaphysics: An Introductory Exposition* (NY: Macmillan, 1958) 22. Whitehead writes: "I refrain from the term 'substance'. . . ." *Process and Reality: An Essay in Cosmology,* eds. David Ray Griffin and Donald Sherburne (NY: Free Press, 1978), 75.

11. Technically, creeds are less detailed than confessions since the latter serve a particular denomination. In the Church of the Nazarene reference is made to the "Articles of Faith" (as given in the *Manual: Church of the Nazarene*) since the church is not one of the traditional so-called confessional bodies.

12. Historically, doctrines have played an essential role for defining the distinctiveness of a denomination. Doctrines, as McGrath points out, have served well in four respects: they give identity by distinguishing between different church groups, they clarify and explain the Christian faith, they articulate the nature of piety, and they provide a group with truth claims. More recently, doctrine has been increasingly played down with the rise of the therapeutic church paradigm.

13. Soteriology is literally the work of the Savior. Attention is given to those doctrines that describe the human condition, the means for alleviating that condition through Jesus Christ and redemption.

14. See, Samuel L. Dunn and Joseph Nielson, "The Theology and Practice of Wesleyan Higher Education," *Faculty Dialogue* 7 (Fall-Winter 1986-87) 71-82.

15. Fichte's actual statement is: "What sort of philosophy one chooses depends, therefore, on what sort of man one is; for a philosophical system is not a dead piece of furniture that we can reject or accept as we wish; it is rather a thing animated by the soul of the person who holds it." Johann G. Fichte, *Science of Knowledge,* trans. Peter Heath and John Lachs (Cambridge, England: Cambridge UP, 1982), 16.

16. Historically. theologians speak of two understandings of faith. There is *fides qua creditur* (faith by which one believes) and *fides quae creditur* (faith that is believed). An acceptable view of faith encompasses both. The problem is that a given era or individual Christian tends to prefer one more than the other. Wesley exhibited both, often giving prominence to *fides qua creditur* (which fits his soteriological emphasis) while many of his peers preferred *fides quae creditur* (which supported creation themes).

17. An example would be classical Fundamentalism, where a few select doctrines are isolated and theological orthodoxy (a person's Christianity) could even be judged on how one stood on a solitary doctrine.

18. World view (*Weltanschauung*) has a distinguished historical background in European thought with Wilhelm Dilthey, Edmund Husserl and others. More recently the term has been adapted by Reformed (i.e., Calvinistic) followers under the influence of the Dutch philosophers, Abraham Kuyper and Herman Dooyeweerd. Two kinds of world view are found in the thought of Dooyeweerd: "that which stems from an obedient faith in the God of creation and grace, and those which stem from apostate 'ground-motives'," so states Arthur Holmes (32). In a Reformed setting, world view focuses on the mind, on philosophical and doctrinal issues as paramount, on epistemology as a pivotal concern. The journal *Faculty Dialogue* has carried a number of articles on world view, among others see esp. Brian J. Walsh, "Worldview, Modernity and the Task of Christian Education," 18 (Fall 1992) 13-31; also Carl F.H. Henry, "The Christian Worldview Imperative," 11 (Spring 1989) 23-32 and Dietrich G. Buss, "Educating Toward a Christian World View: Some Historical Perspectives and Prescriptions," 21 (Spring-Summer 1994) 63-90. As these references show, world view as a term may be treated as one word or two, depending upon individual preference or is it more than preference? That in itself is worth a study on its own.

19. Randy Maddox uses the suggestive language of "orienting concern" with respect to John Wesley's thought, in *Responsible Grace: John Wesley's Practical Theology* (Nashville: Kingwood, 1994) 18.

20. The anthropologist Clifford Geertz distinguishes between ethos and world view in his essay entitled "Ethos, World View, and the Analysis of Sacred Symbols." For Geertz, ethos and world view represent two aspects of religion, with the former depicting the normative or evaluative side and the latter the cognitive or actual state of affairs.

21. John N. Wall quotes Robert Runcie as saying: "Anglican unity has most characteristically been expressed in worship, which includes four essential elements: Scripture proclaimed, creed confessed, sacraments celebrated, and order maintained through an authorized episcopal ministry" (269).

22. The paragraph is suggesting a line of thought to be developed and tested under a different format. Albert Outler's observations on Wesley's as being "eclectic" thinking are worth keeping in mind (44). Outler calls Wesley a "synthesizer of a rich, multifaceted tradition" (58) but goes on to wonder if Wesley's theology is a "doctrinal hodgepodge or actually a higher synthesis" (68) and finally sees Wesley as creating a third way beyond a Protestant *theologia crucis* and a Roman Catholic *theologia gloriae*. The term "conjunctive" as used above is to point out Wesley's ability to deal with East and West, with idealism and empiricism, with piety and learning, with

life and thought. In each case, the poles are not collapsed but maintained!

23. The Reformed use of "world view" is a case in point. People with Reformed credentials use the term frequently, especially in Christian higher education circles. Reformed people are informed by Reformed theology. To assume that one's theology does not impact one's vocabulary is to overlook the implications and assumptions accompanying such discourse. Other terms also come into play with a Reformed world view, including "integration," "foundations," "creation" and the like.

24. The proposed Student Commons Building on the Point Loma campus is a case in point. The layout and design of the building are deliberate attempts to provide an ethos compatible with institutional philosophy and values.

25. "Creation" is used here as an unifying term, drawing together comments on Reformed thought. Reformed thought is singled out for comparative purposes due to the systematic thought given to Christian higher education by Reformed writers. The life of the mind is one of the distinguishing aspects of the Reformed tradition, leading to considerable attention being placed on the intellect. For an outline of Reformed distinctives, see John Leith, *An Introduction to the Reformed Tradition: A Way of Being the Christian Community* (Atlanta: John Knox, 1977).

26. To begin with creation is a reason why some Reformed Evangelicals find it necessary to be definitive on evolution, on whether the earth was created in seven 24-hour days or not, and related matters. In Wesleyan thinking, the focus is on deliverance from sin, with matters of natural science looked at only thereafter. Thus, Wesleyans may genuinely disagree on issues involving natural science without calling into question the integrity of their faith in Christ.

27. At the risk of being unfair to Arthur Holmes, consider his choice of "the biblical and theological mandate for Christian involvement in higher education in general, as well as for the Christian liberal arts college in particular" (*Idea* 13). "Theological Foundations," Chapter 2 covers four concepts: creation, the human person, truth and the cultural mandate. Holmes is to be commended for being consistent with the Reformed heritage in which he stands.

28. An example of this difference is seen in conversation between John Wesley and Joseph Butler. Butler, as a Church of England bishop, urged Wesley to cease his activities. Butler, author of the classic *Analogy of Religion*, was put off by Wesley's views on justification by faith and assurance. See Albert C. Outler, ed., *John Wesley* (NY: Oxford UP, 1964) 348-49.

29. Compare the comments of the Reformed theologians in "Scandal: A Forum on the Evangelical Mind," in *Christianity Today* 39 (August 1995)

20ff with a Wesleyan on the same topic, Donald A.D. Thorsen "The Future of Biblical Studies in the Wesleyan Tradition: A Theological Perspective," *Wesleyan Theological Journal* 30:2 (Fall 1995) 182-202. For a discussion of a Wesleyan starting point, see H. Ray Dunning, *Grace, Faith and Holiness: A Wesleyan Systematic Theology* (Kansas City: Beacon Hill, 1988) esp. Chapter 2 on "Revelation: A Wesleyan Approach."

30. In the earliest editions of the Nazarene *Manual*, the four-fold order of contents covered History, Doctrine, Government and Ritual. Since the 1930s, the order is History, Constitution, Government and Ritual.

31. The historical background is covered in Timothy Smith esp. Chapter 5 on "Phineas Bresee and the Church of the Nazarene."

32. See Reuel L. Howe, *Man's Need and God's Action* (Greenwich, Conn: Seabury, 1953) for an application of the "particularity" theme as it bears on God's dealing with humans as persons.

33. Bangs mentions that for Widney, the name Church of the Nazarene "conveyed nothing explicit about Methodist doctrine or the experiences of conversion and entire sanctification. It was much more an expression of late-nineteenth century Jesus-of-history theology . . ." (197). Bresee, on the other hand, is depicted by Bangs as being more interested in "fashioning a *church* with a theology" [emphasis is Bangs] with a thoroughly Trinitarian position and clarity on sanctification. Within three years, Widney withdrew from the church. See Bangs 197, 212-13.

34. It bears noting that the classic attempt by the Christian Church to define Jesus Christ is framed in terms of substance ("what"). The Definition of Chalcedon (451 CE) states that Jesus Christ has two natures—one human and one divine. Before that is stated, however, a paragraph notes that Jesus is "actually God and actually man, with a rational soul and a body . . . thus like us in all respects, only sin excepted . . . being born of Mary the virgin . . . ." See Leith 35-36.

35. Albert Schweitzer's classic, *The Quest for the Historical Jesus* (1906) details the nineteenth century quest. The rise of historical consciousness impacted traditional Christian claims. The two-natures of Christ was criticized, "substance" was judged suspect. The significant critic Friedrich Schleiermacher writes: "the expression 'nature' is used indifferently for the divine and the human," in *The Christian Faith*, vol 2 eds. H. R. Mackintosh and J. S. Stewart (New York: Harper Torchbooks, 1963): 392. German theologians led the critical parade, due in no small part to German philosophy (especially Immanuel Kant) and the rise of the modern research university as the model for higher education. Numerous lives of Jesus were produced, in some instances for the purpose of emulating the practices of Jesus of Nazareth. It was out of this historical environment with its focus on the Gospels that appeared the influential book of Charles

Sheldon, *In His Steps*, with the question constantly posed for the reader in terms of "What would Jesus do [in this or that situation]?"

36. Bostonian Personalism was an influential philosophy in some Nazarene circles through the 1960s. Two Methodist related institutions, Boston University and the University of Southern California, attracted graduate students who wanted to be theists and philosophically "current." Personalism provided a metaphysic for religion in a time when metaphysics was suspect.

37. Reacting against German Idealism, Soren Kierkegaard (d. 1855) stressed "existence" rather than "essence" for understanding the uniqueness of an individual human being. Jean Paul Sartre later defined existentialism succinctly by stating that "*existence* comes before *essence*" [emphasis Sartre]. See Sartre's "Existentialism is a Humanism," in *Existentialism: From Dostoevsky to Sartre*, ed. Walter Kaufmann (Cleveland: The World Publishing Company, 1956), 289 and Kierkegaard's *Concluding Unscientific Postscript*, trans. David F. Swenson (Princeton: Princeton UP, 1941). The essence/existence issue is related to the what/that relation in the present essay.

CHAPTER FOUR

THE COLLEGE-CHURCH PARTNERSHIP: PAST

Stephen W. Nease

Throughout the years the Church of the Nazarene has consistently maintained a strong commitment to educate its young people in the atmosphere of a holiness college campus. A liberal arts program in Church-sponsored institutions with high academic standards will best serve the Church and strengthen both its laity and its ministry.

In 1915 Dr. Phineas F. Bresee, who participated in the founding of the denomination and was its first general superintendent, stated in his last public address, given in the chapel of the Nazarene University at Pasadena, California:

> The very first thing for this institution and for all our institutions is to see that our students are led into the holy of holies and filled with all the fullness of God. . . . It is not our job to turn out worldly men. . . . There are a thousand institutions in the United States that are engaged in that business; it is our business to turn out men and women of God. . . . The Word of God is taught all through this institution. . . . The very atmosphere of our halls and our lecture rooms is to be pregnant with the divine glory and heavenly presence (qtd. in Snowbarger 4).

Clearly, speaking for the baby denomination, Bresee claimed the University—later to become Point Loma Nazarene College—as "ours," thus identifying a partnership that has endured until this day for PLNC, and for all other Nazarene institutions of higher education. Indeed, the International Board of Education selected the theme, "The Church At Work In Higher Education," for the last General Assembly of the Church.

In the world of higher education much discussion has focused on the partnership between educational institutions which have been established or supported by particular religious bodies and their denominations. The very nature of such "partnership" has been subject to a variety of interpretations. Myron Wicke, in his book, *The Church-Related College*, allows the institution itself to define such a partnership:

> What is a church-related college? For the purpose of this study a church-related college is one which lists itself as such in one or more of three major directories (which he lists) or which in American Universities and Colleges indicates election or nomination of trustees by church bodies. (11)

The 1965 Danforth study *Eight Hundred Colleges Face the Future* states: " . . . there is no single model or definition of a Christian college that is appropriate for all such institutions." The Danforth study suggests three models: the "defender of the faith college," the "non-affirming college," and the "free Christian (or Jewish) college." The Danforth Commission report concludes with the observation "we believe that many more church institutions should aspire to the third model or something like it. . . . [W]e believe that this is the key to the future of church-related higher education in the United States. . . ."

While in some measure each of the first two models defines itself, the Commission writes of the "free Christian college:"

> The "free Christian (or Jewish) college" combines the chief assets of the other two models while it tries to avoid their liabilities. It stands unapologetically for religion and liberal education, but it relies on example, persuasive presentation of ideas, and a climate of conviction, rather than on conformity, to accomplish its ends. (69-70)

The Nature of the Nazarene Partnership

While the partnership of the Church of the Nazarene with its colleges is often expressed as our colleges being "defender of the faith" institutions, and while many in church leadership and elsewhere may view them in this relationship, this writer believes that administrators and faculty members, while deeply committed to the mission of their institutions, and to the theological stance of their sponsoring denomination, more often view their responsibility to their students as "persuasion seeking conviction" rather than an authoritarian effort to hand down "truth" and thereby demand conformity.

Rightly understood, academic freedom is enjoyed by those who teach and learn on Nazarene college campuses. Dr. Willis Snowbarger, an exemplary Nazarene educator, who served as Academic Vice-President of Olivet Nazarene College (now University) for many years, speaks of "academic freedom" for the Nazarene professor:

> In harmony with the terms of their hiring, academic freedom is as real, and is functioning in Nazarene colleges as well as in public universities. . . . Nazarene colleges are real institutions of higher learning, not just agents of indoctrination. That would be short-sighted as a course to follow no matter how tempting to those who think about immediate results only.

While some students, given such freedom of inquiry and final choice, may question or reject their teachers or their church, the experience of the Church of the Nazarene has demonstrated that this method educates a corps of solid laypersons and clergy to carry on the traditions and spirit most meaningful to the Church.

Undoubtedly, potential problems exist in such a partnership. A recent conversation with a loyal churchman who has served as an administrator and faculty member at a Nazarene college for more that a quarter of a century serves as an example. The following excerpts from his letter seem pertinent:

> I myself was not a member of the Church of the Nazarene, nor a believer in holiness when I entered a Nazarene college as a student. One year later I gave my life to Jesus Christ and have sought to follow Him since that time.
>
> In discussions with other faculty members and church members, there is an awareness of an erosion of the influence of the Church of the Nazarene on the everyday lives of current Nazarene college students. I acknowledge that our society as a whole is becoming more secular, and I also understand that commitment to any denomination, political party, or organized institution is not as strong as in the recent past. This does not, however, lessen the importance of maintaining a strong faith, trust, and link between Nazarene institutions of higher education and the supporting denomination. This is a symbiotic relationship; the colleges/universities train and prepare future church leaders and laymen, and the churches encourage their young people to attend the denominational colleges/universities to receive their education in a Christian holiness environment.

It is noteworthy that this writer's experience at a Nazarene college was instrumental in his spiritual growth, and persuaded him to embrace the Church's doctrinal stance. Indeed, he has so much become a part of the Church that he has invested his life in service at a Nazarene college and now expresses concern that a strong partnership continue between the Church of the Nazarene and the institutions she sponsors.

Such seems to be an end result of the "Free Christian College" in the partnership between the Church of the Nazarene and her educational institutions.

Methodology of this Study

In preparation for this study, a letter was sent to forty- five persons who over the years have made significant contributions to Nazarene higher education. Twenty-six responses were received, with representation from each member institution of the U.S./Canada/Great Britain Council of Education as listed in the 1993-1997 Church *Manual.*

Questions posed in the letter were as follows:

1. From the perspective of the college(s) where you have served, what events during both the formative days and the present days of the institution contributed to strong Nazarene connections?

2. The ties of our Nazarene colleges to the Church of the Nazarene both legally and in spirit are important. What legal documents bind the college to the Church of the Nazarene and what narrative of events, or occurrences, drew the college and the Church closer? This may mean that the story of a negative event should be told, counterbalanced by a positive "antidote" to something that threatened to drive a wedge between the college and the Church.

3. Can you supply me with copies of speeches, historical narrative, or any other materials that would underscore the traditional ties between our colleges and the Church?

4. What other research is important to the topic?

5. If you care to, please write a statement—or a letter—reflecting your personal thinking on this matter for possible inclusion in the final essay.

Although some responses were subjective and personal, the scope of the responses and the involvement of the responders in Nazarene higher education yields some indication of the strength of the partnership that has existed between the Church and higher education over the years. Unless otherwise indicated, quotations which follow are gleaned from these responses. All responses have been deposited in the archives of the Church of the Nazarene in Kansas City for future reference.

In exploring the strength and meaning of the partnership between the Church of the Nazarene and its institutions of higher education a number of concerns will be addressed.

The College-Church Partnership: Past

I. **Do the mission statements, bylaws, or other public documents of Nazarene institutions clearly indicate the existence of such partnership?**

Each current catalog of member institutions of the U.S./Canada/Great Britain Council of Education carries a "mission statement" or "statement of purpose," giving in succinct language the identity and purpose of the college or university. A check of catalogs indicates that affiliation with and service to the Church of the Nazarene is in clear and unequivocal language. Two examples of such statements follow:

> **Point Loma Nazarene College** - Point Loma Nazarene College provides higher education in the liberal arts and preparation for service and leadership in selected professions for students who desire such an education in an environment of vital Christianity in the evangelical and Wesleyan tradition....
>
> The relationship of the College and the Church of the Nazarene is characterized by a mutual commitment to the doctrine and mission. In this relationship the College provides quality leaders for Christian service within social, civic, business, and church communities.
>
> **Eastern Nazarene College** - The mission of Eastern Nazarene College is to provide the resources for a liberal arts education and life-long learning in an environment which awakens and fosters truth, righteousness, justice, and holiness as they reflect the life which has been transformed by God's grace through Jesus Christ. We seek to serve the Church of the Nazarene in particular and the Church in general by equipping people for Christian leadership and service to humankind. As a Christian community, we strive to embody academic excellence, personal integrity, and respect for each individual. The entire education program encourages each person to become a creative and redemptive force in the world though integration of the richness of the Christian tradition and the human quest for understanding.

Since these statements from PLNC and ENC—Nazarene institutions on opposite coasts of the United States—seem typical of all Nazarene college mission statements, it seems wise to ask how such statements—developed by members of the faculty and administration—align with the bylaws that originally were developed by each board of trustees, composed of persons nominated to such positions by the Church itself.

> **Point Loma Nazarene College** - Section 1. Trustees: Number and Qualifications: The Board of Trustees shall consist of not more than fifty members, all of whom shall be members in good standing of the Church of the Nazarene and in the experience of entire sanctification.... All nominated trustees shall be elected from nominations made by the

Alumni Association and the various districts of the Church of the Nazarene as the electing body shall determine.

Eastern Nazarene College - Article III. Ownership: This corporation is and shall continue to be a college of the Church of the Nazarene. Article IV. Object: The object of this Corporation shall be to encourage, promote, maintain, and support Christian education through instruction in such fields as classical and modern languages, literature, music, speech, philosophy, theology, biblical literature, biology, chemistry, physics, mathematics, education, history, government, economics, psychology, sociology, and any other fields of education which from time to time it may elect to teach and which are properly taught in a college, university, seminary—all of which shall be in harmony with the doctrines of the Church of the Nazarene as stated in the *Manual* of said Church and issued by its General Assembly in the year 1915 or amendments thereof or additions thereto as authorized by subsequent General Assemblies of said Church.

It thus would appear that both the stated mission of the colleges—PLNC: "The relationship of the College and the Church of the Nazarene is characterized by a mutual commitment to the doctrine and mission . . ." and ENC: "We seek to serve the Church of the Nazarene in particular . . ."—align well with the bylaws adopted by the trustees which in both cases affirm strong ties with the parent denomination.

II. **Has the Church given significant support to its educational institutions?**

While financial support alone may not fully describe the spirit in which support is given, response to the budgetary system of the Church indicates a positive overall support of our educational institutions. While the "educational budget" is assigned to each church on the district level, in conformance to guidelines established by the General Assembly, it is possible for a church congregation or pastor to underpay or even fail to pay the "educational budget." In this sense the budgetary support of the Nazarene college is voluntary. Strong budgetary support would seem to indicate strong support in spirit as well.

Dr. Edward S. Mann, President of Eastern Nazarene College for twenty-one years and later Secretary for the Department of Education for the denomination, said in a 1973 address "The Church and the College as Partners":

In undertaking the support of twelve educational institutions, the Church of the Nazarene has assumed a staggering load for such a small denomination. The delegates at the 1964 General Assembly, of course, had no way of knowing that the establishment of three new Nazarene colleges would coincide with a downswing in the national economy and that these fledgling institutions would be experiencing the travail of birth at a time when other colleges were in their death throes. Neither did they know that the period to follow would be characterized by widespread restlessness on college and university campuses which would also make its appearance at Nazarene colleges. Yet despite reports of campus turmoil, frequently overstated, despite changes in dress style and life style which have affected college students along with other young people in general, and despite garbled rumors of campus activities which have been recklessly (and sometimes maliciously) bandied about by thoughtless people, Nazarenes have increased their giving to higher education each year from a total of $2,000,000 in 1967 to more than $4,000,000 in 1972! Nearly $13,000,000 was invested in Nazarene higher education during the last quadrennium.

Statistics for the decade 1985-1994, released by the International Board of Education list total financial giving to the U.S./Canada/Great Britain Nazarene Institutions totaling $153,881,332.

Dr. Willis Snowbarger, who also served as Secretary for the Department of Education for the denomination, sums up Church financial support as follows:

> Financial support from the denomination has been remarkable since 1950; ... sporadic before that time. I think only Missouri Synod Lutherans may have given more on a per student basis. The idea of a living endowment has been accepted by accrediting bodies. Additional campaigns for buildings, debt reduction, and scholarships have been well received time and again. With rising costs, government financial aid, aid for buildings from government or foundations, the total budget for the college has grown so much faster, that church contributions, generous though they are, are only about twelve percent of the total and the churches don't realize it.

Dr. B. Edgar Johnson, longtime General Church Secretary states:

> My belief is strong that we are doing a pretty good job with the College-Church partnership. There is no denomination of which I am aware that matches, on a per capita basis, the financial support for higher education that is found in the Nazarene system.

Nazarene colleges are dependent on their sponsoring church to supply adequate support to enable them to keep costs to their students relatively low in comparison to like institutions. While invested endowment funds are in their infancy, the stability of church support has led accrediting agencies to accept the regular denominational support as a "living endowment." Over the years the "living endowment" has enabled Nazarene colleges to operate without incurring significant deficits.

III. **How do elected members of the board of trustees and faculty and administrative personnel impact this partnership?**

The Constitution of Canadian Nazarene College contains language regarding the election of members of the Board of Trustees, that is typical of all Nazarene institutions surveyed.

> The Membership of this Corporation shall be the supporting members of the Church of the Nazarene within the Canadian Nazarene College educational region as set forth by the *Manual* of the Church of the Nazarene.

Nazarene colleges surveyed accept the names of persons nominated by Nazarene districts of their region, and allow the board of trustees itself to elect such persons to membership. While this would seem to conform to the requirement by accrediting agencies that such boards be "self-perpetuating," experience has proven that Nazarene college boards nearly always vote such nominees into membership. This writer is not aware of any deviation from this norm.

One who responded to our survey states:

> The other important foundation for College-Church relationships and stability is the Board itself. As far as I recall there is nothing in college bylaws to keep any college from going its own direction, except the strength and loyalty of the Board itself. It appears to me that the college foundation board must be careful to watch its membership so that disloyalty does not creep in.
> - Dr. L. Guy Nees, former president of Mount Vernon Nazarene College

The fact that no Nazarene college has ever seriously given consideration to severing its denominational affiliation would seem to indicate that Nazarene college governing boards have demonstrated exceptional stability and loyalty to the sponsoring denomination.

IV. **Do the numbers and percentage of students enrolled from the Church demonstrate such a partnership?**

Nazarene colleges clearly state that enrollment is open to all academically qualified persons who find themselves in harmony with the principles of the school attended. A typical statement reads:

> Olivet Nazarene University policy prohibits discrimination on the basis of race, sex, religion, age, color, creed, national origin or ethnic origin, marital status, or disability in the recruitment or admission of students and in

the operation of all college programs, activities, and services (1995-1996 *Catalog*).

While recent statistics indicate that young people from other church backgrounds are taking advantage of the excellent, relatively low cost, educational opportunities in Nazarene colleges, statistics released by the Institutional Board of Education indicate that in 1993, 6,367 or 62% of a total undergraduate enrollment of 10,318 indicated a "Nazarene preference." Since the data does not isolate the various new programs such as "degree completion programs" which attract large numbers of non-church members, the percentage of Nazarene students enrolled in traditional academic programs is probably considerably higher.

V. **Have Nazarene Colleges Provided an Educated, Informed and Spiritual Clergy and Laity to the Church?**

In the opinion of this writer the answer to this question is an unqualified *yes*! However, since no definitive study of the numbers and influence of clergy and laity in the Church who have attended a Nazarene institution is known to us, personal observation must suffice.

Dr. E. S. Mann states in his 1973 address, "The Church and The College as Partners,"

> ... It is most significant that at this early stage in our denominational history, eighty-two percent of today's church leaders—general and district superintendents, seminary and college presidents, executives and general board members—are alumni of Nazarene institutions of higher education. It is equally impressive to know that seventy percent of our missionaries on the field are also alumni of our own institutions.

No one who has been present in a General Assembly education service where those who attended a Nazarene college are asked to stand can fail to be impressed with the great numbers who are in attendance during the quadrennial legislative sessions of the Church.

Recently when a layman objected to the need of supporting his Nazarene college financially, the responding general superintendent reminded him that in the ordination service that evening every pastor and wife ordained to the Nazarene ministry had attended a Nazarene college.

Perhaps a doctoral candidate should be encouraged to quantify these indisputably subjective impressions through a research project.

VI. **What is the "Indefinable but Real" Partnership in Spirit?**

General Superintendent Emeritus Dr. Eugene L. Stowe tells of a conversation with the late General Superintendent Dr. Samuel Young. Dr. Young stated that all of the constitutional and bylaw protections would not keep the institution closely tied to the church if the president were not dedicated to this basic purpose.

In essence, Young is saying that the strongest link in the partnership between the Church and its colleges is not legally imposed, rather it is a spirit of commitment of the leadership of the school to the ideals of the denomination. This writer, who served in a leadership role in four of our colleges and then as Education Commissioner for the Church, observes from a first-hand acquaintance with all Nazarene college presidents for two decades that this commitment has never been greater or more meaningful.

In his response to the questionnaire Dr. Mark Moore, former president of Trevecca Nazarene College who later served as Secretary of the Department of Education, noted:

> Since our colleges/universities are autonomous, the strongest ties are not legal. This bond exists when both are dedicated to the same mission. . . . Mission binds us together more than the law. . . .

Perhaps in quoting others the reader will allow me to quote from a 1986 report I gave as president of Eastern Nazarene College to the Board of Trustees. I wrote, with help from Dr. John M. Nielson,

At ENC the Spirit Makes the Difference . . .

There are lots of other colleges around. Many of them are closer to home, a few of them are less expensive, some of them are more famous. So why is ENC so important to you?

ENC is important to you because of . . . *its Mission*.

ENC is not a trade school. It is not primarily a research institution. It is not coming from a secular orientation. It does not leave the teaching to graduate assistants. . . .

ENC is important to you because of . . . *its Ownership*.

ENC is sponsored by the Church of the Nazarene and is loyal to its doctrine and practices. That makes ENC your college. You pay for the campus. You subsidize the education of her students. You pay the salaries of her faculty. You elect her Board of Trustees who choose her leaders and set her policies. Many of you are her alumni or are parents of her students. ENC really is your school.

ENC is important to you because of . . . *its Ministry*.

ENC alumni are serving God, the Church, and the World all over the Earth as ministers, missionaries, teachers, doctors, social workers, public officials and more. That's because ENC seeks to do more than provide training to make a living. It always endeavors to challenge young people to lives of commitment and service—to find the Master Design for their lives. Most Nazarene pastors and missionaries are alumni of Nazarene colleges. . . .

ENC is important to you because of . . . *its Environment.*

ENC provides a value-oriented and redemptive environment that challenges every student to develop to his or her full potential in Christ. Standards of conduct, chapel services, revivals, Bible studies, counselors—all are directed toward this same purpose.

At ENC the Spirit Makes the Difference . . . And the Difference is Worth It!

It is true for all of our colleges—the Spirit *does* make the difference.

VII. What conclusions and guidance can the church and the college draw from this "study" to support their increased mutuality and strength?

Five years ago, Arthur J. DeJong, President of Whitworth College, wrote the book, *Reclaiming a Mission, New Directions for the Church-Related College.* He states,

> . . . after World War II the church-related liberal arts colleges lost their uniqueness, their *raison d'etre* and began to model themselves after the large universities. To begin with, the secular winds blowing in these universities began to blow in the church-related colleges as well. Second, the structure of the universities, based upon a distinct separation of the academic disciplines and specialization in those disciplines, was adopted by the church-related colleges. Instead of attempting to influence the total lives of their students as they had in the past, the church-related colleges adopted from the universities the concept of a "value-free" approach to the educational process; as a result, the impact of the church-related colleges on the moral and spiritual dimension of the students was greatly diminished. During these years many of the colleges and their denominations parted company, or at least grew far apart . . . (Introd. x).

Thankfully, the partnership between the Church of the Nazarene and the institutions sponsored by the Church remains strong. May it ever continue so! Several suggestions are in order for this to be so:

For the sponsoring denomination—

Understand your Nazarene college as "The Church at Work in Higher Education"—as vital to our denominational mission as every other endeavor of the Church.

Continue strong support of your Nazarene college in spirit and in finance. It has been rightly said of church-related colleges, "Where your support comes from, therein lies control." In a day of concern about our church budgetary system, payment of the educational budget should be on the same priority level as any other budget, for example, the General Budget for World Missions. After all, where do our missionaries and pastors receive their education and preparation for service—and indeed, often settle God's call?

Carefully select persons to be nominated by the District Assembly as members of the Nazarene college board of trustees. Traditionally—and rightly—the Church has not nominated such persons solely on the basis of financial resources and potential for giving to the college. Let character, academic background and commitment to the mission of Nazarene higher education be given priority consideration. Persons nominated primarily because of popularity seldom make good trustees!

Encourage and support the brightest Church young people as they prepare for an educational ministry in the church.

There was a time when nearly every young person in a local Nazarene congregation readily assumed that she/he would attend their regional Nazarene college. The Church, in cooperation with pastors, Nazarene Youth International, and the college must work to make this so again.

For the Nazarene College—

Review the "mission statement" of the college. Be sure that in addition to more general statements (such as "in the Wesleyan-Arminian tradition")—that may well express the basic commitments of the institution—warm and persuasive reference is included regarding the church connection of the institution. It is noteworthy that early in his administrative days at Eastern Nazarene College, Dr. Cecil Paul, in whose honor this *Festschrift* is offered, instituted a thorough review and rewriting of statements regarding the mission of the College.

Maintain close contact with "grassroots" Nazarenes in every possible way. Visits to local congregations by college ensembles, students, faculty members and other representatives are vital. It is probably a mistake for our colleges to add an additional percentage to the annual educational budget for capital building projects. Send college personnel to present the college and its needs in a personal way. Let it be the college goal, regardless of extra time and effort involved, to have some *personal* representatives of the college in *every* church on the college educational region each year if possible —every other year at the very least. Encourage personal financial contributions to the college programs. A "small pledge" or gift carries with it a commitment to the mission of the institution. Those who now give in this manner will be more likely to increase their giving as their financial resources increase.

In a day when competition for qualified faculty members is intense, as new professors are recruited attention must be given not only to their academic preparation, but equally to their personal lives and testimony, and to their philosophy of education. Will they be comfortable serving on the campus of a "holiness college?" Are values—academic and spiritual—of equal concern with scholarly presentation of course material?

Assure the congregations of the local churches—and individuals who give to the college—that their support of the institution is appreciated, accurately accounted for, and expended in a spirit of careful Christian stewardship.

A Final Word—

As our Nazarene constituency—in local churches throughout the land—view the ministry of our colleges as a *partnership*, understanding them to be "The Church at Work in Higher Education," and as we view these institutions at their best, the *partnership* between our Nazarene churches and the Nazarene colleges will continue to deepen, and our colleges in turn will fulfill their part of this *partnership* by providing hundreds of well-educated, adequately-trained young people to take their places of ministry— both lay and clergy—"until Jesus Comes!"

> . . . When your children shall ask their fathers in time to come, saying , What mean these stones? Then ye shall let your children know. . . . (Joshua 4:21-22)

TRIBUTE

It is said that we see by the light that enters our eyes. In the presence of Cecil R. Paul often we say by the light from his eyes. Each of us saw potential in ourselves just a bit more clearly. It was not the sounding of trumpets nor the waving of flags. It was that light shining forth from his eyes, imparting something of his spirit to us. It shined from his eyes to the depth of our souls, a light that searched out recesses of our beings where unrealized potential lay, where discouragement clouded our vision. Penetrating but not invasive, those eyes spoke . . . you can do this. A big smile, a friendly laugh . . . I knew you could. That light was cultivating the spirit, sometimes prodding but always encouraging. Cecil was an enabler of persons.

How often the lens of our eye magnifies the flaws in others. How rarely does our eye reflect the light from our Master to enable a colleague or friend?

Lowell H. Hall
Professor of Chemistry
Chair, Division of Natural Science
Eastern Nazarene College

TRIBUTE

A man with a vision for Christian education . . . an outstanding professor who could stimulate and captivate the student's mind . . . a colleague, mentor, and friend with the uncanny ability to uplift and motivate others . . . Dr. Paul was this and more.

Matilda "Tillie" Casler
Director of Graduate Studies
Assistant Professor, Chair, Department of Psychology
Eastern Nazarene College
(first met Dr. Paul as a student in 1962)

CHAPTER FIVE

THE COLLEGE-CHURCH PARTNERSHIP: PRESENT AND FUTURE

Tom Barnard

Richard John Neuhaus, in a 1993 commencement address to the graduates of ENC, said:

> A genuinely pluralistic society requires not only individuals but also institutions that are truly different. . . . That this is a Christian school is not an accidental leftover from history; it is a necessary part of its constituting claim and continuing purpose. This college is free to be itself because it is bound by a truth greater than itself (*Christian Scholar*, ENC, Summer 1993).

The College-Church Partnership: The Present

From the point of view of the Nazarene college officials who are responsible for maintaining relationships with the churches of the Nazarene on their region, the present state of church-college relationships within the Church of the Nazarene is excellent. No informed Nazarene academics would rise in protest over the fact that the Nazarene liberal arts colleges receive annually, as a group, millions of dollars from Nazarene churches on their region in support of their institutions and the students who attend them.

The statistics are impressive. On the average, each of the Nazarene liberal arts colleges in the United States receives annually about $1.6 million from the churches on their region through payment of what is called the "educational budget." In terms of 1995 revenues paid by the churches to the eight liberal arts colleges of the Church of the Nazarene, totals per college ranged from about $1.4 million. For six of the eight liberal arts colleges in the Church of the Nazarene, 1995 church gifts amounted to about ten percent of the college's total annual revenues.

Since Nazarene colleges are non-sectarian, they continue to attract a growing number of non-Nazarene students who elect to enroll, particularly those transferring from community colleges and those enrolling in degree-completion undergraduate programs or graduate programs. Nevertheless, more than half of the freshmen who arrive each fall at Nazarene colleges and enroll in traditional baccalaureate programs report their religious preference as "Nazarene." The term "traditional" here refers to the typical four-year baccalaureate programs of the colleges, as opposed to the non-traditional, degree-completion programs which have sprung up within the past few years on or near Nazarene campuses. Statistics indicate that a very high percentage of students enrolling in degree-completion programs and graduate programs come from religious backgrounds other than Nazarene, or profess no religious affiliation at all. The question of whether or not these degree-completion programs fit comfortably within a Nazarene college's mission is a matter discussed elsewhere in Chapter 6. The authors have chosen not to discuss the efforts Nazarene colleges make to link with non-Nazarene, evangelical churches for the purpose of expanding the potential freshmen pool.

Nazarene liberal arts colleges are similar in the types of students they enroll, the programs they offer, the faculties they attempt to recruit, the mission they strive to fulfill, and the relationships they seek to foster among the churches of the Nazarene on their regions. Creating a link between the Nazarene colleges and the churches is a central focus of every college president serving Nazarene colleges and universities. For example, Eastern Nazarene College's current president, Kent R. Hill, like his other presidential colleagues, attends district assemblies each year on the region and many of the pastors-and-mates retreats as well. To say that there is a positive relationship between the President of ENC and the members of the Board of Trustees is an understatement. And that could be said of Dr. Hill's immediate predecessor at Eastern Nazarene College—the late Cecil R. Paul—as well as other presidents before him.

Each of the Nazarene liberal arts colleges employs persons whose responsibilities include the oversight of activities and programs which intersect with the churches on the region. For some of these persons the work of Church Relations constitutes their primary responsibility. This would be true at Mount Vernon Nazarene College, Northwest Nazarene College, and Eastern Nazarene College. At Point Loma Nazarene College, Southern Nazarene University, Olivet Nazarene University, MidAmerica Nazarene College, and Trevecca Nazarene

University the individuals employed to head up the work of church relations carry additional responsibilities (beyond church relations).

Whatever the staffing plan, the college must be sensitive to the needs and concerns of the churches on the region. The person who serves in a liaison role between the college and the church will keep the president informed about matters impacting church relations, i.e., informed opinion about the college's impact on students from the churches; complaints or criticism about the college that surface on the region; questions about college policies; student financial accounts; changes in patterns of church payments to the college.

Church-relations personnel at Nazarene colleges should treat pastors in the same way college development personnel treat major donors. Pastors are key persons in establishing a pattern of payment of the church's educational budget as well as recruiting prospective students for the college. Pastors often have more ideological connection with the college than some major donors, but it is easier for development personnel to cater to a relatively small donor pool than to cultivate relationships with a large pool of pastors who are more likely to be taken for granted and treated with less importance than major givers. However, if one were to multiply by ten the annual gifts from a local church to the educational budget of the college, the total sum would be impressive. For example, a Nazarene church of 50 members contributing $3,000 per year to its educational budget will donate over $30,000 to the college during a ten-year period. What college development officer would spurn a donor list of 500 or more persons who are willing to give that amount to the college over a ten-year period? What college admissions officer would ignore a group of potential recruiters whose influence could positively impact a college's annual new-student pool? Pastors *are* key persons in the revenue-generation strategy of every Nazarene college. Thus, pastors should be seen as "very important persons" in helping the college fulfill its mission.

The College-Church Partnership: The Future

In an effort to construct an agenda for a discussion of the future relationship between the colleges and the churches, selected administrators with church-relations assignments at each of the eight liberal arts colleges of the Church of the Nazarene were asked to respond to a Spring 1995 survey about their perceptions of the current status of that relationship, together with predictions of some of the future challenges.

Both the College *and* the Church have a huge stake in what the other does or does not do. However, the question must be asked: What will this partnership look like twenty-five years from now? Fifty years? One hundred years? If one considers the direction many church colleges in the United States have taken beyond their first century of existence, the future of college-church relations in the Church of the Nazarene could be bleak. But must it (or will it) be so for Nazarene institutions? An honest answer might very well be: it depends.

The late Cecil Paul, president of Eastern Nazarene College from 1989 until his death in 1992, was gifted at engaging people in dialogue by asking thought-provoking questions without revealing at any point along the way what he thought the outcome should be. He believed strongly—no, *passionately*—in being direct and honest with people (and he did both equally well), but he often allowed the individual (counselee, student, faculty colleague, administrator) to wrestle with him over a problem without coming right out and saying what he believed the solution should be. Not that he feared making decisions. He preferred joint ownership. Thus, in strategic planning, he often elicited ideas from people in whom he had confidence. Then he engaged them in dreaming, planning, and working jointly toward a desired goal.

If Cecil Paul were writing this section, I believe that he might say that forecasting *anything* in a time of political, social, and religious uncertainty is a dangerous exercise. Then he would gather a few friends together and ask, "If you were to forecast what the College should be like twenty-five years down the road, what questions need to be answered now?" He would avoid making predictions until the right questions were asked. So, instead of setting out a series of prophetic declarations here, perhaps a more scholarly (i.e., a more "Paul"ine approach) would be to propose a series of questions, the answers to which may depend upon the choices our successors make about themselves and their colleges in "Century Two" of Nazarene liberal arts education.

As a starting point, it might be appropriate to address questions to those who are directly responsible for the future of the liberal arts colleges of the Church of the Nazarene—i.e., faculties, administrators, and boards of trustees.

To what extent will the College commit its resources toward cultivating a bond between the institution and the churches which support it?

In terms of staffing for church relations, survey results from college administrators revealed no consensus about the way colleges structure their church-relations efforts. Several Nazarene colleges have moved toward establishing full-time positions in church relations, i.e., providing personnel and operating budgets adequate for putting college representatives "on the road" in an effort to build relationships with pastors and churches. The decision about how much a college is willing to commit to church relations may, in fact, determine the future strength of the college-church partnership. A fair question to ask is what is it worth to an institution to foster a relationship with a consortium of donors (i.e., local churches) that contributes almost $2 million annually to the college, in addition to providing a pool of prospective freshmen each year? In a heartbeat, the answer should be, "A great deal!"

To what extent will a college commit institutional resources for need-based scholarships and grants to ensure that young people from the supporting constituencies are able to afford the escalating costs of a Christian liberal arts education?

One Nazarene college currently matches, seven to one, gifts from churches (up to $250 per student) in support of their undergraduates attending that college. Other Nazarene colleges offer incentives to districts and churches when they meet certain levels of payment of their educational budgets. At least one Nazarene college sets an annual budget for college-funded scholarships (institutionally known as "unfunded scholarships")—an amount about equal to the educational budget receipts from the region during the most recent fiscal year. In the future, Nazarene colleges will be expected to make significant efforts to recruit children of pastors and missionaries, as well as other Nazarene youth. This could be called a strategy of reciprocation—giving back to the churches through scholarships and grants a significant portion of revenues received from them. Regardless of what they are called, all such efforts will send a message to the churches that the regional college is trying to support the churches (and their college-age students) by making a Nazarene college education more attractive and affordable.

To what extent will Nazarene college officials be open to the concerns expressed directly or indirectly by pastors, parents and trustees regarding subjects addressed in courses required of all undergraduate students?

It is not uncommon for incoming freshmen at Nazarene colleges to bring with them certain limited perspectives about life at college. They may be surprised or confused by what is taught in certain college courses, e.g., in natural science courses, biblical literature classes, etc. To complicate the situation, college admissions advisors may not be adequately informed about what is taught in the classroom, e.g., whether "creationism" or "evolution" is taught in lower-division college courses. If college recruiters assure prospective students (or their parents and pastors) that what is taught in the college classroom is identical with what they have heard from their pastors or Sunday school teachers, some freshmen will no doubt be in for a major shock. *There must also be dialogue among faculty, administrators, and admissions persons at Nazarene colleges so that consistency is maintained between what is promised and what is delivered in the classroom.*

While most would agree that faculty persons need to be protected from unfair (and perhaps unscholarly) criticism from those outside academia, listening to the concerns from "outside" and cultivating opportunities for dialogue with those who are most responsible for encouraging students to attend the regional college may be a factor in reducing the tensions which can undermine satisfactory college-church relationships. To ignore such contact and dialogue could have serious implications for church support in the future.

To what degree will college governing boards support college administrators in spending money to improve college facilities and services?

Visual impressions, particularly first impressions, are not only lasting, but they also affect the decisions students make in the selection of a college. Prospective Nazarene college students from earlier generations (i.e., prior to the 1980s) looked to the Christian college as the logical place to spend four years following high school and prior to going out into the workplace. Going to a Nazarene college was nearly a given–something everyone in the youth group wanted to do. Being assigned three to a room at college was no problem then, at least in the minds of most students. In the 1990s (and beyond), the expectations of college-bound students and their parents have changed. Anticipations are greater for things as advanced technology, modern libraries with on-line accessibility, attractive buildings, consumer-friendly services, and comfortable residence halls. While not wanting to yield to a crass consumer mentality, Nazarene college officials understand that the way they market themselves—programs, course titles, and special services impacts the decisions which lead to the choice of a college. With colleges everywhere becoming more consumer sensitive and with competition for students increasing at both Christian and non-Christian colleges, Nazarene schools will undoubtedly continue to find creative ways to attract more students to *their* campus, rather than to another.

To what extent will the Nazarene liberal arts colleges be sensitive to the special financial problems faced by undergraduate and graduate students who are preparing for full-time ministry in the Church of the Nazarene?

Currently there is considerable dialogue and concern expressed (but no concrete plans underway denominationally) about offering major financial assistance to Nazarene students who intend to enter full-time ministry in the Church of the Nazarene following completion of their undergraduate and/or graduate training. Unlike students preparing for professions which offer substantial salaries almost immediately following completion of their graduate training, e.g., law, medicine, business, engineering, students entering the ministry usually earn beginning salaries well below the national average. Most will never earn high salaries as pastors. If a ministerial student (or spouse) accumulates a large debt through student loans in the process of completing his or her education, it is likely that entering full-time ministry will have to be delayed until most of the student loans are repaid.

College presidents and general church leaders are examining options to assist pre-ministry students toward the cost of college and seminary tuition. One Nazarene college is considering a proposal to subsidize ministerial students through special scholarships which basically reduce tuition costs in order to keep within reasonable limits their accumulated tuition debt. If the Church of the Nazarene hopes to attract bright students called to ministry, some creative programs must be developed.

Will Nazarene liberal arts colleges continue to maintain their Wesleyan-holiness roots as Nazarene higher education enters its second century of existence?

A commitment to required chapels, prayer before classes, and standards of modesty will not guarantee that a loyalty to the Church's theological roots will survive.

In the early years college administrators in the Church of the Nazarene recognized the importance of maintaining a theological linkage between the liberal arts colleges and the Church. In 1920 Dr. H. Orton Wiley, the gifted theologian who served as college president at Northwest Nazarene College and later at Pasadena College, expressed these strong views:

> Christian education is not Greek learning baptized, nor worldly education rechristened. Placing the Bible in the schools does not make education Christian, neither does the transplanting of current education to a "spiri-

tual environment" make it any less (secular). The fundamental principles are wrong, the motive is wrong.... Herein lies the difference between ... the education of the world, and true Christian education. The one seeks to find grace at the end of a system of truth; the other seeks first the personal knowledge of Christ through a gracious transformation into the moral image of God by the Spirit, and then plunges deeply into the search after truth as it is in Christ, the eternal Word.... (*Herald of Holiness*, January 14, 1920)

Bertha Munro, dean at Eastern Nazarene when secular education was on the rise in Christian colleges, wrote a position paper as background for a 1952 Education Commission report to the General Assembly of the Church of the Nazarene, in which she stated:

> The core of our educational system ... should remain the traditional liberal arts curriculum, so directed and channeled and expanded as to meet individual needs and fulfill social responsibility. It is peculiarly adapted to the use of the Christian faith and the achievement of our specific goals. (Sanner 6)

Picking up on Miss Munro's position, the Commission included in its report to the 1952 General Assembly the following statement:

> They [the Nazarene colleges] are to consider their educational task as an academic program of standard quality, interpenetrated with Bible holiness, and their educational objectives as assisting young people to achieve a fusion of holy character and sound education. (Sanner 8)

Among the "Distinctive Features" of Nazarene colleges, recorded in the Summary Report of the 1964 Education Commission Report to the General Assembly of the Church of the Nazarene, were these succinct lines:

> Nazarene colleges are church colleges and not merely church-related colleges.... All fields of study in Nazarene colleges must be viewed through the eyes of faith grounded in Scripture; all theories of life and its meaning, must be subjected to the test of biblical truth. (Sanner 9)

Without question the early leaders of Nazarene colleges clearly understood their mission to include the necessity of combining an aggressive pursuit of Christian faith and character among students, concurrent with an honest search for truth.

Current leaders in Christian higher education have also underscored the importance of uniting faith and learning on the Christian campus. In his baccalaureate message (which was also the setting for his installation as President of Eastern Nazarene College) Cecil R. Paul said,

> A Christian liberal arts college experience has, at its heart, the mission of service to God, the church, and humanity. Within this context, we are called to teach and model servanthood (*Christian Scholar*, ENC, Summer 1990).

In his 1993 inaugural address ENC President Kent R. Hill noted,

> Christian higher education . . . at its best . . . is not a hothouse for ideology, but a vibrant and bracing encounter with competing conceptions of truth and reality, but an encounter within a distinctly Christian context. (*Christian Scholar*, ENC, Summer 1993)

Will Nazarene liberal arts colleges find creative ways to support the churches in addition to sending out summer travel groups and providing leadership for district camps and retreats?

Thirty years ago the primary public relations efforts of Nazarene colleges were limited to college quartets traveling throughout the educational zone in the summers, singing in as many churches as could be scheduled, usually accompanied by a college "rep." This strategy worked well in recruiting, fund raising, and generating good will. However, today's pastors are looking for greater access to Nazarene higher education than that provided by traveling student teams and music ensembles. Colleges may be in the unique position of being able to provide resources for pastors in their efforts to confront some of the contemporary issues facing the church—i.e., worship trends, changing music styles, new expectations in pastoral counseling, etc. This may require larger college operational budgets and additional staff to successfully interface with churches in creative and collaborative ways to make the college-church partnership work.

Does new technology offer special opportunities for the colleges to expand their educational services to the churches on their regions?

The technology frenzy in the United States and Canada in the last five years—spawned by adventures into "cyberspace" and a national preoccupation with things new and different—has resulted in serious discussions within higher education about ways the college can link with the churches through distance-learning technology without physically transporting personnel and services to sites many miles from the campus. Technology will undoubtedly advance—and advance quickly—to the point where distant sites can cost-effectively access the college campus for programs and instruction for individuals unable to enjoy such services personally on campus.

Now let's ask a few questions of church leaders, i.e., those responsible for establishing the network within which students are encouraged to attend their regional college, as well as for the establishment of annual educational budget allocations in support of the liberal arts colleges.

How can the local church be more proactive when it comes to advising its young people where they should attend college?

A recent survey of students attending Nazarene colleges revealed that the influence of a pastor or youth pastor ranked higher than the influence of family or friends in making the final choice of a college.

Nevertheless, for a variety of reasons the majority of college-bound Nazarene youth today choose a secular college over a Nazarene college. And two of the most-often-heard reasons Nazarene youth give for their choosing not to attend a Nazarene college are these: cost and distance (from home). Some parents prefer that their children attend a public college close to home—a choice that on the surface solves the dual problem of cost and distance. Thus, many Nazarene young people choose a community college or state college over a Nazarene college because of factors which side-step the primary reasons that make a Christian education most attractive, i.e., Christian values taught, relationships established, lifestyles embraced, and the quality of classroom instruction offered at a Nazarene institution.

Furthermore, in Nazarene college circles it is generally believed that both the college and the church are negatively influenced by non-denominational, or even anti-denominational, sentiment which has become widespread in American religious culture in recent years. In some cases this results in a mind-set that places Nazarene higher education in a secondary position *below* secular education in terms of student preference. It is not uncommon to meet economically successful Nazarene adults who are willing to pay *more* to send their youth to other private colleges than it would cost to send them to a Nazarene school. The status of a non-Nazarene college education may be more attractive to them than that provided by their own church-related college. Ruling out a Nazarene-college education on grounds like these may well be a short-sighted perspective.

If the choice of a college were made on the basis of the qualities outlined above, i.e., values, relationships, lifestyles, and quality classroom instruction—rather than on the basis of distance, cost, and anti-denominational sentiment, all of the Nazarene colleges would enjoy growth and continued church support well into the third millennium.

Nazarene colleges cannot solve every problem prospective students face when making decisions about where they will attend college. Establishing local scholarships to aid students attending the regional Nazarene college would help. Some churches use their Nazarene college alumni to counsel with high school seniors who are on the threshold of a decision. Once a student has enrolled, annual visits to the campus by parents and pastors have a lasting impact on students who leave home to attend the regional college. If a local church is fortunate to have one of its own youth enrolled in a Nazarene college, featuring that student in an annual Nazarene College Day worship service might encourage prospective college students in finalizing their choice. Clearly, in order for a partnership to work, both sides need to be effective recruiters.

To what degree will Nazarene churches and districts continue to take seriously their role in giving financial support to the regional college, particularly in terms of the payment of the educational budget?

Statistics indicate a leveling trend in church financial support for Nazarene colleges. To the degree that financial support from churches remains flat or declines in the years ahead, Nazarene colleges will be forced to replace such funds through other means and from other sources. Typically college administrations face this issue through two sources of income growth available to them—funding through private and corporate gifts, and through raising tuition and fees. No college wants to be more tuition-driven than it currently is, but when pushing stops and shoving begins, one viable source of funds is student tuition. Cutting operational expenses is only a temporary solution because most college budgets are quite lean. In order for Nazarene colleges to maintain their Nazarene identity, continued financial support from the churches is vital.

To what degree will college governing boards—which constitutionally are made up of members of the Church of the Nazarene—cultivate and elect candidates who not only have a strong loyalty to district and general church leadership, but who also are willing and able to help develop a network of donors who will be responsive to the endowment and capital needs of the regional liberal arts college?

Most independent colleges and universities screen prospective trustees to insure that they have significant financial resources themselves or have connections with individuals who are capable of making major gifts to the institution. Nazarene colleges do not have this luxury. The quality of a candidate's churchmanship has more bearing on being elected to trusteeship than a person's ability to either pledge large gifts to the college or facilitate the reception of large gifts.

It is inevitable that some Nazarene college graduates—whether they work in service professions or are highly successful in business or other enterprises—eventually are elected to serve on a Nazarene college governing board. Participating in college life as trustees should require more than *pro bono* work for the school—specifically, trustees should be expected to set an example in their financial support of the college. Sadly, highly successful alumni/ae or other prominent lay people on college boards may enjoy a lifestyle which leaves little room in the family budget for making significant gifts to the college. Consequently, development officers at Nazarene colleges are often forced to go outside the college constituency to locate donors who can be persuaded to give significant sums to the college.

As a result of these and other economic factors, i.e., the lack of financial strength in smaller churches, church members with little sense of commitment to Nazarene higher education, etc., Nazarene colleges possess modest endowments and relatively small donor pools. However, college trustees who are not in a position themselves to contribute significant financial resources to the college may still be in a position to be contact persons with key individuals of means who *are* financially able and willing to give financial support to Nazarene institutions.

Conclusion

In the future, administrations and boards of trustees must develop creative ways to maintain denominational loyalty and financial support while at the same time controlling the spiraling costs which have characterized American higher education for more than a generation. To accomplish this, Nazarene colleges will need to be more proactive in three areas:

1. Increasing the number and amounts of annually-funded scholarships;

2. Holding annual tuition increases to a modest percentage

3. Exploring new opportunities to service the continuing education needs of pastors and lay people through distance learning.

The president of a prestigious independent college in New England has stated that the yearly tuition increases at his college must never again rise more than two percent above the regional cost-of-living index, if the college hopes to continue to be competitive in the academic marketplace. One thing seems very clear: Nazarene college and church leaders must face prayerfully and responsibly the challenges facing the college-church partnership in the decades ahead.

Without doubt, the future of Nazarene higher education will be influenced by concerns beyond those discussed in this chapter. Federal and state funding for students attending church-related colleges is a concern being monitored currently by organizations like the Washington-based Coalition for Christian Colleges and Universities. Other institutions serving independent colleges and universities are also lobbying with governmental groups to make sure that spending cuts will not seriously impact students whose unmet financial needs are greater than they can handle, without government financial aid. Other issues, such as the need for advanced technology on Nazarene college campuses, will demand funding well beyond that being projected by some of the liberal arts colleges. The changing role of faculty—from being the "campus experts" in an academic discipline to becoming facilitators in the retrieval of knowledge through technology—is inevitable.

Cecil R. Paul served as president of Eastern Nazarene College for less than three years. His premature death in August, 1992 left a huge void at the campus and in the community he loved. Although as a college president he was concerned about many things, he was above all committed to mission and to what he believed to be the strong future of the college. He was intensely goal oriented and was impatient when progress was slowed through indecision or lack of commitment of others. He wanted campus growth to occur everywhere, concurrently. He saw challenges as "wonderful new opportunities," to quote him directly. He feared "the phenomenon of creeping inflexibility, what might be called (institutional) sclerosis—precisely the loss of that ability to change and adapt."* He cared a great deal about Eastern Nazarene College and the Church of the Nazarene, but he cared more about people. All kinds of people. He applauded cultural diversity and lobbied hard for leadership roles for women and minorities.

Although he predicted for himself a short tenure as president—he often talked about early retirement and what he would like to do with the rest of his life—Cecil Paul very much wanted to be part of planning that would affect the future of the college. He did indeed improve his present moment, and he would have been the first to face squarely the challenges and opportunities of church/college collaboration in the years ahead.

Cecil Paul was committed to equipping pastors and congregations for their work of ministry. He longed for the day when the college and church would be seen as partners together in ministry. I believe that had he lived, he would have liked what has developed in church relations at Eastern Nazarene College. He would have challenged us to grasp the benefits to both church and college of distance learning through advanced technology.

Theologically, Cecil Paul expressed concern over the tendency of some in the church and college to embrace a narrow mind-set which he characterized as inflexibility (See chap.2).

In his presentation to Nazarene leaders he said, "We have something to say to this age that is not easily accomplished within the narrow parameters of fundamentalism."* (While Cecil Paul did not define "fundamentalism," he spoke of it in the context of what distinguishes Wesleyans from people of other theological persuasions, particularly those who are "reformed fundamentalists in their world and religious views.") That "something" to which Cecil Paul referred above is what the church and college should be addressing in the decades ahead. Cecil Paul argued that the effort—if it is to be genuinely Wesleyan—must be based on Scripture, reason, experience and tradition.

Cecil Paul was convinced that the church and the college *together* share a worthy mission, one which changes the lives of all who are engaged in the process. Faculty, students, pastors, and parents are all principal players. I believe that if he were alive to speak to us today, he would press us to continue the task of "improving the moment"—both present and future.

CHAPTER SIX

Non-Traditional Education and the Nazarene College: Issues of Mission-Fit, Distinctiveness, and Survival

Wayne Dunlop and Steve Pusey

In his 1991 address to the Eastern Nazarene College governing board, President Cecil Paul noted that cultural and socioeconomic changes "create a new context for the college and the church in which to operate." And while Paul was quite aware that there are some who will "panic in the face of dramatic changes and will mistrust us as we endeavor to create strategies for addressing these times with new methods," he boldly proclaimed that these changes "should not threaten us, but bring out the best of our individual and corporate courage to be." Paul's willingness to accept change rested in his sense of assurance that such change could be the basis for "rediscovering our mission and . . . creating new methods for expressing and operationalizing the mission." He was convinced that ultimately "the source of our confidence and hope is the consistency with which we articulate and model the distinctiveness of our mission."

A recent example within Nazarene higher education of the type of accommodation to which Paul referred is the development over the past decade in several colleges, including ENC, of a diversified range of innovative undergraduate and graduate level programs of that which are directed at adult learners. This "non-traditional" population is characterized as being working adults, age twenty-three and older, with work experience and some college credits earned, and typically non-Nazarene in faith affiliation, who meet for classes at non-traditional times, and in some cases, at off-campus instructional sites. The programs themselves are non-traditional in their emphasis on an "androgogical" approach to the teaching-learning dialogue, and in their offering of curricula which is most often modularized and accelerated in format. As of Fall 1995, Nazarene colleges were offering more than twenty non-traditional for-credit programs, with total non-traditional undergraduate and graduate enrollments of nearly 3,000 students, or better than 22% of their combined student enrollment.

This paper will review the emergence of non-traditional education in Nazarene colleges in light of the historic mission of Wesleyan higher education, along with the forces and rationales supporting their development, and will suggest that such programs have strong potential for assuring the ongoing distinctiveness as well as the survival of the Nazarene college into the twenty-first century.

Changing Student Demographics and the Nazarene College Response

In 1992 the College Board reported that as many as seven million adults, twenty-five years of age or older, were enrolled in for-credit college programs across the United States, and that only 20% of the total college population was then full-time, in residence, and under 22 years of age (Aslanian 12). While this increase in the number of adult students is largely the consequence of changes taking place in society; in workplace realities and expectations, in technology, and in personal adult life situations, many of which occur outside the individual's control, a number of adults continue to show up at the doors of academia out of an intrinsic motivation to improve their lives. It is predicted that by the turn of the century, 50-60% of the students in American colleges and universities will be over age 25, translating, according to the National Center for Educational Statistics, into more than 16 million adult learners by the turn of the century, and contributing to a "multi-age" campus environment (Aslanian 15).

Typically, programs designed for adults are non-traditional in their delivery system, providing for-credit coursework that is convenient, accessible geographically and/or electronically, and combined with credit-for-life experience. Dunn and Miller have referred to this evolution in higher education as the shift from the "industrial" to the "virtual" university and argue that schools of the future will continue the trend of being client-centered, serving both traditional and non-traditional students at the site, time, pace, and style desired by the learner (Dunn and Miller). Such universities will be the norm and will offer curricula that are flexible, marked by a focus on quality, and accessible through multiple modes. The institutions which are thus willing and able to adapt to the changing environment will be the ones which will survive. Dehne noted that the adaptable college will appeal to a variety of groups and will look quite different from most small colleges of the past, most notably in the enrollment blends of age groups and publics (Dehne 5-7).

Nazarene institutions of higher education have been affected by the same societal forces and the resulting changing student demographics and programming trends that have affected all of higher education. Nazarene colleges have discovered new opportunities to embrace and extend their historic mission while staking a claim for goodness and righteousness in diverse segments of society. Adjusting to these changes has not been easy or without debate, as witnessed at one of the colleges where more than two years of oft-heated deliberations between the faculty and the administration occurred prior to a final decision to proceed; however, leaders such as Cecil Paul have been willing to take bold steps to assure that their colleges are able to meet the needs of an ever-expanding element of American society which is in need of Christian-centered higher education.

While "non-traditional programs" have only taken shape within the last decade, "adult education" among Nazarene colleges appears to have gained its first foothold as early as 1949 when the North Central Association urged Olivet Nazarene University to place an increased emphasis on adult education and opportunities for lifelong learning, particularly for returning war veterans and local school teachers. These initiatives were non-traditional by contemporary terms only in the age of the students served since neither adult learning theories nor other than conventional delivery methods were then developed.

The present era of non-traditional programs can likely be identified as having begun in 1966 when Trevecca Nazarene University started to offer alternative summer for-credit continuing education classes for teachers, and appointed its first adult program director. For a short time in the 1970s, Trevecca also maintained some off-campus sites for delivering other academic programs. In 1980, Olivet began a degree-completion program for an associate degree in practical ministries in conjunction with the Salvation Army, with classes taught both on the main campus and at the Officers' Training School in Chicago. The largest expansion of adult education programs, however, came in the mid to late 1980s at a number of the institutions in fields as diverse as nursing, ministry, business, and education. Olivet developed a degree-completion track for registered nurses and Southern Nazarene was the first to develop a degree-completion program in the management of human resources (MHR), a modularized, accelerated program for adults offered at satellite sites in addition to the campus. By decade end Trevecca and MidAmerica Nazarene College had also developed MHR programs, and Southern added an undergraduate major in family studies and gerontology. MidAmerica also offered a degree-completion program for graduates of the Nazarene Bible College and expanded its offerings to include a teacher re-certification program conducted at various sites in the greater Kansas City area.

ENC joined these schools in 1990 with its appointment of a full-time director of its Leadership Education for Adults (LEAD) degree-completion program which initially offered a bachelor of science in business administration and later associate degrees in business, general studies, and liberal arts. In 1994 Mount Vernon Nazarene College gained Ohio Board of Regents' approval to offer business administration courses in the greater Columbus area as well as on campus through its newly-founded executive center for life-long learning (EXCELL) program for working adults. During this same time, Olivet expanded its programs. The Salvation Army associate degree program was discontinued in 1990 and substituted with a bachelor of science in practical ministries. Olivet also developed a human resource management degree-completion program and restructured the nursing degree-completion track to offer a bachelor of science in nursing program specifically designed for working adults. Coursework in general education or elective credit became available in non-traditional formats at Trevecca, MidAmerica, Olivet, Eastern, and Mount Vernon. In each case where non-traditional programs were offered, the institutions added a full-time director or directors of adult education to oversee the new initiatives.

Non-traditional offerings have not been limited to undergraduate students. Graduate programs at many of the colleges have taken on formats that are considered non-traditional. In 1984 Trevecca developed a graduate program in education which was offered at sites throughout the state of Tennessee as well as on the Nashville campus. By the end of the decade, Olivet was offering a master of arts in education in a non-traditional format, Southern had added a master of science in management, and MidAmerica expanded its offerings to include an on-campus master of education. During the 1990s there has been ongoing development of non-traditional graduate programs at each of these colleges, particularly in the fields of business, education, and counseling.

Rationales for Non-traditional Programs

Much debate continues over whether or not Nazarene colleges should be involved in academic programs which are designed to focus on other than the traditional 18-22 year-old Nazarene student. Nonetheless, the fact is that Nazarene institutions are successfully offering such programs and their reasons for doing so are justification in themselves for the benefits of such programs to the college. Most important, however, is the question of whether or not non-traditional programs are consistent with the mission of the Nazarene college.

A review of official documents submitted to regulatory bodies and boards of trustees of Nazarene colleges reveals little variation in the initial reasons and purposes behind the development of these non-traditional programs. These seem to focus on two major issues: (1) To serve the needs of Nazarenes and other adults from the surrounding local communities through distinctive Christian-based professional programs and (2) To help promote the college within the local community. MidAmerica's proposal statement for its master of management program is representative: "to serve the management and business community in the greater Kansas City area . . . with a quality program in the context of MidAmerica's commitment to Christian excellence" (Metz 262). Mount Vernon's objective for its degree-completion program, while somewhat more broadly cast, "grew out of the basic mission to serve the supporting constituencies of the College in central Ohio by expanding its services to meet the needs of adult learners" (Proposal for a B.A. Degree, MVNC 8). SNU reported that its MHR program had "produced excellent public relations and support for the college" (SNU MHR Unpublished Document 5).

At the same time, the success of adult programs at the colleges has led to strong justifications for continuing to develop and expand the programs. Donald Metz, in his history of MidAmerica, reported that a dramatic reversal in the pattern of enrollment in the late 1980s at his institution could be traced directly to its adult education programs (Metz 16). In his summary of the impact of the development of these non-traditional courses of study at the college, he writes "innovations have become a vital part of the institution's operation. Among the significant innovations of recent years, an adult education program has proved beneficial to the student and helpful to the College" (Metz 384). Kent Hill, the successor to Cecil Paul as president of ENC, observed in his 1995 "State of the College" report that "it is certainly possible that ENC's witness on the South Shore and in the Boston area will be increasingly the product of our non-traditional undergraduate program." And, in a strong appeal for support of such programs, Hill concluded that ". . . perhaps there is no need in Christian higher education so pressing at the present time as to devote serious thought and study on how to be faithful to mission and serve the adult learner."

Reflected in these statements are the common rationales of service to the community, enrollment stabilization, extension of mission, innovation, and Christian witness. It has also been argued that non-traditional programs provide the college with the opportunity to be on the cutting edge of teaching methodology and of learning theory development and practice. In addition, the schools are finding their traditional student population positively impacted through enhanced name recognition in their geographical areas, through referrals by the non-traditional students, through mentoring programs by which adult students team up with traditional students, and through active alumni chapters of non-traditional program graduates.

In no case has the intent been to develop a proverbial "cash-cow," although taken together, such programs annually provide the colleges with millions of additional revenue that, in effect, support and enhance the mission of traditional liberal arts education through increased dollars for operations, capital improvements, and building expansion and upgrading, all of which contribute to attracting traditional-age students. Not so apparent in the initial implementation of these programs has been the academic benefits of faculty development from contact with adult learners and innovative teaching methodology. One instructor reported a higher level of participation occurred among day students when an "innovative" teaching method was used from the evening class. Some faculty are experimenting with restructuring their traditional courses to move them toward a more modular format or with computer-enhanced instruction.

Non-traditional Programs and Institutional Mission

Nazarene institutions of higher education, as all colleges and universities, are shaped organizationally and functionally by their mission statements. Whatever reasons are given for offering non-traditional academic programs at Nazarene colleges, there can be no justification for doing so unless such programs are supportive of the mission of the college. While mission statements are concerned more broadly with such issues as characteristics of the student and with curriculum organization, the core of the mission is in what the college seeks to accomplish.

This paper has attempted to this point to document what changes in educational programming have taken place in several Nazarene colleges as a response to a changing socioeconomic context; however, it also recognizes that some things do not and must not change. Hubbard aptly reminds us that "it is the institution, not the mission, that adjusts to the changing environment" (Hubbard 5). Of most importance, the core mission of the Nazarene college has not been altered in the implementation of programs for adults. In fact, a review of Nazarene college mission statements over a period of years does not reveal that there is or ever has been a conflict between the intrinsic goals of Nazarene colleges and alternative forms of education. First, centrally and fundamentally, the core mission of the Nazarene college is to equip individuals in the church for service to God and society through providing a Christian environment in which life-long learning is modelled and launched. Second, the Nazarene college also seeks to impact society through an educational experience characterized by a Wesleyan-holiness ethic made available to any individual with qualifications to enroll in college. These notions appear to be the enduring ones while other mission goals, more extrinsic in nature, are appropriately revised in language from time to time to reflect changes in approach or mission implementation.

It seems to be true that non-traditional students represent the same people that Nazarene colleges have always sought to serve: the Nazarene constituency, Christians of all faith communities who desire a liberal arts education within a distinctively Christian context, and those from the local community. An overview of the mission statements of the Nazarene colleges, as revealed in its published statements in catalogs and official reports to regulatory groups, reveals that it is not and never has been exclusive in who is served, even though the opportunities and challenges unique to Christian higher education have been generally limited in the past to the traditional-age student. Consequently, while the primary focus is on intellectual and spiritual development, the Nazarene college generally seeks to develop the total individual, both as a person and as a member of her community, regardless of differences in race, gender, creed, nationality, culture, or age.

This view is consistent with the Wesleyan view of higher education discussed by Dunn and Nielson in their article "The Theology and Practice of Wesleyan Higher Education" and is reflected in catalog mission statements where an emphasis is placed on developing "a sense of self-worth and achievement" and being prepared for "service to humanity." Likewise, the Nazarene college seeks "to develop compassionate individuals" with "character" who love their neighbors and enemies as self and are socially and culturally aware.

Dunn and Nielson argue that this characteristic is a central component of Wesleyanism and note that Wesleyan colleges have always "tended to move with society as a whole, to move in response to pressures, and to develop programs where there is demand and need." And, because Wesleyans take seriously the commitment to a just society, they desire to see each student prepared as completely as possible to "carry on the work of creation, culture and redemption." Wesleyan educational practice, then, conclude Dunn and Nielson, is largely shaped by a theology which emphasizes "a desire to learn from and serve the greater society, the search for truth wherever it may be found, [and] preparation for lives of dedicated service" (Dunn and Nielson 72-80).

What has changed has been the creative programmatic and curricular adaptations on the part of the colleges to increase their relevance to society. In the words of Bertha Munro, Dean Emerita of ENC, "Our gospel must find people where they are; it must work with people as they are" (Wolfe 83). "Actively addressing culture" captures for John Bowling, President of Olivet, the relevance and mission-fit of their graduate and adult studies programs: "By offering education to a growing population of adult students, Olivet makes the natural response to a change in the educational environment. . . . Traditional and non-traditional education work together as legitimate expressions of the Christian university's mission—they build upon one another" (Bowling 8).

At the same time, it must be recognized that the Nazarene college cannot be expected to meet the higher education needs of all people. Specifically, there are issues which each institution must address with respect to providing education for adults who come from outside its faith confession or who do not practice the college's lifestyle standard. It must provide for those who seek an education in a Christian environment, asking, in turn, for acknowledgement and respect for the institution's values and commitments.

The Question of Survival

Sam Dunn has predicted that 25% of the colleges which are operating in 1995 will be closed by the year 2025 (Dunn). While it may be somewhat of an exaggeration to proclaim that institutions of higher education will survive into the next century only if they are willing to change to meet the needs of an escalating older student population, the implications are clear that the chances of survival for the private college particularly are greatly enhanced if initiatives are taken to address this population.

George Dehne explored a number of trends that he believes will have major impact on small private colleges and universities in the next decade, and he concluded that there will be five types of institutions of higher education in the future: (1) The high prestige and highly-endowed; (2) The distinctive small colleges with unique and special programs; (3) The successful small colleges that are adaptable, having recognized that the era of colleges populated only with traditional 18-year-olds is over; (4) The colleges which are a hybrid between the adaptable and the distinctive; and (5) Those that will be significantly smaller or closed (Dehne 5-9). Dehne noted that the adaptable college will appeal to a variety of groups and will look quite different from most small colleges of the past, most notably in the enrollment blends of age groups, a combination of programs, and being open virtually 24 hours a day. These colleges will not be judged by the success of their traditional undergraduate population, but by their ability to provide a quality education to a variety of publics.

It is not likely that Nazarene colleges will ever participate in the first category of Dehne's categories of schools, and it could be argued that they do not wish to fall into the second, given that to be distinctive in this sense would mean to be exclusive. Only the third group, and possibly the fourth, if "distinctive" is viewed in the context of mission, would appear to be attractive and realistic for Nazarene institutions. Consequently, if one places faith in Dehne's predictions, the Nazarene school that survives must clearly promote its own real distinctiveness and be proactive in adapting to changing demographic and technological realities.

Implications for Non-traditional Education in the Nazarene College

As the Nazarene college develops the best structure and programs to help accomplish its goals, several significant concerns must be considered. The following are offered as representative:

- How will mission be communicated to and effected in adult students in the absence of such functions as chapel and student ministries?
- Should there be a concern if the majority of students in adult education programs do not have a Wesleyan affiliation, or at least an appreciation for the fundamental premises and mission of the institution, and may be only enrolled for convenience or as a result of aggressive marketing strategies?
- How will faith be integrated with learning? How will non-traditional programs promote the Wesleyan distinctive?
- What impact will non-traditional programs have on the identity of the institution as a liberal arts college?
- How is faculty governance over non-traditional programs to be maintained?

- How important is it that academic programs be housed on campus?
- Is there a concentrated effort to resist the temptation to be needs driven rather than needs sensitive, such as getting caught up in competition or becoming budget driven?
- What effect will non-traditional programs have on faculty work practices?
- Can traditional faculty be re-trained to teach adults? Is the institution willing to make the commitment to re-train faculty?
- How relevant is prior learning and how will previous learning experiences brought by the adult learner to the program be assessed?
- How is academic quality to be monitored?
- What demands on the college's infrastructure can be predicted and accomplished?
- How will the questions of growth be handled?
- Will the college be ready to tolerate flexibility in academic policies and procedures to accommodate to the realities of the adult learner?
- What will be the mission-fit standards for adjunct faculty recruited and contracted to teach in the non-traditional programs?
- How will the outcomes of the adult learner programs be assessed?

Conclusion

The debate as to whether Nazarene institutions of higher education should be in the business of offering non-traditional educational programs will not go away and will, in fact, intensify.

As an institution that values both tradition and change, the Nazarene college must continually strive to be faithful to its distinctive mission, yet relevant and available to its constituency. Cecil Paul's call for the Nazarene college to have the "courage to be" as it rediscovers its mission and creates new strategies for expressing that mission captures well the vision necessary to assure that the Nazarene college will remain relevant and redemptive as a moral force well into the twenty-first century.

CHAPTER SEVEN

THE SYMBOLIC VALUE OF PLACE

Maxine E. Walker

> For 'tis your thoughts that now must deck our kings,
> Carry them here and there, jumping o'er times,
> Turning th' accomplishment of many years
> Into an hour-glass. . . .   Prologue, *Henry V*

It is commencement day at the Regional Christian College. As the candidates march across the platform, Professor Brilliant whispers to Professor Gifted, "I don't know a fourth of the graduates. Who are these students?" Such observations, especially in a period of expanding off-campus sites, discussions on the liberal arts canon, and the proliferation of graduate programs in Christian liberal arts colleges, renew debates about the centrality of "place" in conveying the mission of a Christian college. In Nazarene institutions of higher learning, nearly four generations of students and professors experienced and recognized the ethos, spirit, and mission of the college within the intimacy of a small academic community. (Those who were not of this mind may have found themselves asking "what does it mean to be a part of a community of faith" in ways similar and dissimilar to Stanley Hauerwas' "resident aliens.") The academic circle enclosed undergraduates with primarily liberal arts majors; the few professional and graduate programs (if any) were limited to religion, Christian ministries, and education. It was the daily interchange in faculty offices, on the sidewalk, in chapel and classes, and in the residence halls that reinforced loyalty to the "place."

An event such as homecoming elicited the affirmation of territorial symbols that helped unify the past and present and set the stage for future loyalty and support of the college. The commencement ritual confirmed and strengthened the social identity and posited the distinctiveness of the academic community; the medieval regalia proclaimed the college's long connection with the great universities of Europe even though the college was located in the most rural American town. These two symbolic events were incorporated into the fabric of Christian college life and were repeated with familiarity and certainty among persons that had known each other for four years on a small campus. The Christian college culture from the early to mid-twentieth century laid down a perceptual, even cultural, template on reality that for better or worse lasted a lifetime. The rituals and the symbols reinforced and affirmed the community's boundaries.

Multiple forces in all higher education have decreased institutional loyalty and support, and thus the ability of colleges, in particular Nazarene colleges, to convey their mission through images, symbols, rituals, and place deserve closer consideration. This closer consideration is needed because symbols about place contribute to the mental construct "community," and those symbols can either operate to unify or to divide. As the social anthropologist Anthony Cohen noted, ". . . the symbolic expression of community and its boundaries increases in importance as the actual geo-social boundaries of the community are undermined, blurred or otherwise weakened" (50). What essentially has happened to Nazarene colleges is a movement away from unity and uniformity that occurs in isolation and commonality toward multivalent places, a movement grounded in the inherent characteristics of Nazarenes' "theology of place."

By "theology of place" for Nazarene colleges, I mean a conceptual mapping of either the natural landscape or man-made structures that reflect how the colleges and its sponsoring denomination think about God's revelation in various places. The history of Nazarene college locations as well as the purpose and placement of buildings frequently expose a contradiction within this theology of place. This contradiction evolves from both the emphasis on the work of the Spirit in "full salvation" experienced "anywhere" by "anyone" and a religious experience that may require a "sheltered retreat" for its preservation. This "contradiction" is not unique to Nazarenes, but Nazarene colleges are at a juncture in their collective history where such variances may lead to community disruption or to a renewed vision, a dilemma that Cecil Paul understood in the spirited discussions on the *raison d'etre* for "adult learning."

Studies of Christian spirituality throughout the centuries affirm the continuing tension between place and placelessness—in what place or enclosed space can God be found? God is both known by reference to concrete images formed from the fabric of the world and also known by His elusiveness, mystery, and transcendence; even absence from place (Lane, "Landscape and Spirituality" 10) God is encountered where He is and is not, and God is also encountered at "home" and in wandering and exile. Within the Wesleyan tradition and its permutations manifested in the American revivals of the nineteenth and early twentieth centuries, this pull between finding God in a sacred place such as the established church and the *mysterium tremendum* of all other places is evident. This awareness of the mystery of God did not appear for early American Wesleyans in the wild forces of the natural world as it did for the early Puritans as they read an inscrutable God in thunderstorms and the rugged rocks and high gray Atlantic waves ("Puritan Reading" 105). For American Wesleyans, preaching in the fields and on the circuits, setting up tents for camp meetings, locating a storefront to establish a church, sitting with the poor in urban-industrial settings, women studying the Bible in Victorian parlors, preaching that embraced the central images of the "sawdust" trail and the rough-hewn altar conditioned seekers to find God in places outside the established and permanent parish. These commonplace settings became a symbolic locus for the working of God.

"Called unto Holiness" meant encountering a holy God and living a holy life in places that were not only culturally and socially marginal but also without much sublimity. The mystery of God's presence could be found in the impermanent revival tent. Belden Lane notes in "Liminal Places in the Evangelical Revival," [the revival] was the place where I discovered a God who was too . . . unpredictable to be contained in the cultivated interior of a traditional sanctuary. Just sitting in [the shoe store in front of the large glass windows] was a defiant proclamation to the world that God had supplanted all merchandise and usurped every claim to stubborn secularity" (155). Caroll Smith-Rosenberg comments on this abandonment of the traditional places and practices that characterized a religious life for the revivalists: "time-honored liturgies no longer seemed relevant; individualism reigned" (200). Smith-Rosenberg also suggests that the boundless possibilities inherent in revivalist "perfectionism" and the immediate experience of the Holy Spirit contributed to this rejection of the customary places of worship.

The experience of entire sanctification, a doctrinal tenet that appeared to firmly hold the early Nazarenes both educated and uneducated together, could be received in any location where God's grace was present. Not only the "uncommon" place but also the experience "itself" became the literal and symbolic understanding of how the community held together. Viewed in this perspective, what happens within a person connects her to the interior world of other persons, and the distinctive of the community and the reality of the boundary more firmly resided internally than in the structural forms of community. When Dr. J.P. Widney in 1895 (wealthy Methodist, President of the University of Southern California, and friend of Phineas Bresee) wanted to make his point that the essence of Christianity was not the recitation of a creed nor the observance of rituals, he referred to the novelist Tolstoy who had left his position to serve the peasants in a remote Russian village. The mission of the new "Nazarene" church and, one might say the "place" to be honored by that church, was any place where the "battle of life has been sore, and to every *heart* that hungers for cleansing from sin. Come" (Smith,*Called* 110-111). The experience of sanctification became in the Durkheimian mode an "integrative force" from which a particular academic culture emerged (Cohen 20). In this view of the "commonality" found in early Nazarene college communities, *all places* and all persons are fit for God's chosen people. The distinctiveness of the community was indigenous, i.e., the meaning of their existence as a community did not come from imposition nor from a physical place but was attributed and "experienced" by its members in entire sanctification. This part of our "placelessness" in denominational heritage makes it easy to think about hotel rooms as sites for "non-traditional" students to take classes with "non-traditional" delivery in "non-traditional" programs. The business-conference-room-turned liberal arts classroom distant from the campus poses no problem for a God to come as he came in a storefront 100 years ago. After all if God is not confined to the sanctuary, why should a graduate education class or an undergraduate history class be confined to a building on a campus that may historically have been built for a military building or a wealthy family's parlor?

The other feature of the Nazarene's theology of place is the appearance of a "center," a physical center that is single and unifying. Symbolism of a center such as a Mount Zion or a Jerusalem in the history of religion is not uncommon as Mircea Eliade has noted; the spot "constitutes a break in the homogeneity of space" (37). A site becomes a symbol of the spiritual for extraordinary perceptual changes occur there, and the symbol in turn shapes experience. For example, Dr. H. Orton Wiley, past president of both Northwest Nazarene College and Pasadena College believed that the desert landscape suited the development of character. "If the desert and its loneliness stand for communion with God, and the necessity of faith alone in God and His grace to transform the human heart; so likewise the mountain vastnesses are conducive to communion through their solitude, but they inspire us with the thought of the eternity of the Godhead and the immutability of the promises" (qtd. in Price 8). For the Puritans in New England, the symbolic center of the village was the meetinghouse. Lane in "The Puritan Reading of the New England Landscape," points out that the covenant relationship between God and man in New England is evident in the spatial model of the village. At the center was the meetinghouse designed for community worship, a meetinghouse symbolic of the medieval *roland* or *cosmic axis* (111). Around the meetinghouse, a village green and houses of congregation members were "orderly placed to enjoy comfortable communion" (112). Beyond the safety of the village lay the vast swamp that symbolized chaos and disorder.

The *cosmic axis* for Nazarene colleges was chapel, a place that complemented the classroom for building inward spiritual strength in order to resist external cultural pressures. Chapel would be the ". . . place which lends structure, contextuality, and vividness of memory to the narrative of spiritual experience" ("Landscape" 6). The early philosophy of education, as stated by the Church of the Nazarene leaders, was closely linked with denominational goals, and formed the rhetorical context for such a "center" in Nazarene colleges. H. Orton Wiley writes, "On every school, on every book, on every scholastic exercise should be stamped, 'Holiness unto the Lord'" (qtd. in Kirkemo 22). In the original master plan of MidAmerica Nazarene College, for example, all buildings were planned to frame the chapel. The chapel was to the colleges what periodic revival meetings had been to the denomination, and the chapel became the symbolic locus of much that holiness educators held in common. This connection of spiritual life to academic life rings clearly in the histories of the colleges. James Cameron reports "The college had opened in Wollaston with a revival. . . . On the day that school was scheduled to dismiss at noon for the Thanksgiving vacation, the Lord visited the morning chapel service. . . . As they finally dispersed to their homes, the students carried the revival fires to the churches all over the Eastern Educational Zone" (153). Ruth Vaughan recounts in *Fools Have No Miracles* that it is the revival [in chapel] every semester that encourages "confrontations with God [so that] our students find opportunity to open themselves to His power and to observe His miracles firsthand" (15). Even in the "new" colleges established in the 1960s, chapel remained essential to college life. The construction of the Mount Vernon Nazarene College chapel in 1989-1990 "marked the coming of age" for the institution. Donald Metz in his history of MidAmerica recounts the crisis when the Kansas attorney general declared that required chapel made MANC students ineligible for the Kansas Tuition Grants. In a chapel service describing the action, an administrator stated that "MidAmerica was not about to sell its *spiritual birthright* for a mess of Kansas tuition pottage" (qtd. in Metz 276).

If chapel was the symbolical vertical shaft, then the classrooms and dormitories existed in spatial and spiritual relationship to that center. Those relationships were most frequently expressed in the images and language of "home" so that the suggestive symbolic significance of chapel had preserving and stabilizing effects. Thus, as the discussions in the late twentieth-century have centered on "family values" and the sociological (even spiritual) reasons why home has lost centrality in modern culture, Nazarene educators may want to look at the symbolic relationships between chapel and academic and student development as studies in our own small contribution to cultural conditions—for good or for less than the good. It is clear, however, that early Nazarene college leaders viewed their physical setting as an intimate spiritual and academic community. These were communities of faith, perhaps not as "visible" or as "confessing" as Hauerwas and Willimon advocate, but ones that believed they were "living out the story together" (78).

For example, the new building in 1947 at Canadian Nazarene College housed offices and classrooms on the main floor, dining hall and kitchen were in the back and plans called for a chapel above the back wing. When the dining hall was relocated from the basement of the girls' dormitory, the space was renovated into apartments for faculty families (Thomson 24-25). As Nazarene colleges were established throughout the world, the same sense of intimacy and "home" connection was maintained. Students and faculty studying, eating, and living together was not done exclusively for financial reasons but also in the belief that "[t]here is no substitute for living around other Christians.... [people who live aright the traditions of home]" (Hauerwas 102). The first stage of building at European Nazarene Bible College was space for an adequate library, chapel, rooms for Sunday school, and a large student lounge (Dudney 84). C.E. Thomson notes in *The Story of Canadian Nazarene College* that even though the college had no building plan in its early days, dormitory space was deemed necessary (3). Lectures were in a church auditorium or in the college president's office, but it was essential to have a place for students to live. Point Loma Nazarene College has consistently maintained for example that the College can best be described as "a liberal arts College, an instructional College, a *residential* College, a transformational institution, a denominational College . . ." (1985 Self-Study 51) even though the enrollment statistics show a large number of non-residential students. It is an important symbolic proclamation of the College's heritage.

The metaphor of home also suggests the experiences and relationships that are formative in our identities. C.S. McClain in his personal history of Olivet Nazarene College identifies closely with John Henry Newman's view of the spirit of college life:

> ... [the University or College] will constitute a whole, it will embody a specific idea, it will represent a doctrine, it will administer a code of conduct, it will furnish principles of thought and action. It will give birth to a living tradition, or a *genus loci* (Spirit of place), as it is sometimes called, which haunts the home where it has been born, and which imbues and forms, more or less, one by one, every individual who is successively brought under its shadow. (qtd. in *I Remember* 25)

The "coming in" and living in a close sheltered environment appeared to be essential before students could go out into the world "fully prepared" with the distinctives of the denomination. The culturally inscribed traditions and the religious or ideological traditions that captured the imagination found rest in a matrix of symbols of "home."

As a way to think about the college as a symbolic "home," consider the "dispersal" effect noted by Ron Kirkemo when Pasadena College moved to San Diego, 120 miles away in a different community. In 1970, 57 of 72 faculty lived within a 1.5 mile radius of the campus. Those 57 faculty families in addition to other faculty attended either Bresee Avenue Church or Pasadena First, both within the same radial distance. Kirkemo also observes that whereas nearly all faculty offices were in three closely located buildings, in San Diego each academic division and even some academic departments had separate buildings. The culture of the campus after the move was influenced by the location of dormitories at either end of the 90-acre campus (in comparison to 17 at Pasadena) and no specific building existed at that time for a chapel or student commons. As a consequence of the move, Kirkemo posits important questions "What parts of the campus community and organizational culture were crucial to the mission of the college?. . . . Replication was impossible" (320-321). However, as shall be noted later, the cultural changes that occurred at Point Loma College (1973) are not just unique to a college that "died" along Interstate 5 South but also are latent changes in nearly all Nazarene colleges' understanding of their philosophy of education.

In 1917, J.B. Chapman pointed out that the aims of the colleges had "scarcely been altered through the years . . . [and] those aims . . . were to protect young men and women from the apostasy growing in the world around them, and to raise up a holiness ministry for the church" (Smith *Called* 323). The moral and religious confusion and the pull between fundamentalism and modernism led to a vigilance against campus "worldliness." This kind of enclave, as Wheaton College professor Lisa McGinn reports in her 1995 analysis of secularization in Christian colleges, is a way to "regulate which external influences they will conform to as a part of necessary change for survival and which influences they will reject as compromising their primary mission" (101). The idea that a Nazarene or holiness college must be a sheltered retreat for the preservation of the Nazarene distinctive call to entire sanctification had several corollary thoughts. First as Chapman noted, holiness seminaries provided an education "too late" to mold students' minds; second, a Bible school did not have enough training in "substantial liberal arts" to prepare Christian students for leadership (324). Not all agreed with Chapman, of course, but his notions held the day, and they essentially identified the need for a sheltered if not isolated academic community for young people ready to leave their birth home and to take up the heritage of their spiritual birth.

In the first 100 years of Nazarene colleges, discussion about students "called unto holiness" centered on "called from the world with its idols to flee," a flight that claimed to assure its pilgrims and witnesses of the primacy of liberalizing education and simultaneously to claim that core values would not be subject to secular influences. Various college seals symbolically appear to reveal the parallel strengths of faith and learning, and simultaneously that parallel is not entirely clear from the symbols. Not that the symbols *must* coincide with the academic life lived over the decades, but the current response to Mark Noll's indictment that profound connections have not been made between theology and other forms of learning as well as our own conferences on Faith/Living/Learning may suggest that the symbols may or may not have expressed reality. One might even ask, are good symbols important when charges are made that "evangelicals . . . have not won the right to be heard by twentieth-century intellectuals . . . [and evangelicals] are often suspicious of the methodical poking around of the scholar, and the intellectual's characteristic nuance, qualification, and suspension of judgment" (Hatch and Hamilton 409-10)? For example, consider the college seal of Madonna College, a Catholic college attempting to define how it is indeed "Catholic" in meaning and practice. The seal is used on all official documents, and on the chief ordinary is an open book, the symbol of learning. Across the pages are inscribed the words *Sapientia Desurum* (Wisdom from Above), "symbolizing the Holy Spirit, the source of all knowledge. The red of the escutcheon stands for the love of God, the aim and crown of all learning" (Grusczynski 3). The emblem is the starting place for examining how Madonna College is a witness to the Church's apostolate of teaching.

The seal of Eastern Nazarene College, recommended by President Gardener, incorporated the college motto *Via, Veritas, Vita*—the Way, the Truth, and the Life (Cameron 220). The lamp of learning stands on an open book with the world in the background. The Northwest Nazarene College seal also is shaped in a circle with laurel leaves, a cross, a torch, a triangle (Riley 107); the designer of the seal, Helen McMichael Robbin, stated that the emblems represent peace, the shield of salvation, the triangle as the high attainment of spirit, mind, body, with the help of the Trinity, the torch of knowledge and enlightenment, and the cross overshadows the entire seal (Archives letter 1960). MidAmerica Nazarene College's institutional crest identified the major images that tied the American heritage theme to the church and the college. The crest changed over the years, and now the central symbols are laid within a circle and the eagle, much larger, stands above the Christian cross and an open book. Should the colleges articulately interpret their symbols in the twenty-first century to stir and deepen the imagination?

The preservation of scholarship and holy living occur in the circle as they do for Madonna College, but it is perhaps not so clear what relationship exists between the intellectual and spiritual values of our own colleges. The circle was sufficient to experience God in the center and at points where the radii touched the outer ring of the circle. The problem for us is that the ring of the circle has been rubbed and blurred by the very forces that early traced it. The colleges, their leaders, and their constituencies turned to face culture in order to survive financially and to accomplish their own educational and spiritual goals. Nazarene colleges whether located in more rural areas such as Nampa, Idaho or Mount Vernon, Ohio or enmeshed in an urban setting as Trevecca Nazarene University set their course, however tentative, to enter "the world." Mildred Bangs Wynkoop in *The Trevecca Story* understood this call of the colleges to a "truly dynamic, a wholesome tension between a conservative organization and a liberal operational aspect:" (255)

> Can Trevecca College justify her existence in this new world? Can she survive financially? But, more important, can a Christian College enter the new world as a responsible involved entity, capable of speaking with and speaking to the new situation, but in the front line, not hiding in a corner. (254)

In the colleges' early history, urban culture seemed to epitomize all that was "evil" in American society. On the other hand, it was, according to historian James Cameron, the appeal of Quincy as a center of "history, culture, and education" that helped to influence the move of ENC from its early location in Rhode Island in 1919 (148). Cameron also notes the rich resources of the Boston Public Library and other university libraries in the greater Boston area. Graduates of the college could easily be encouraged to pursue graduate studies in the area.

The theme of MidAmerica Nazarene College's "American Heritage Education" was expressly established because traditional values in the country were scorned and institutional priorities were replaced by individual preferences; thus, the ". . . total campus atmosphere shall demonstrate a dynamic social awareness, a consistent appreciation of the American heritage, and a practical application of both Christian and democratic principles" (qtd. in Metz 166). Who was going to determine the features of "American heritage" and to define how both "kinds" of principles are implemented practically was not directly stated, but the potential did/does exist for a continued cultural isolation in order to make secure "American heritage." On the other hand, the college's theme strongly urges a "dynamic social awareness" that equally suggests contact if not dialogue with society. Dr. Curt Smith, with accurate understanding of past Nazarene educators, early commented that the criteria for selecting a location would be climate, job opportunities, accessibility, student population, and control of surroundings" (qtd. in Metz 94). According to Dr. Metz, "the College . . . became known as a center of conservative, dynamic spiritual expression," and as the academic dean he strongly urged making academics an "adventure of ideas" (111). The tension between "control" and "adventure" paradoxically pulls the circle with both centripetal and centrifugal force.

Concomitant with the motivation to keep true to the doctrinal standards in behavior and belief by establishing a connection between an academic, secluded "home" and the students' birth home was the inculcation of both positive and negative attitudes toward the liberal arts curriculum. Phineas Bresee, in 1915 at his last address to a college audience, set the rhetorical "stage" for the inclusion of liberal arts in Nazarene colleges.

> We have not forsaken the old classics. . . . We do not fear philosophy. We delight in mathematics. We cultivate the sciences. But in all of these matters the rule of life [is] the Word of God. It is appealed to, honored, studied. . . . It is the standard of experience, morals, life. (qtd.in *Called* 263)

This philosophy of education drafted by Dean Bertha Munro in 1948 (authorized by General Assembly) was anchored by a commitment to "an academic program of standard quality interpreted with Bible holiness, or as the best in faith combined with the best in education . . ." (qtd. in Cameron 371). As Nazarene faculty throughout the colleges were pursuing terminal degrees in liberal arts disciplines to fit them and to prepare students for service, who could foresee the forces of Wesleyan fundamentalism that saw "godlessness" in places as Harvard and the University of Chicago (*Called* 308-09)? The "incidental" nature of education in comparison to the supreme objective of building "holy character" caught the imagination of Pasadena's second president, E.P. Ellyson. The boundaries between liberal arts and professional studies, between the social sciences, the natural sciences, and the humanities, between undergraduate and graduate programs were subject to the all-consuming "larger" mission of preparation for evangelizing the world for Christ. However, the centrality of the liberal arts curriculum in Nazarene colleges' educational philosophy, variously interpreted, remained strong. The liberal arts tradition then and now was utilized to assist in the formation of character as an ideal education for leaders; in this sense that curriculum bound the college to a tradition and to a classical past.

Viewed this way, the liberal arts curriculum inevitably moored the Nazarene colleges to a programmatic posture that gave a certain credibility to their recent appearance in American education. It was an analogical counterpart of the traditional established "sanctuary" with its renowned reputation of academic "liturgy" that historically had shaped the best and brightest educated, and Christian, leaders. Conversely, the second tradition of liberal arts gained strength by its continuing search for truth. "It assumes no truth in the past, but is critical, constantly looking for new truths; it *liberates* individuals rather than binding them to a tradition" (Nord 82). This kind of investigation and confidence in the pursuit of truth on the frontiers of knowledge becomes a rough analogical counterpart to the "storefront church" and field preaching that took early holiness groups out of an established tradition. In both kinds of "frontiers," marginality and even isolation characterize the adventurers, and it is the "domestication" and application of knowledge or experience that brings a certain safety to the place where they research or worship.

Curiously enough, the most spirited discussion about non-traditional programs and off-campus sites has occurred among liberal arts adherents. This is, of course, not to suggest that liberal arts faculty are more attuned to preparing students to evangelize the world for Christ than their professional studies or graduate-faculty counterparts. In addition to the dual tradition inherited by liberal arts faculty, their own graduate training and gifts in either legacy are best exercised in the kind of isolation that early characterized Nazarene colleges. Nearly all liberal arts faculty as well as liberal arts adherents would agree with a recent scholar who told a faculty group that his way of serving is to study for four hours and write for four hours. The research project between chemistry professor and student in the laboratory—hours of working and building together—sitting together occasionally in chapel—meeting with other science students late in the summer for collaboration and coffee—narrowing in on a problem that might turn into a co-authored publication—writing and rewriting graduate school applications in an undergraduate classroom with the board full of art history dates as a backdrop—how different from the hospital conference room or teacher's lounge in an elementary school turned into a place for consultation between professor and student. Those intimate contacts and close relationships also occur for the professional-studies student and professor but the physical, academic, and spiritual communication—especially at the upper division level—frequently occurs off-campus. The contradiction inherent in "theology of place" surfaces again. The Nazarene colleges cultivated the symbols of "home" to keep the environment predictable and nurturing in faith and learning and at the same time this attachment to the locus of the college exists with a co-equal diasporic adventurous impetus.

What shall we say then? To not accept the contradictions in theology of place is also not to accept the mysteries of grace. Neither the move into the margins of place and society nor the preservation of a specific and sacred place will adequately define the experience of "called unto holiness." I wanted this essay to conclude with certainty that the historical ethos of a Nazarene college and the symbolic value of place cannot be transplanted to distant sites with new programs and adjunct faculty. In a narrow interpretation of the past, such transplanting would be possible and even necessary to remain faithful to the heritage. In a narrow interpretation of the past, the close nurturing of the religiously faithful as they study is also possible and even necessary to remain faithful to the heritage. However, a retrieval of the past, as Gerald Bruns notes, will inevitably "unmask" the past and force us to acknowledge alien categories both then and now (210). What Christian college whether an isolated enclave or one allegedly open to diversity and pluralism either historically or at present has not struggled to decide what and how much accommodation should be made to the secularizing trends—in chapel requirements, in faculty hiring practices, in conduct codes, in writing the mission statement, in defining what, who, where, and how a Christian academic community exists? On the other hand, as George Marsden reports, current research and analysis designed to define the distinctives of a Christian college already indicates the "triumph of academic over clerical values" (qtd. in *The Soul of the American University* 416). Bruns also notes, any reflection on tradition will require us eventually to consider the "nature of authority" (211). And that "authority" may be far more entrenched and powerful that first imagined.

Our "theology of place" as a denomination and as educational institutions has had contradictory impulses throughout, and the use of place and symbol both support and undermine any singular reading of the past and present. The temptation is great to listen to church historian, Timothy Smith, and to assume that his observation on compromise will *return* us in a revivalist spirit to what we claimed to be through the decades; in the "five principal elements of compromise," Smith states that historic Methodism was led away from its Wesleyan mission [by] the decline of the *doctrine of holiness* [italics mine] in Methodist colleges and theological seminaries" (*Mission* 8). The assumption that an historically linear and homogenous ascent to the experience and theology of entire sanctification existed collectively and individually is uncertain. PLNC Professor John Wright would say there is no "one horizon" in any category, past or present. Dr. Frank Carver, Professor of Philosophy/Religion, submits that "there are many dwelling places available to the disciple when the Paraclete comes." As Carver continues, "there are many surprising rooms awaiting discovery in the life of the Spirit" ("My Three Johns"). No room nor place is privileged over any other. However, it is to privilege "life in the Spirit" that both pulls into the center and allows the radii to break the circle. Amid the discussion by off-campus and on-campus faculty about programs that claim to fracture the community inside or outside the pale, the conversation may in fact be nothing more or less serious than what the institution views as academic quality and financial strength. (I am astonished by the raw irony of this observation.) Or the dialogue may be (should be?) "rifted" by the rupturing question that always characterizes Nazarene education: How will the symbols and rituals, the faculty and students, the chapel and the curriculum—in whatever place—tell the stories of prevenient, justifying, and sanctifying grace—stories of women and men "called unto holiness" in the academic community?

TRIBUTE

Kenosis

*What happens to a person's life when they leave
the place where that life was lived?
Does it end, like the waves of the ocean that reach
the limit of their race to the shore, drifting back
into mere memories of a time that was,
places that were, people that I once knew?
Or does it continue, like the persistent lap of those
same waves, making their mark on an ever-changing
shoreline of time, place, and people?
As I walk down this familiar beach, unfamiliar
with time, the place, and the people, I realize
that this existential question is really a question
about Incarnation.
And in Jesus, I find the answer is "yes;" and I'm
comforted in the pain of my separation, and given hope
in the search for the continuity I so deeply desire.*

> *Douglas S. Hardy*
> *Assistant Professor of Psychology*
> *Eastern Nazarene College*

SECTION TWO

CONFRONTING THE CENTRAL QUESTIONS

Does the Christian define personhood and pursue answers to the identity question in distinguishing ways? Will we take full advantage of a Christian liberal arts education to prepare us for an enlarged understanding of life?

Cecil Paul, from *First Message to Students*

CHAPTER EIGHT

THINKING ABOUT ECONOMICS AND ETHICS AS A WESLEYAN

Samuel M. Powell

The purpose of this essay is to contribute to Wesleyan thinking about ethics in one field—economic activity and policy.

However, the attempt to develop Wesleyan ethics provokes a couple of questions: What are the prospects for devising such an ethics? And, is the notion of distinctively Wesleyan ethics desirable? Responses to the first question are provided by several recent Wesleyan theologians who believe that John Wesley's theology gives some guidance for reflection on the ethical issues. James C. Logan has characterized Wesley's theology of culture as transformation because of Wesley's belief that the doing of God's perfect will is a realizable goal within history. This belief is, capable of unleashing "an ethical dynamic" (Logan 368). His point about the ethical optimism of Wesleyan theology is endorsed by Theodore Runyon, who has developed the idea of cultural transformation by annexing to it Wesley's concept of sanctification. He holds that for Wesley

> sanctification [is] the active presence of love expressed not only in word but in deed. . . . This is the power of the Kingdom that begins to exercise its humanizing impact in the present age. . . . Sanctification is the enlisting of the individual in God's own work—the redemption of his creation. (Runyon 34)

For Wesley, human ethical activity is an indispensable part of the divine salvation that is being worked out within the world (Runyon 28).

So the prospects are promising for developing Wesleyan ethics. The entire direction of John Wesley's theology and ministry points to the importance of ethical inquiry. However, the development of Wesleyan ethics has not yet been accomplished, especially as that ethics is to be applied to economic activity. Wesley himself did not fashion one. Although he occasionally made pronouncements on economic issues, they are helpful today mainly for their humanitarian spirit (Madron 115). His specific analyses are out of date, being responses to the economic systems of his day, systems that were chiefly mercantilist in character and only incipiently capitalist (Haywood 314-321). Wesley's followers have not fashioned one; their zeal has been more evident in social action than in social theory (Schilling 197 and Wogaman 391), an imbalance that suggests the need of more intellectual work to match the often impressive practical endeavors of Wesleyans.

As to the second question (Is the notion of distinctively Wesleyan ethics desirable?), one salient fact is that John Wesley made no claim to originality and, far from seeking a distinctive theology or ethics, sought only to be faithful to the heritage of Christian faith and practice. In other words, it is most "un-Wesleyan" to seek distinctively Wesleyan ethics. Wesley's idea of the catholic spirit impels the Wesleyan to recognize the ecumenical character of theology and to eschew narrow parochial approaches. As a result, Wesleyan ethics draws on the wisdom to be found within the entire Christian tradition.

What, then, does Wesleyan ethics when applied to economics, look like? Above all, love must be the central concept, for if Wesleyan theology stands for anything, it stands for the centrality of love (Hynson, *Reform* 56; Madron 105-6). The New Testament, especially 1 Corinthians, insists that love is a matter of seeking the common good. In particular, love guards against a selfish view of economic activity. Love also points toward the proper goal of economic activity—human good. Economic activity and policy must be constantly directed toward the satisfying of human needs and the securing of the material conditions of human good.

However, love is not sufficient as an ethical principle. In fact, it is more than a little bit vague, for it does not specify how to calculate the common good—whether all should receive equal amounts of the common good, or whether some may receive more than others. It is better to conceive of love as a compendium of values such as justice and stewardship. These supplementary values give specificity to love and are far more useful for directing ethical activity.

Justice, as applied to economics, compels recognition that every person is due the minimal goods necessary to conduct human life in a way befitting a being created in God's image. Of course, no one knows in advance what this minimum is; justice demands that there be public discussion and agreement on this issue. Also undecided in advance is how the goods that a society produces beyond its needs are to be distributed and used. In other words, what sort of gap, if any, between rich and poor can justice tolerate? It is an open question whether justice requires that every member of society receive equal shares of that society's goods or only equal opportunity to acquire those goods.

Love also comprises stewardship, which suggests duties toward God and future generations. Because of these duties, humanity bears a responsibility for the wise use of the earth's resources. Here Wesleyan ethics touches on environmental ethics, that is grounded in duty to God the Creator and that also implies the importance of using the world's resources in such a way that future generations will be able to enjoy a standard of living consonant with beings created in God's image. The principle of stewardship is an alternative to merely humanistic ethics and provides a universal context for Christian ethical inquiry—universal in space because it relates Christian ethics to the material world as well as to human society; universal in time because it forces consideration of future generations, both of humans and other living beings.

Wesleyan ethics must also take into account the doctrine of sin. This is the case not only because without sin there would be no need of ethical inquiry, but also because, in a sinful world, none of these values—love, justice, stewardship—can be maximally achieved without diminishing the others. That is, in theory there is a perfect harmony of these values; in practice there is no harmony. The implementing of one value necessarily involves the diminishing of another. As a result, decisions must be made as to which values will be subordinated and which will be emphasized.

This fact introduces another aspect of Wesleyan ethics—its pragmatic character. The adjudication of values and their implementation in the practical sphere are political decisions; they always involve negotiation and compromise. On the one hand, Wesleyans, with their perfectionist heritage, may be repelled by the idea of compromise; on the other hand, John Wesley's well-known pragmatic attitude toward the practical affairs of church and life suggest that Wesleyan ethics is the sort of ethics that stands for accomplishing as much good as is possible in any given situation. As a result, Wesleyan ethics is essentially political ethics, for it is concerned with actualizing certain values to the extent that they can be actualized. It does not remain content with describing the ideal realm of values but is instead prepared to use appropriate political means to bring about good.

In this essay I will review the following issues: first, how the Bible should be used in ethics; then the central values that compose love—stewardship and justice—and their application to the subject of human labor; next, a case study in the conflict of values—the debate about the merits of the free market and its relation to secondary values like freedom and private property; finally, some directions for further inquiry that are necessary if Wesleyan ethics is to be more completely articulated.

The Use of the Bible in Ethics

Wesleyan ethics is forthrightly based on the Bible. Scripture remains a storehouse from which the Christian ethicist takes new as well as old treasures. However, it is one thing to assert the importance and authority of the Bible; it is another thing to have a coherent account of the precise way in which the ethicist should employ the Bible. On this point ethicists extensively disagree. Nevertheless, there are some constants in the Wesleyan tradition that provide for a measure of agreement. Wesleyans acknowledge that the Bible provides the point of departure for ethical thinking. Further, Wesleyans agree that Scripture can be understood and confirmed only when tested with experience and reason and with the help of the larger Christian tradition. This appeal to experience, reason and tradition underlies some characteristic features of Wesleyanism: First, Wesleyans will refuse to be dogmatic about a supposed teaching of the Bible if it cannot be confirmed in the experience of the people of God. Second, the Wesleyan ethicist will not hesitate to use his or her critical and rational abilities in order to discern Scripture's meaning and to test interpretations of the Bible. Third, the Wesleyan will have an ecumenical openness to insights from other streams of the Christian tradition and will be eager to learn from the history of Christian thought.

These general principles will probably command widespread acceptance in Wesleyan circles. However, they do not offer much in the way of specific prescription for ethical activity. The question of how the Bible is to be used in specific cases is still unanswered. Wesleyans may be tempted to adopt the opinion of some Christian writers who assert that biblical prescriptions can be applied directly to modern economic issues without much interpretive fuss. They argue that the Bible is nothing less than a blueprint for national economics (North 27, 33-34). Others less obdurately insist that the Bible provides at the very least a particular direction for a nation's economic policy (Gish 138-140, 145-146).

However, Wesleyans should resist this temptation to find in the Bible a blueprint for national economic and social policy, lest they rashly assume that employing the Bible in ethics is an easy and direct matter. Economic realities change over time with the result that biblical precepts appropriate to ancient economic realities may not be directly and specifically helpful today (Halteman 36-37). For example, there has been a great change in the idea of wealth since biblical times. Ancient people

> thought there were only so many goods and services available to be distributed to the people. Increasing the economic pie by expanding productivity over time was not part of their thinking. . . . They thought this constant pie of production was fixed permanently at roughly an amount equal to what it took to keep the population alive and well but not expanding. (Halteman 54-55)

Because of this view, wealth was regarded as "hoarded future consumption that contributed nothing to future production." What ancient people lacked was the capitalist notion of wealth that produces new wealth (Halteman 56). As a result, the teachings of an ancient document like the Bible should not be lifted, without further consideration, out of their original social context and forced into a modern context.

In summary, while no one can know in advance what the Bible will say about this or that issue in economics, we can at least be sure that Wesleyans will take the Bible with the utmost seriousness and use all available resources to understand it rightly. Following John Wesley's lead, they will refrain from wooden literalistic interpretations of the Bible and will keep in mind the overall purpose of Scripture instead of fashioning precepts on the basis of isolated bits of the Bible.

Ethical Norms Commonly Used in Christian Ethics Today

Instead of seeking to apply particular scriptural passages to today's ethical issues or nostalgically longing for a return to biblical law, Wesleyans will most likely draw certain ethical norms from the Bible that indicate God's will generally for humanity.

Contemporary Christian authors and denominations appeal mainly to two such norms: stewardship and justice. Protestants are especially attracted to the idea of stewardship, perhaps because of the predominance of the idea of covenant in Protestant theology. Roman Catholics tend to use the idea of justice more than stewardship since their ethics relies on the ideas of natural law and the social nature of human beings. In general Protestant ethics rests more on humanity's obligation to God while Roman Catholic ethics rests more on human beings' obligation to each other.

Where do Wesleyans stand on this subject? That is not easy to determine, for neither covenant nor natural law has been a mainstay of Wesleyan theology. Besides that, John Wesley himself engaged in no sustained ethical thinking and his followers have historically proved quite eclectic. However, in view of the claim made by Wesleyans to be neither Roman Catholic nor Protestant exclusively, perhaps the wisest policy, or at least the most Wesleyan, will be to acknowledge the claims of both stewardship and justice as leading norms and to give up the attempt at a single dominant norm that should characterize Wesleyan ethical thinking.

Stewardship

Stewardship implies that responsibility for something has been delegated by one individual to another. Familiar examples of it include the oaths of office taken by public officials and the appointing of trustees to oversee an estate. In each case the steward is given a duty to perform on behalf of another. In moral discourse, stewardship implies that the steward does not have absolute authority over the object of his or her care. So a trustee has discretion in the disposition of an estate but not the freedom that comes from ownership.

The Bible neither defines stewardship nor applies it systematically to economics; however, there are Scriptures in abundance that presuppose the idea of stewardship. The most notable of these is Genesis 1:28 according to which God, having created humans in the divine image, commanded them to rule over the world. The idea of stewardship is present in the notion of delegation; God has delegated rule over the earth to humanity. Therefore, human use of the earth lies within the bounds of God's providence and is subject to God's moral demand. This point is reinforced by Psalm 24 which asserts "The earth is the Lord's." Genesis 1:28 and this Psalm together imply that while ownership belongs to God, use and its concomitant responsibility are given to humanity.

This responsibility makes humanity answerable for the use of such gifts as freedom and power, a responsibility that places moral limits upon their exercise. It is also a matter of wisely using the resources of the earth to provide materially for humanity's material well-being. Since humanity has the use but not the ownership of the earth, it should not use the earth's resources in any arbitrary way. Instead, God establishes limits on what may legitimately be done with the created world and demands that its use be in accord with God's own desires. Furthermore, not only the redeemed people of God bear this responsibility; stewardship pertains to humans as created beings, not as redeemed beings and so it is a universal duty. Everyone must answer to God the creator for the use of what God has provided.

The idea of stewardship finds a clear resonance in Wesleyan theology's emphasis on human responsibility. Admittedly, Wesleyans have more often exercised the idea of responsibility as a buttress for the notion of freedom than as a means of discerning our ethical duty. Nevertheless, there are resources here for Wesleyans to exploit for constructive thought about economics and ethics. Human responsibility and responsiveness suggest both our ethical duties and our interconnectedness with God and with each other.

Justice

However, the idea of stewardship in itself, apart from other norms, does not indicate *how* to allocate resources or in what measure, or to what extent it is permissible to exploit natural resources, or which goods and services to produce. In itself stewardship functions mainly as a limiting concept in economic analysis by disclosing that there are moral limits to actions. It prohibits certain actions (e.g., selfishly squandering what God has provided), but does not expressly state what should be done. Other norms such as justice are required for more specific ethical prescriptions. Wesleyans, with their renowned and socially progressive activism, should be naturally inclined toward issues of justice.

The problem is that justice is a much controverted subject among Christian ethicists. The disagreement extends even to the meaning of the word justice. Some hold that, in Scripture, justice is a *virtue* that the *individual* exercises (e.g. by helping the poor), not a *prescription* for a *nation's* economic policy. Such a definition would discourage the state from entering the economic arena with the aim of ensuring a predetermined distribution of goods. This definition likens justice to individual righteousness and rejects its application to politics and the idea of distribution (Nash 21-22).

However, most Christian ethicists embrace a wider meaning of justice, acknowledging that it includes the proper distribution of goods. For these ethicists, the question is, "Which economic system comes closest to bringing about this proper distribution?" Some display considerable confidence in the free market, stipulating only that it can ensure justice when supplemented by such Christian virtues as concern for the poor and simplicity of life (Diehl 91, 102). Others are more guarded about the free market's ability to bring about justice. Their reservation is based on the observation that, while the market may allow rational agents to transfer goods fairly, it excludes those who, because of past injustices, have no goods to transfer. In other words, the market is merely a mechanism of transfer; action by the state is required to redress the effects of unjust distribution of the past (Beversluis 40, 46). The contemporary debate about affirmative action illustrates this problem. If the state merely ensures that current economic transactions are fair, justice may still not be served, for unequal possession of wealth in the present may result from unjust acts of distribution in the past. Guarding current transactions could serve only to protect the results of these unjust acts. So, according to this view, the state should seek to compensate those in the present who suffer from past unjust acts because the market is unable to provide compensation. Others are even more critical of the market, holding not only that the market cannot ensure justice, but also that it is an obstacle to justice—that it is an instrument of injustice (*Gathered* 84, 86, 90).

Wesleyans have historically been sympathetic to the call to justice; however there has never been a consensus among Wesleyans as to the precise meaning of justice or its social consequences. A recent book by Theodore Jennings, Jr. has sought to remedy this lacuna in Wesleyan ethics by stating in unequivocal terms that Wesleyan theology should attack "the principles of capitalism and the ethos of accumulation and consumption of wealth" (Jennings 116). Wesley, he suggests, questioned the identification of the church with the propertied and powerful and thus opened "the way to a fundamentally radical socioeconomic ethic" (Jennings 43). Wesley's ministry to the poor indicates that "the welfare of the poor should be the litmus test of *all* activity" (Jennings 66). Holiness, in this view, consists in standing apart from the world, especially in its addiction to wealth (Jennings 148-149). Holiness also implies evangelical economics, because it is a matter of devoting to God the whole of life and because the economic sphere is "the sphere of human agency *par excellence*" (Jennings 154-155). This opinion holds wealth to consist in whatever goods one possesses beyond what is required for well-being. Jennings asserts that such wealth in truth belongs to the poor—keeping it for oneself is in fact theft (Jennings 106-110).

There is no question that Jennings has represented an idea that was important to John Wesley. Wesley was concerned not only for the material condition of the poor but also for the spiritual condition of the wealthy. He shared the New Testament's teaching that wealth is a great spiritual danger and wanted Methodists to embody monastic simplicity and even poverty. However, can Jennings' otherwise laudable view serve as the basis of Wesleyan social ethics? Can it serve as a national social policy? If all Christians or even all citizens acted according to this prescription, would the pressing national problem of poverty be alleviated? Regrettably, the answer is probably "No." The redistribution of wealth to those with need for the purpose of raising their level of consumption would result in the postponement but not the elimination of poverty. Jennings scores some good points with his criticism of a consumer-oriented society; however, his admonition that Christians give away their surplus wealth may save them from the perils of riches but will most likely not bring an end to poverty.

For the most attractive treatment of justice, the Wesleyan ethicist will turn to Roman Catholic theology. The Roman Catholic view is that a society's prosperity cannot be measured simply by the sum of its produced goods. Instead the index of prosperity must include justice, that is, the way in which the goods are distributed throughout the society. This is because all economic activity aims at the development and perfection of each individual within the community. Justice demands the removal of immense economic inequalities. It implies that individuals possess the fundamental rights that are essential for dignified life in community. It is, finally, measured by our treatment of those who are powerless—society's treatment of the powerless is the yardstick of its level of justice (*Justice* 119; *Building* par. 86).

Roman Catholic thinking about justice is grounded in the created dignity of human beings and the predominant importance of the human person for economic ethics. Two foundational statements are found in the Vatican II document, *Gaudium et Spes*:

> The subject and goal of all social institutions is and must be the human person, which for its part and by its very nature stands completely in need of social life. (*Justice* 174)

> There is a growing awareness of the exalted dignity proper to the human person, since he stands above all things, and his rights and duties are universal and inviolable.... Hence the social order and its development must always work to the benefit of the human person if the disposition of affairs is to be subordinate to the personal realm. (*Justice* 175)

The idea of human dignity complements the idea of stewardship and provides direction for action. It affirms the centrality of human good in ethical considerations and emphasizes the importance of justice.

Justice, then, is one of the concrete forms that love takes. It deserves the Wesleyan's highest attention because of John Wesley's own special concern for the poor. Of course, it is one thing to be concerned about the plight of the poor and even to take active steps to alleviate their pain; it is another thing to develop a sound theory of justice. Wesleyans have been a bit slack on the theoretical aspect, but it is precisely to this aspect that requires attention if we are to discern the forms that justice should take.

Human Labor

As a way of showing the application of stewardship and justice in the sphere of economics, I will consider the subject of work from Roman Catholic and Protestant perspectives.

The Roman Catholic view associates the idea of work with the image of God and thus with human dignity. Because humanity is created in the image of God, it seeks to actualize itself through work. In a remote way human labor imitates the creative activity of God. For this reason the value of work depends on the person who works and not on the kind of work performed (*Justice* 298-299). Further, because the value of work has its origin in the worker and not in the product, labor is more important than capital; labor is the primary efficient cause in production, capital is merely an instrument. Capital is simply the accumulation of human labor (*Justice* 308-309). The point here is that capital is not an autonomous factor in production with magical properties but rather a means for humans to actualize their nature. Protestants have a slightly different view of work. They hold that work is good because it is a means by which stewards use the creativity that God has given to us. They also emphasize the social nature of work, the fact that cooperation is necessary for God's gifts to us to be expressed (Graham 99-100). Work is far more than a means of obtaining material goods for the sustaining of life. It is also a spiritual activity by which we make ourselves into truly human persons. So, work or working conditions that diminish a person's humanity or which do not allow for the expression of our creativity conflict with Christian ethics.

As noted above, a Wesleyan theory of labor will draw on both sides of the Roman Catholic-Protestant divide. Wesleyans, neither exclusively Protestant nor Catholic, will gladly appeal to both stewardship and justice in fashioning a view of human labor.

Wesleyan pragmatism will concern itself with bringing the conditions of labor into conformity with these principles. In a modern economic situation, jobs are so specialized that the individual's contribution to a product may be small and work may consist of restricted and repetitious acts. What does it then mean for work to express our created dignity? Some work is so menial as to frustrate the process of becoming truly human through work. At the very least, Christian ethical considerations compel us to support social policies that ameliorate the mind-numbing and body-deforming aspects of physical labor. Examples of such policies include vigorous governmental inspection of the workplace, insuring compliance with safety laws, and the enforcement of child labor laws overseas.

Capitalism: A Case Study in the Conflict of Values

In this section I will illustrate the point that in a sinful world there are inevitable conflicts of values. All values cannot be simultaneously affirmed to the same degree; choices must be made and hierarchies of values established, some assuming a superior position, others a subordinate position. The merits of the capitalist system of economics presents a case study in this conflict, for arguments for and against capitalism hinge on the choice between *freedom* and *justice.*

Supporters of the free market claim on both historical and logical grounds that only the free market can guarantee individual freedom from undue governmental encroachment. They thus elevate freedom to the highest rank. Critics of capitalism argue that freedom must be balanced by or even made subordinate to justice.

On the one hand are those Christians who advocate capitalism as a bulwark of human freedom (Griffiths 89-90). First, they define freedom as absence of unnecessary governmental intrusion into the private sphere. One can observe here the classical liberal fear that unless there is some counterweight (like the free market) to the state, the result will be governmental totalitarianism. Second, they support their association of capitalism and freedom by criticizing the post-World War II communist regimes of eastern Europe. That is, they draw attention to those countries where private property was most thoroughly eliminated and individual freedom minimized and draw the conclusion that there is an inseparable connection between politics and economics. They regard the totalitarian communist regimes as proof of the demerits of socialism and of the need of a free market.

On the other hand are those Christians who are critical of the classical liberal notion of freedom, holding it to be incompatible with biblical values. They want freedom to be balanced by an emphasis on social obligations (Hay 162). Some go so far as to reject the liberal valuation of freedom by contrasting it with the kingdom of God's emphasis on the total welfare of all people. They point out the contrast between the free market's auction-based system of pricing goods and the need-based voluntary sharing characteristic of God's kingdom (Halteman 51).

The dilemma is that neither freedom nor justice can attain a maximum without diminishing the other. Complete freedom would threaten justice by allowing the powerful and wealthy to establish their own rights at the expense of others. Perfect justice could only occur by a presumably coerced curbing of freedom. As a result, an adjudication of this conflict of values is necessitated, an adjudication that must remain an open question as long as people disagree on the relative values of freedom and justice.

This question of freedom and justice is given concrete form by the idea of *private property*. Advocates of the free market commonly associate freedom with private property. They argue that freedom from the overweening power of government can be maintained only if individuals possess wealth-making property and the power that results from it. Christians who agree with this view offer biblical arguments for private property. They assert that the right of private property is supported by Old Testament law and custom, which granted to each family autonomous use of their property within the limits of stewardship responsibility (Griffiths 56). The fact that land was the principal means of producing wealth in ancient Israel confirms, the advocates assert, Old Testament support of private property.

Other Christians have attacked the priority of property rights, arguing that such rights are not absolute. Although conceding the right of private property, they deny that it is so important that it should be the foundation of economic ethics. Instead of emphasizing the prerogatives of private property, they stress the obligations of stewardship (Hay 78-79). Further, they challenge the assumption that present-day distribution of property rests on just distributions in the past. Finally, they believe the Old Testament idea of the Jubilee (Lev. 25) refutes the thesis that property may be owned absolutely by stipulating that land was eventually to revert back to its original owners (Hay 161).

The Roman Catholic document *Gaudium et Spes* provides a balanced view of property rights and freedom. It denies absolute freedom with respect to private property. It teaches that all material goods including property should be used in light of the fact that God created the earth for the common good. Material goods have a social, not merely a private, function. Even the right to private property is violable, for those in extreme poverty are morally justified in taking what they need from the riches of others (*Justice* 190-191).

However, it also recognizes the value of private property, which contributes "to the expression of the personality" and furnishes the individual "an occasion to exercise his function in society." It also safeguards the autonomy and freedom of the person and is a condition of civil liberties. Consequently, it can be appropriated by the state, in socialization, "only by the competent authority, according to the demands and within the limits of the common good and with fair compensation" (*Justice* 192). The Roman Catholic church is here stating that neither governmental authority nor private property is absolute: private property is a legitimate check to governmental power, but must be relinquished if the interests of the larger political community are compelling.

The dilemma between justice and freedom is at work in the current debate about governmental foreclosure of private lands needed for ecological restoration and the need to provide fair compensation for lands so designated. Wesleyan pragmatism compels recognition that in an imperfect world, every political decision will involve a compromise of values. Wesleyans will attempt to bring about as much good as is possible under these conditions while maintaining the vision of the perfect realization of God's will even in the midst of hard choices and difficult decisions.

Concluding Wesleyan Postscript

In this postscript, I will sketch out some of the issues that Wesleyans should address if Wesleyan ethics is to attain completeness.

One issue is deciding which theological doctrines Wesleyans should employ as the basis of Wesleyan ethics. Scholars are undecided as to whether John Wesley's ethics is based mainly on the doctrine of creation and concomitant ideas as the image of God, natural law and prevenient grace (Hynson "Implications" 380-381; Logan 365) or on the doctrines of redemption and Christology (Schilling 205, 208; Hynson *Reform* 52, 56). Fortunately, there is no need of an either-or choice between these options; however clarity is needed regarding the foundation of Wesleyan ethics.

Another issue concerns certain theological issues that are troublesome. Two that are especially problematic to Wesleyans (because they have never been the object of sustained reflection) are the kingdom of God and the interpretation of the Old Testament. Understanding of the kingdom is important for clarifying the motivation for ethical Christian activity in the world; greater appreciation of the Old Testament is required because the Bible's teaching about justice and stewardship is located almost exclusively in the Old Testament.

Wesleyan theology must come to terms with the idea of the kingdom of God and the theological issue of eschatology. Wesleyan denominations have wisely avoided making pronouncements about the end of the world; however, Christian ethics must build on some conception of the kingdom of God. In particular, a tradition's view of the kingdom and of eschatology at least partially determines the tradition's stance toward social and political issues. For example, apocalyptic sects have been understandably reticent to become involved in political action and economic issues because of their conviction that all such things will soon pass away. So Wesleyans, if they are to contribute to Christian ethics, must think hard about eschatology and the consequences of their eschatology for social and political involvement. I suggest that we regard the kingdom as those occasions when people do what is pleasing to God. The kingdom is already present to the extent that people obey God; however, the full measure of its presence lies still in the future because we do not obey God continuously and consciously. Further, the kingdom can be found outside the bounds of the Christian churches, just as the good Samaritan (Luke 10) and Cornelius (Acts 10) were pleasing to God while standing outside the historic people of God. According to this view, the political arena is not cut off from the kingdom—indeed, the kingdom may be just as present in government as in the church. This does not mean that political activity is equivalent to building the kingdom. It does mean that the church should not ignore the potential presence of the kingdom outside the boundaries of the visible church and should recognize political activity as a legitimate expression of the ethics of love.

Wesleyans must also come to terms with the Old Testament's concern for justice. This presupposes a grasp of how the Old Testament relates to the New. Some streams of the Protestant tradition, notably those of the radical reformation (the "Anabaptists") have emphasized the New Testament's differences from the Old; others, especially Reformed Christians, have regarded the Old and New Testaments as two forms of the same covenant. Anabaptists have been somewhat suspicious of the Old Testament; Reformed Christians have regarded the Old Testament as a fully valid source of revelation. Not surprisingly, Christians of the radical reformation have tended to eschew direct political involvement while Reformed Christians have eagerly encouraged involvement in social activism and political efforts.

Wesleyan churches, especially the smaller ones, have uneasily combined these two historic traditions, leaving to the individual the decision as to what sort and level of social and political involvement is appropriate. There is a certain strength to this position, for a denomination as such should not be directly involved in the political sphere. Such involvement would constitute ecclesiastical encroachment on public policy-making. Nevertheless, by leaving the matter up to individual choice entirely, the churches risk giving the impression that social and political involvement is unimportant. For this reason, it is imperative that the Wesleyan churches consider their corporate responsibility to inquire into social and political matters; however, before this can happen there must be some understanding of the relation of the Old Testament to the New. The point of departure should be the fact that the New Testament writers regarded the New and the Old as different, yet continuous. The New does not cancel the Old; it continues and perfects the Old. As a result, we should regard the Old Testament's concern for justice and stewardship as fully a matter of revelation as any teaching of the New Testament.

In broad outline, then, Wesleyan ethics as applied to economic theory and practice begins with the Bible. It seeks there its foundations. It is also sensitive to the difficulties of interpreting the Bible and applying it to present-day ethical issues. It accordingly takes into account the importance of rational coherence in ethics, the role of experience in confirming the results of biblical interpretation, and the wisdom of the Christian heritage. It avoids narrowly provincial approaches and instead makes common cause with Christians of other traditions, seeking agreement wherever possible.

At the center of Wesleyan ethics is the command to love God and neighbor. However, it implements love concretely by attending to the Bible's message of justice and stewardship. Thereby it avoids abstract theses and keeps in mind the importance of fashioning ethics in the context of contemporary issues.

Wesleyan ethics is also pragmatic. On the one hand, this pragmatic character implies mindfulness about the need of practical involvement and activism—ethics is not just theory; on the other hand it suggests recognition of the fact that in political activism compromise is inevitable. Wesleyan pragmatism always seeks the greatest amount of good possible, using its principles of love, justice and stewardship as guides. It tempers the optimism inherent in the Christian view of the kingdom with a sober acknowledgement of the imperfection and sinfulness of the world.

Thus conceived, Wesleyan ethics can be just the sort of apologetics that the church today needs. Gone are the days when theologians could imagine that intellectual arguments for Christianity were the main task. Today, in addition to the necessary job of defending Christianity intellectually, the church must open up another apologetic front—a practical one, consisting in good works and love of neighbor and based on sound theory. Such practical apologetics should be part of the face that the church presents to the world and a means by which it may compete against the religious challenges of the day.

TRIBUTE

When I think of Dr. Cecil Paul, I picture a kind, gentle giant—not large in stature, but large in heart and compassion, absolutely committed to equality among people. He inspired all who knew him to reach greater heights in the workplace, in their relationships, and in their personal lives.

Norene Pfautz Fiacco
Associate Professor of English
Eastern Nazarene College

CHAPTER NINE

FROM "BARELY" TO "FULLY" PERSONAL: ON THE THERAPEUTIC ACTION OF PREVENIENT GRACE *WITHIN* THE PERSONALITY

G. Michael Leffel

Once a prince went crazy and convinced himself that he was a turkey. He took off all his clothes and sat naked under the table, and refused to eat any real food. He put into his mouth only some oats and tiny bits of bone.

His father, the King, brought all the doctors to cure him, but they could do nothing. Finally, one wise man came to the King and said, "I take it upon myself to cure your son."

Right away the wise man took off all his clothes, sat under the table next to the prince and began collecting oats and bits of bone, and putting them into his mouth.

The prince asked him, "Who are you? What are you doing here?" The wise man responded, "Who are you? What are you doing here?" The prince answered, "I am a turkey." The wise man said, "I also am a turkey."

The two turkeys sat together until they got used to each other. Once the wise man saw this, he hinted to the King to bring him a shirt. The wise man put it on, and he said to the prince, "Do you think that a turkey isn't allowed to wear a shirt? He is allowed, and if he wears one, he is not any less a turkey." These words the prince took to heart and he agreed to wear a shirt, too.

A few days later, the wise man hinted to the King to bring him a pair of pants. He put them on, and said to the prince, "Do you think that a turkey is forbidden to wear pants? Even if he wears pants, he is still a full-fledged turkey." The prince admitted that this was true, and he too started wearing pants.

This went on, step by step, until finally, having followed the wise man's instructions, the prince was wearing a full set of clothes. Later, the wise man asked that human food be served on top of the table. He took some of it and ate it, and he said to the prince, "Do you think that a turkey is forbidden to eat some good food? One can eat the best food in the world and still be a true-blooded turkey." The prince accepted this, too, and began eating like a human being.

Once the wise man saw this, he said to the prince, "Do you really think that a turkey must sit under the table? No, not necessarily so! A turkey can walk around wherever he likes and no one holds it against him." The prince pondered this and accepted the wise man's view. And once he stood up and walked like a human being, he began acting like a real human being and forgot that he was a turkey.

This story of a *person who became a turkey who became a person again*, drawn from the homiletic tales of one of the Chassidic rabbis, Rabbi Nachman of Bratzlav (qtd. in Roth 41-42), may be interpreted as a narrative of Christian transformation. A familiar interpretation of this story might sound something like this. Human creatures, "fallen" from their princely place in the Kingdom, have become "lost" to and disoriented from their true destiny, and are now living lives that no longer could be regarded as "personal." While our biblical interpretations of original sin do not tell us exactly how the prince has fallen into this lower, less advanced form of life, the King, unwilling to abandon his son to this state of sub-personal existence, sends his representative to restore the son to his princely status. He takes upon himself the shape of fallen existence, meets the fallen creature with wisdom that appears as foolishness, and step-by-step restores the prince to his original destiny.

To Christian eyes, this story is a reasonably complete parable of Grace, including a few insightful lessons about how wise human guides might participate in the restoration of lost persons. I would like to suggest, however, that this parable (and the accompanying interpretation), like more familiar narratives of spiritual transformation, tells only part of the story, and, in fact, has a tendency to obscure part of it. Ludwig Wittgenstein (29) once observed that:

> The aspects of things that are most important for us are hidden because of their simplicity and familiarity. (One is unable to notice something because it is always before one's eyes.) The real foundations of his inquiry do not strike a man at all. . . . And this means; we fail to be struck by what, once seen, is most striking and most powerful.

What this story of transformation does not, indeed cannot say to us, given the more familiar theological emphasis on God's "transcendence" more than "immanence," concerns the transformative activity occurring *within* the prince which made it possible for him to be changed by the King's emissary. This is the story of the immanence of Divine activity within the personality, in distinction to (but certainly not opposed to) the transcendent activity of the transforming Other "outside" the personality.

Toward a Psychology of Prevenient Grace

> I am more convinced than ever that the basic substance of the Wesleyan view of man's incredible journey from the "barely" human to the "truly" human to "fully" human is one of the richest of all available options.
> —Albert Outler

One of the Wesleyan tradition's fundamental and perhaps distinctive contributions to the spiritual formation literature is its vision of what it means to be "person" and what it means to be characterologically transformed. Using concepts from contemporary psychotherapeutic psychology that pertain to characterological change, this essay will suggest a direction for constructing a psychology of Prevenient Grace that is consistent with an Anglican-Wesleyan anthropology and theology of character transformation. The essay outlines a central theological organizing principle for thinking about Prevenient Grace in immanent terms: *character development as transformation of the capability to create and the freedom to express generative love.* Concepts from contemporary psycho-therapeutic literatures potentially useful in describing the therapeutic action of immanent Prevenient Grace are introduced, particularly the concept of generativity.[1]

From an Anglican-Wesleyan point of view, Prevenient Grace is not to be seen only as the action of a gracious God standing outside human personality acting upon it to initiate change, but also and more fundamentally, as developmental and transformative (restorative) processes immanent within (i.e., built into) the personality. Thus viewed, this proposal is an attempt to expand upon certain Eastern Orthodox anthropological understandings that Wesley incorporated into his theology of the "dynamics of the Divine-human relationship" (Maddox 65). In particular, it emphasizes the Eastern Orthodox idea that what it fundamentally means to be a person, and to come to a "knowledge" of God, is to *truly* share in the Divine nature of God. Sharing in the Divine nature means that a person more *fully* participates in the "energies" of God. Lossky (87) summarizes this position:

> In receiving the gift—the deifying energies—one receives at the same time the indwelling of the Holy Trinity—*inseparable from its natural energies* and present in them in a different manner but none the less truly from that in which it is present in its nature. . . . The union to which we are called . . . is a union with God in his energies, or *union by grace making us participate in the divine nature*, without our essence becoming thereby the essence of God.

Thus, this proposal builds upon an interpretation of Wesleyanism (Maddox 67) which holds that "Wesley's understanding of human nature and the human problem gives primacy of place to therapeutic concerns, as those more characteristic of Eastern Christianity."

Recent developmental and psychotherapeutic psychology literatures, particularly the contemporary psychoanalytic tradition (Greenberg and Mitchell), has the potential to help deepen our Wesleyan understandings of Christian transformation. Wesleyanism's identification of "love" with spiritual maturity (deemphasizing the intellectual "belief" component of Christian faith that is more heavily emphasized in the Reformed tradition), makes it especially imperative that Wesleyan anthropology understands something of how love develops, becomes malformed, and is transformed. Many psychotherapeutic constructs may be seen as an "alternative language system" for expressing theological truths. Essentially, this essay argues that when the concept of Christian transformation is viewed through a central Wesleyan hermeneutic, *the capability to create and the freedom to express generative love*, personal developmental goals typically relegated to the realm of the "therapeutic," become fundamentally the same goals of spiritual development for all persons. If we affirm with St. Irenaeus, one of the fathers of Eastern Christianity, that, "The Glory of God is man (*person*) fully alive," then God's transforming activity in the lives of persons must surely encompass processes which psychotherapists recognize to be essential to the maturation of capabilities which make us persons. Grace must make us *persons*, even as (or perhaps before) "it" makes us spiritual persons (i.e., a *person* also living at a functional level called *spirit*).

The theological construct of Prevenient Grace, most reviews suggests that the term represents both a general description of God's all-encompassing activity in the lives of persons, and a more specific meaning having to do with the preparation of a person for the acceptance of the gospel of salvation proper. Concerning the general meaning, Outler (8) writes:

This is the true meaning of God's prevenience: not only that God loves us no matter what (although he does), but that God's grace anticipates us at every turn—from conception and birth through all our crises to destiny's climax, creating and holding open possibilities of health and growth and self-fulfillment, never imposing mere arbitrary determinants of character or moral action.

And again, emphasizing prevenience as the ever-present, sustaining activity of God, he concludes:

Men are not just what they will and choose . . . they become what they will and choose within the atmosphere and options of God's grace (prevenient, cooperative, encompassing). Thus, *no man is on his own at any point in development*, and no man can "save" himself apart from God's ever-present activity.

Following Outler's general meaning of the Wesleyan notion of Prevenient Grace, I propose that Prevenient Grace involves the developmental and therapeutic immanence of God in the human personality: *Prevenient Grace within the personality is God's way of extending to us the opportunity to become persons, and to accept our responsibility to participate in that process. The attainment of "personhood" itself, and in particular, the transformation of a person's capability to create generative love, is a developmental and therapeutic achievement made possible only by the transformative processes of immanent Grace at work in the human personality.* To say that Prevenient Grace is both developmental and therapeutic suggests two things. First, immanent prevenient grace is to be observed both in the developmental construction of the personality itself, and secondly in its innately therapeutic (restorative) functioning. From either vantage point, personality is animated by a movement towards its own transformation, even if this movement is not acknowledged or responded to by the individual. Stated another way, this position suggests that the theological term Prevenient Grace names transformational processes inherently built into the functioning of the human psyche. These processes are understood to have their fullest therapeutic effects when persons willingly and consciously participate in and with them; but processes, nevertheless, which have their origin outside powers of conscious deliberation and will power. Since these processes can be understood to exist as part of the inherent functional workings of the personality, objections from the social constructionist theory of knowledge notwithstanding, they could be referred to as *transformative processes of Prevenient Grace*. While this position does not suggest that Prevenient Grace should be thought of only as inherent developmental and therapeutic processes, I am proposing that our understanding of Prevenient Grace should be inclusive of these processes. To the extent that these inherent processes are understood to be expressions of the Creator working in the fabric of human personality, Christian growth and development may be viewed as the life-long activity of participating in the processes of Prevenient Grace. Participation in these processes can be construed as part of the revelatory and sacramental activity of God in the lives of persons; activity designed for our continued transformation from developmental states which are *barely* personal, to *truly* personal, to (more) *fully* personal.

Attempting to be suggestive and invitational, rather than definitive and sufficiently systematic, this essay outlines a "vision" of characterological transformation that is consistent with an "Anglican consciousness"(Holmes), a theological consciousness that seeks to preserve both Catholic and Protestant insights about the relationship between nature and grace. Methodologically, this understanding of Prevenient Grace draws on concepts found within familiar interpretations of Wesleyanism (Maddox; Wynkoop), while attempting to extend them to encompass "personalist" anthropological understandings (Brightman), and psychoanalytic assumptions about the nature of personality development (Erikson) and therapeutic process (Loewald; Settlage).

Before discusssing these ideas it may be useful to first consider both some of the potential contributions and controversies that identifying Prevenient Grace in immanent terms may raise. First, identifying personality itself as a natural province of Prevenient Grace has the potential to assist us in understanding characterological transformation in several ways. It identifies certain "means of Grace" which have infrequently been recognized within the scope of God's activity (e.g., the therapeutic aspect of transference, liberation-mourning, internalization). As such, it specifies different ways in which a person can actively be involved with God in their own transformation (i.e., *an asceticism of characterological transformation*). It also specifies clearer roles for those who are acting to assist believers in the crisis and process journey of spiritual development.

Within Wesleyan thought there presently exists a wide "gap" between our anthropology which stresses the need for an affectional-motivational change in the "heart" of the person, and our theology which tells us how this is to be accomplished. In the absence of scholarly and popular writing on the practices of transformation, almost by default, contemporary Wesleyanism uncritically accepts most of the more "rationalistic" principles and practices of spiritual change that are more a product of Reformed thinking than the "lost" Anglican heritage of Wesleyanism. For example, we have almost entirely abandoned teachings and spiritual practices from the "apophatic tradition" within our Anglican heritage that, in some sense, informed Wesley's own vision of transformation. Ironically, many psychotherapeutic understandings practiced both by secular and Christian therapists are essentially apophatic in nature. For example, the importance of suffering, grief, and sorrow in "heart change"; the "purging" of the power of early memories by telling and re-living them in the therapeutic relationship; the importance of "detachment" from false self-esteem-enhancing motivations and relational patterns; and the need for a movement away from culturally-determined "centers" of meaning and identity to a more authentic foundation, are all apophatic practices reminiscent of early Eastern (Allen) and Western (Leech) Christian spiritual direction practices. Despite our anthropology, Wesleyan practices still tend to be based on "rationalistic" assumptions about spiritual formation, emphasizing matters of conscious thinking, belief, and "will" (understood rationalistically, not as "affections" as Wesley did).[2] This emphasis, useful as it is in some ways, has the unfortunate effect of limiting us from thinking more deeply about one of the central distinctives of Wesleyanism, the capability to love and its restoration from the "powers of canceled sin," powers which reside in (at least, in part) the workings of human character. From the vantage point of psychotherapeutic psychology, present Wesleyan thought, unlike some historical Anglican thinking, seems to operate without much understanding of the importance of unconscious mental and emotional processes in the development and transformation of love. Thus, we are not drawn to certain historical spiritual development literatures that understood something of the unconscious determinants of love and its distortions (e.g., the writings of St. John of the Cross). I believe that Wesleyanism would better find its place of distinctiveness in the Evangelical world and would better serve the twenty-first century tragic person by placing more emphasis on the immanent activity of the transcendent God in the human personality, and in our "apophatic" response to this activity, than is presently emphasized.

Several important objections to a proposal of this nature should be briefly noted and addressed. A first objection argues that an emphasis on the process, developmental, and "naturalistic" understanding of God's activity undercuts the Christo-centric nature of Wesleyan theology, making non-believing but loving persons virtually equivalent with "spiritual persons," thereby diminishing the importance of Christ's redemptive life and death. I would argue that this "strong version" of the argument, while it does have some historical precedent, is not the inevitable nor logically necessary conclusion. An understanding of personal transformation that emphasizes the immanent activity of God does not need to wed itself to a completely deterministic, "closed universe" assumption that makes the need for a transcendent Word of revelation unnecessary. There is "room" for transcendence, I would argue, precisely because of God's immanence. The "fallen turkey" was able to receive Emmanuel and internalize the life transforming wisdom, precisely because of the prior operation of Prevenient (preventing) Grace operating invisibly *within.* As Wittgenstein reminds us, the invisibility of a phenomenon does not make it less real; once seen it may be more "*striking and powerful.*"

What this greater emphasis on immanence does suggest, however, is a greater need to think about Christology in immanent terms, the importance of a *Christology of immanent Grace.* Related to this, I believe the immediate challenge for scholars within our tradition is to construct a theology of characterological transformation which addresses the psychological finding that mature identity construction almost inevitably leads to an disjunctive crisis of personal meaning, and subsequent need for the development of and "leap" into (some kind of) "philosophic faith" or "search for transcendence" (Jaspers). In this regard, there are developmentally-minded psychotherapists who have already anticipated us, and who, in some sense, await the response of the Christian community (Chessick). The sincere "secular" psychological community asks: "What does 'religious faith' add to psychology's 'own' developmental understanding of the need for mature love and (some form of) philosophic faith? Why is a religious faith important in restoring the person to *fullness*? Or are you saying that religious faith offers something more or different from the developmental goal of full (loving) personhood?"

A second and related objection is that such a position "psychologizes Christian faith" (again), and makes the crisis/process experiences of justification and sanctification virtually equivalent to the therapeutic processes available to anyone, regardless of "faith." What an "integration" of theological and psychological understandings of the person really means, may be found in substantive areas of mutual concern, particularly at the juncture of the meaning and practices of character transformation. *There are significant convergences in the goals and methods* of contemporary psychotherapeutic and Christian transformation practices, even when individuals on both sides do not *look* in order to *observe* them. Christian theology must be ever mindful that while individuals who have lived as turkeys have since been "proclaimed" to be princes again, and are genuinely viewed as such by the King, may still view themselves and continue to interact with others as turkeys. Psychotherapeutic practices, particularly when viewed though a theological hermeneutic, have an important role to play in facilitating the invisible processes of Prevenient Grace which will make the transformation from *barely to fully* a reality, not merely an "optimism of Grace." Following Browning, I would suggest that it is precisely the task of the developmental and psychotherapeutic psychologies to assist theological anthropology to keep in view the interactions between biology, early parental and social influences in the formation of character, and the processes involved in transforming these influences. What human character is, how it develops, and how it is transformed is particularly important in a Wesleyan view of salvation, precisely because of Wesleyanism's belief in the possibility of *real* character transformation as the ultimate journey for all persons. On the other hand, it remains the task of theology to conceptualize those issues of *meaning* concerned with the goals and expressions of a (relatively) well-formed identity.

Generative Love and Characterological Transformation: Central Organizing Principle for a Psychology of Prevenient Grace

The developmental and therapeutic goal (intent) of Prevenient Grace is the transformation of a person's capability to create and the freedom to express generative love.

This underlying organizing principle suggests a direction for constructing a theology of characterological transformation.[3] Characterological change may be seen as the development and therapeutic transformation of a primary potentiality of the person; the *capability to create* and the *freedom to express* a particular kind of love (*generative love*). Prevenient Grace can be seen as the immanent activity of God in the form of personality processes which have as their "final cause" (Aristotelian sense) the development and transformation of this foundational potentiality of the human. In this view, the "incredible journey" of personal and spiritual development is not to be seen as separate movements (one as psychological, the other as spiritual), but rather as a single and continuous line of development in the human progression from a barely to truly to a (more) fully developed capability to live as persons. The "saving grace" of justification and the "sanctifying grace" of entire sanctification are not different goals, nor is Grace aimed at different times at different aspects of the personality. As Wynkoop has suggested, speaking of the distinctions between justification, regeneration, and sanctification:

Each has an element of truth that must not be confused with the others. But these are not different events which may be separated in experience. They are different aspects of *one event*. . . . Justification or forgiveness is an essential element but incidental to the central purpose of salvation, which is freedom from sin, or holiness of heart. Sanctification must include all that regeneration and justification mean to save it from humanism. (193)

From this perspective, the *one event* which is the *central purpose of salvation* is the restoration of the potential capabilities of personality to their original purpose. Wiley speaks to this issue:

The self is not only essentially active, but was created for unlimited progress. Under grace this becomes an ever increasing advancement in the divine likeness—a change from glory unto glory (II Cor. 3:18). In sin the increase is "unto more ungodliness" and hence a descent from shame to shame. It must be remembered, however, that sin is but an accident of man's nature, and not an essential element of his original being. He retains his personality with all its powers, but these are exercised apart from God as the true center of his being, and are therefore perverted and sinful. Sin is not some new faculty . . . infused into man's being. . . . It is rather the bias of all powers. (2:402; cited in Wynkoop 196)

This organizing principle suggests three inter-related ideas: (1) that generative love is the central issue in a Wesleyan spiritual theology; (2) that the capability to create generative love is a possibility of the personality which must be developed and transformed in order to be realized; and, (3) that the expression of generative love requires an inner (subjective, experiential) freedom. First, I propose that use of the term "generative", as a qualifier for the term "love", holds promise for helping us rescue the term "love" (including Christian love) from the semantic ambiguities and overly-romanticized cultural conceptions which enshroud it. Originally proposed by the psychologist Erik Erikson (*Childhood*) as the central psychosocial issue of middle-age adult development, generativity is now conceptualized more broadly as one of the central developmental destinations for all mature personalities (McAdams) and a developmental progression which predates middle adulthood. Erikson (*Childhood* 267) defines "generativity" as "primarily the concern in establishing and guiding the next generation." Not confined to procreation and child-rearing, it also encompasses the generation of "new products and new ideas" as well as the generation of "new beings" (*Cycle* 67). Thus, for Erikson, the term "generativity" not only is it the *capacity to create*, but it is the *capacity to care* for that which one creates. "Care," he says, "is the widening concern for what has been generated by love, necessity, or accident" (*Insight* 131). Thus, generativity includes both the capabilities to create and care. Since creativity can be unconcerned with caring for that which it creates, generativity not only creates, but it also maintains and nourishes as well. If past developmental deficits and intrapsychic conflicts inhibit the development of this generative potentiality, then, in Erikson's terms, individuals fall back into the dilemma of making themselves "their own . . . one and only child" (*Childhood* 267). The generativity concept is discussed in a similar manner in some theology-psychotherapy discussions (Browning) and Christian development literatures (Whitehead and Whitehead).

In the present context, generativity is thought of as a particular developmental "level" or potential mode of functioning (living and loving) which an individual may, but not necessarily attain; theologically, a portrait of the "destiny" of the created creature. Second, it is regarded as an innate "developmental thrust" within the personality, a life-organizing motive in the functional workings of a *truly* developing person. Third, extending the meaning of generativity to encompass one of Wesley's theological constructs, the idea of "motivating affections" (Maddox 69), generativity could also be reconceptualized as a particular affectional-motivational disposition of the "heart." In this regard, generativity can be characterized by certain affective and motivational action tendencies: (1) a desire to move beyond culturally-defined productivity and role-defined living, towards greater authenticity and creativity in work and relationships, (2) a desire for life involvements where personal and distinctive sets of talents and experiences can be given self-expression, and (3) a desire to use personal power responsibly in the service of interests which go beyond mere self-interest (Whitehead and Whitehead). Where this "impulse to generativity" is experienced and can be seen to operate within an individual, I propose, is Prevenient Grace "calling" the individual to higher levels of personal organization, to a truer and more full participation in the purposes (processes and energies) of God.

This implies that the individual-would-be-person has developed and can recognize her own talents, ideals, and personal power. A central distinguishing feature of generativity is the experience, *a sense of responsibility* to express one's vision of reality, using one's own identity, for the good of a larger community. To be generatively responsible is to assert one's own vitality, vision, and mastery for the enrichment and continuity of the surrounding culture. Weisman calls this subjective responsibility:

> Subjective responsibility . . . accords primacy to man as the initiator of acts instead of to man as an object acted upon. It recognizes the reality of

choice, freedom, consciousness, motivation, and the capacity to control the consequences of purposeful action. These realities are a man's private property, and he cannot barter, share, or surrender them . . . Subjective responsibility corresponds closely with the sense of reality for what we are and what we do. Existentialists call this authenticity; psychoanalysts call it identity. (167-168)

Some contemporary developmental psychologists (McAdams) and psychotherapists (Chessick) believe that the dynamisms (processes) of movement towards generativity are inherent within the human organism, but are more salient at particular times in the life span (e.g., the identity crisis of young adulthood and the mid-life crisis of middle adulthood share certain generativity features). The experience of the inner developmental "call" to generativity does not do away with other (appropriate) desires to prove myself, to pursue excellence, or to be needed by others, but rather focuses these desires around more of how I may uniquely contribute myself as "gift" to the larger community. Similar ideas are to be found in theological literatures, while not always referring to the generativity concept *per se*. In Wynkoop's understanding of Wesley's "psychology of holiness" she suggests that "one who has not become a true self will never be able to take his place in a society of selves," and that "the basis of spiritual living is the whole self in wholesome integration with all the uniqueness of personality intact, positive and strong" (203). Likewise, Ernest Becker beautifully articulates a theological vision of generativity: ". . . man links his secret inner self, his authentic talent, his deepest feelings of uniqueness, his inner yearning for absolute significance, to the very ground of creation and . . . begins to posit creatureliness vis-à-vis a Creator who is the First Cause of all created things . . ."(90). In Christian existentialist terms, the generative mode of personal existence may be said to involve a Kierkegaardian leap from the merely "ethical" sphere of living to the truly "religious" sphere with an act of self-transcendence which does not obliterate the self (i.e., self-effacing meanings of "self-sacrifice" or "self-denial") but rather situates the self in a larger Cosmic narrative which has greater significance than a narrowly-defined cultural vision.

In this central organizing proposition, I suggest that generative love be thought of as a portrait of the *truly personal* human being; as a "higher" developmental realm of functioning where *princes* are inwardly "called" and "destined" to live. *While Christian theology may mean more than this when we refer to a person as "spiritual," I submit that it cannot mean less than this, if we are to speak in any meaningful way about Christian character involving mature love.* This suggests that for a human being to live at this organizational-motivational level of personhood, he/she must have achieved prior developmental capacities which make the capability for generative love possible. A human being must first attain the capability to function in the realm of *personal,* even as (or perhaps) before the individual lives as *spirit.* Here I am following the lead of Brightman who in his chapter on "Spirit as Developing" writes:

> . . . all the changes in level of the spiritual life are changes within personality. . . . The soul of man who has become spiritual to any degree has been raised to a higher level. Habits of attention are different; interests are transformed; different goals are chosen; different achievements are valued . . . Action and invitation to action—this is the essence of Spirit, giving life from the very start of creation an impulse to higher levels . . . To raise the level of life is to change its leading principles, and the only change that is an elevation is a change in the direction of the divine purpose. (160-164)

Second, the offering of a generative love life presupposes certain character qualities of the person. Pastoral and psychotherapeutic experiences alike confirm that we should not assume that these prerequisite qualities of self have been developed in every individual, nor in every Christian who has come into a "saving knowledge" of Christ (faith). Rather, this organizing principle suggests that we regard generative love as a *functional* potentiality of the developing person, not as a "given" quality "residing in" human nature. It is a developmental affectional-motivational potential not an innate human characteristic, nor a "gift" automatically given upon entering into faith. Thus, while individuals-not-yet-persons have the potential to develop the capability for generative love; it is not a guarantee that they will do so. In Wesleyan terms, the development of this *potentiality for the personal* becomes an "optimism of Grace."

From a psychotherapist's vantage point, it is my observation that what appears to be underemphasized in many theological treatises on moral or character development (certainly not limited to Wesleyan thinking), is an appreciation of the fact that this capability (the abilities to create and care), is in actuality, an enormous relational-developmental achievement having a unique history for each individual. That is, the presence of generative capability, where it can be seen to operate, is itself the result of a "good enough" (Winnicott) relational-developmental history with early caregivers. Unfortunately, what marks the personalities of growing numbers of post-modern *barely* persons seen on our college campuses, in local congregations, and in psychotherapists' offices is precisely the absence of the developmental precursors necessary to create and express generative love. Such persons are typically diagnosed with a *character disorder* or *self disorder*, clinical categories which refer to characterological disturbances having their origins in less-than-good-enough, and in many cases exceedingly debilitating relational-developmental backgrounds.

Meissner, a Jesuit psychoanalyst and one of the leading contemporary integrators of psychoanalytic therapy and religion, has suggested that there probably is no issue more important for us to clarify in constructing a psychology of grace than this issue of the functional capacity for and the freedom to love. Theologians and psycho-therapists have had a tendency to talk past each other on this issue, thus, obscuring an important mutual concern in understanding characterological change. Briefly summarizing his position, he argues that for the most part, theologians in the Christian tradition have almost universally taken human freedom as an established fact, regarding it as one of the distinguishing features of *imago Dei*. The capacity to choose between alternatives, to will, even to accept revelation is seen to depend on the person's innate freedom to choose and especially freedom to choose to love. Their subsequent discussions then assume that most individuals function with a relatively well-developed generative capability intact as part of their personality. However, within our society, at least Western society, this is no longer a tenable assumption about what constitutes a "person." Meissner suggests that this stand on freedom implies that the person possesses certain qualities of the self which the developmentally-minded psychotherapist does not take for granted about the individual-not-yet-person (pre-generative person). Rather, depth psychotherapists generally view both the *capability to create* and the *freedom to express* mature love as a hard-won struggle whose existence as a capability "within" the person is always precarious and subject to sometimes tragic reversals. Individuals who emerge from "barely personal" environments surrounded by individuals who themselves never achieved generative capability, and therefore, knew little about facilitating its development in their children, or worse yet, obstructed its development, are far more likely to live tragically. Thus, it is not "given" that an individual will attain that *developmental organization of personhood* that makes them capable of choosing, creating, and sustaining a generative life.

This first proposition suggests, that when the task of spiritual development is seen from this central hermeneutic, it is the capability to create generative love itself that is primary, antecedent to, and developmentally prior to other concerns (even when those other concerns look *to all appearances* to be more "spiritual"). That is, since it is possible for a person to "love" others, self, and God, in a distorted (pre-generative) way, concern must first be given to the person's capability for generative love itself. Deficits and conflicts which impair this fundamental capability must be given priority. A theology of characterological transformation, mindful of the tragic characterological conditions of a growing number of persons in contemporary society, must be able to address the issue of how this *transformation of the tragic person* is to be effected and do so in ways that incorporate our best psychological knowledge about how the potential to love is diminished and transformed. I believe our own quadrilateral-based epistemology asks this of us.

A third notion in the above proposition concerns what psychotherapists refer to as *inner (subjective) freedom*. As used in some psychotherapeutic literatures (Johnson) the concept of inner freedom refers both to a *freedom from* obstacles which limits an individual's capability for mature love itself, whether these limitations derive from external sources or from inhibitions imposed by defects of character, and a *freedom to* express this functional capability. "Freedom from" relates to the capability to create mature love itself, and therapeutically involves helping to diminish character *defects and deficits* resulting from relational-developmental "holes" in the life of the individual. Develop-mentally speaking, it is understood that some persons arrive in adulthood with defects and deficits as a result of relational experiences which failed to adequately facilitate the development and maturation of qualities which form the foundation for generative loving (e.g., experiences of basic trust in self and others, security, esteem, value formation, etc). "Freedom to" involves diminishing the effects of inner characterological *conflicts* (many of which involve defect and deficit problems) which inhibit the expression of mature love.

For example, the inability to trust in and feel close to another person because of early relational absences (experiences of emotional unavailability and betrayal) is a typical and wide-spread relational-developmental deficit. The situation of conflicting desires to enter into a marriage relationship and the simultaneous wish to avoid further pain (e.g., an intense and perhaps paralyzing fear of commitment related to early parental betrayals), involves the issue of intrapsychic conflict. In developmental characterological thinking, some individuals are said to be inhibited (theologically, "enslaved") more by defects and deficits in the ability to create mature love; others are said to be inhibited more by inner conflicts which obstruct the expression of a capability which has been developed but is for some reason not presently functional. From the perspective of characterologic psychotherapists, individuals live to a greater or lesser degree in a relative state of *diminished capability* to create and freedom to express mature love. Thus, the central psychotherapeutic task is the restoration of both the capability to create and the freedom to express mature love. This involves participating in the processes which can restore, and in some cases construct for the first time, the ability of the person to respond to self and/or other person (or God) in a manner which is more mature than a pre-generative love.

I have in mind three therapeutic processes immanent in the "natural" workings of personality which a characterologic and developmentally-minded therapist aims to facilitate: *transference, liberation-mourning,* and *internalization.* So fundamental and essential are these processes to affectional-motivational personality changes, they could be referred to as the *triad of characterological transformation.* Briefly summarizing the therapeutic actions of these processes, *transference* has the primary effect of making unconscious, un-loving affections-motivations of the "heart" more visible (conscious), thus making it possible for individuals to become more responsible for their feelings and actions. *Liberation-mourning* has the "subtractive" function in characterological transformation. It is a primary means of "dissolving" strong affective attachments to intrapsychic experiences and charcterological conflicts which inhibit the expression of generative love. *Internalization* is the primary "additive" function in characterological change. It is the principle means whereby defects and deficits in the "relational deep structure" (Jones) (theologically, "heart") of personality are filled in. Overall, the three-fold therapeutic action of these processes in the lives of persons is to *illuminate* unloving motivational intentions of heart, to *diminish* internal relational experiences and characterological conflicts which inhibit and distort the expression of mature love, and to *construct* an under-developed capability to love made deficient primarily because of early relational deficits.

On Becoming Wise Guides to Tragic Persons

To the extent that the theological vision of human fulfillment cannot be achieved without some measure of characterological maturity, theological anthropology can benefit from certain contributions from psychotherapeutic psychology. As a community of Wesleyan scholars, constructing a theology of character transformation around the central hermeneutic of *capability for generative love,* I am hopeful that more serious attention will be given to (1) how the capability for generativity is developed, (2) how it is malformed, and (3) how it is transformed. Many of our teachings and practices about character formation would look quite different if the focus of transformation was understood to concern (in part) participation in personality processes of Prevenient

Grace which are "aimed at" the transformation of our capability for mature love. Without both the theological and psychotherapeutic perspectives, we may "fall" guilty of imagining ourselves to be living as "princes" even as we actually live, and appear to others to live, as *barely* persons, or worse yet, as "turkeys."

NOTES

1. This essay is a brief version of a more extensive manuscript in progress by the author initiated as a Center Scholar (Spring, 1995) and Center Fellow (Spring, 1996), Wesleyan Center for 21st Century Studies, Point Loma Nazarene College: "Transformation of the Tragic Person: Wesleyan Thought in the Culture of Psychotherapeutic Care." The author wishes to gratefully acknowledge the funding, time, and support provided by the College and the Wesleyan Center to undertake this project.

2. *Transformation of the Tragic Person* addresses the difference between "constructivist" and "rationalistic" models of change, both of which are to be found within contemporary therapeutic and Christian formation approaches. It is my observation that within the Wesleyan tradition, while our anthropology may acknowledge the need for a depth and constructivist type of change (a legacy of our Anglican heritage), most of our practices of spiritual formation do not "target" this level of change. Rather, our view of transformation, and subsequent spiritual formation practices, tend to remain predominately rationalistic in their focus and intent. Ironically, as Maddox (69) has recently reminded us, Wesley himself quite deliberately attempted to distance himself from the rationalistic tradition which was gaining prominence in Western psychology.

3. In *Transformation of the Tragic Person* I take up four additional organizing principles for constructing an Anglican-Wesleyan theology of characterological transformation in immanent terms. In addition to this first proposition concerned with the *goal* of Prevenient Grace, these additional propositions are concerned with the *focus, actions, processes,* and *means* of Prevenient Grace. The *focus principle* asks the question: What is the focus (target) of Prevenient Grace within the personality itself? The *actions principle* asks: How are characterological deficits and conflicts in the "heart" healed? The *processes principle* asks: What are some of the therapeutic processes which themselves may be regarded as Prevenient Grace? The *means principle* asks: How are therapeutic processes of Prevenient Grace made operative within the person?

TRIBUTE

Every once in a while, a person emerges from among the common crowd and so inspires a group of people that the vision which he or she formulates seems to have a life of its own. Like Caleb and Joshua in Numbers 13, Cecil Paul stood against those who only saw giants and fortified cities in their quest to take what God had promised. He was a Caleb—no, a Joshua, a capable leader who focused on creating a vision for Christian education that defied giants and walls and struggle. He was the type of person who could inspire and motivate with one flash of those dark eyes. Those who knew him best knew that one of his personal quests was to create a Christian educational community that would have no cause to be apologetic for any phase of its mission, staff, program or facilities. I count it a personal privilege to have participated with Cecil in his all too brief administration. He would be pleased to be honored by the content of this publication.
—*from* The Christian Scholar, *52:1 Fall 1992*

Clifford B. Hersey
Associate Professor of Communication
(Under Cecil Paul, Executive Director
of Communication and Development)

CHAPTER TEN

ECUMENISM IN NAZARENE HIGHER EDUCATION

George Lyons

Most Nazarenes are familiar with the dictum of Phineas F. Bresee, founding father of the Church of the Nazarene: "We are debtors to every man to give him the gospel in the same measure as we have received it" (Redford ch. 6). This quotation has characteristically motivated us to the mission of world evangelism. But what of our debt to the mission of education? And what has education to do with that other "e-word"—*ecumenism*?

The very notion of ecumenism in Nazarene higher education seems at first glance to be an impossible oxymoron. Can there be such a thing as ecumenical, denominational education? Ecumenism implies inclusiveness and emphasizes the generic features that all Christians share. Denominations exist to perpetuate the specific traits that distinguish one Christian group from another. Is it possible for a Nazarene college or university to remain faithful to its core identity as an institutional expression of one of the denominations of the Wesleyan-Holiness tradition and still be genuinely ecumenical?

Institutional Ecumenism

Few Christians today cling to the romantic ecumenical dreams of the fifties and sixties, despite the efforts of the Ecumenical Movement.[1] Institutional ecumenism—full organic union of all churches—is passé today. It has suffered the same fate as Martin Luther King's dream of racial integration, despite the moderate successes of the Civil Rights Movement. More strident voices on both extremes—White Separatists of the so-called Christian Identity Movement and Black Muslims of the Nation of Islam—celebrate our diversity.

The recent trend of local Christian congregations to omit references to denominational affiliation in their advertising should not be misinterpreted as evidence to the contrary. This is less an expression of ecumenism than an anti-institutional assertion of local autonomy. The "grass-roots" recognized long before denominational headquarters that a "McDonald's style" approach to franchising churches simply did not take seriously differences in local tastes. What has emerged is the exact opposite of institutional ecumenism. The churches of the 1990s have been non-denominational and *independent,* but hardly ecumenical. And the growing movements have been those of special interest groups (such as Pro-Life) that have tended more to polarize than unite Christians.

There is yet another recent trend that might be mistaken as ecumenically motivated. Many Nazarenes (and Christians of other denominations, as well) seem eager to identify themselves as evangelicals rather than as Wesleyans or Holiness people. But this willingness to diminish our denominational distinctives is less motivated by ecumenical conviction than by accommodation. It is not the unity of the Church but upward mobility that drives us. Evangelicals have become the new religious mainstream within American Protestantism. Tired of our marginal status, we seem anxious to emulate these successful Christians. Never mind that generic evangelical Christianity is theologically incompatible with many of the central convictions that brought us into existence as a movement. Is tepidness about doctrine the essential prerequisite for ecumenical cooperation?

Mission-Driven Ecumenism

Beyond the ancient, so-called "Ecumenical Creeds" — the Apostles', Nicene, and Chalcedonian—Christians have found little else they can agree upon theologically. Somewhat greater consensus on the sacraments has emerged in the recent "Faith and Order" consultations sponsored by the World Council of Churches. Whatever others mean by ecumenism, I use the term here to refer to catholic or universal cooperation in the Church's mission. Evangelism and education come together in what is generally accepted as the Church's central "Mission Statement"—the "Great Commission." It is, as Matthew 28:19-20 puts it, the mandate to make disciples of all kinds of people by teaching them to observe the words and ways of Jesus.

Denominations may be ecumenical if ecumenism is not confused with homogeneity in opinions or practices. To be ecumenical in mission is to find community in heterogeneity. It is not to compromise principle in pursuit of some theological or ethical lowest-common-denominator. Nor is it to accept a relativistic pluralism in which everything is true, but only in the eyes of the beholder. Mission-driven ecumenism refuses to imagine that any denomination is the sole proprietor of all truth. Nazarenes are not the only true Christians. This kind of ecumenism compels us to acknowledge our indebtedness to other Christian traditions. Because we have learned from others, we are obliged to share what we have learned with all who are willing to listen.

Although modern sensitivities make us wish Dr. Bresee had said "all persons," rather than "all men," who would deny the ecumenical scope of his vision? Like John Wesley, who saw the world as his parish, Bresee refused to make gender or social class or ethnicity the basis for Nazarene identity. "We are debtors to every man to give him the gospel in the same measure as we have received it." "The gospel"—granted, a distinctive interpretation of the gospel—was to be the bottom line. Bresee claimed no originality, acknowledging, instead, Nazarene indebtedness to the rich tradition of the larger Christian Church.

The historical statement in the *Manual* of the Church of the Nazarene recognizes the indebtedness of our denomination to a wide range of religious traditions. The earliest Nazarenes were largely disaffected Methodists, whether "come-outers" or "put-outers." Other denominations and theological traditions also contributed their fair share to the fledgling denomination. Of course, there were those with no church background, converts from the ranks of modern pagans. This heterogeneous early membership often shared little more than an unwavering commitment to spreading abroad the message of "scriptural holiness," particularly to the "down-and-outers." Other differences were inconsequential in comparison to this common mission of holistic evangelism.[2]

Among other things, holistic evangelism motivated early Nazarenes to sponsor Christian liberal arts colleges. This educational mission set us apart from the fundamentalist denominations with which we have sometimes been mistakenly compared. They founded Bible colleges intended for ministers only. Our colleges recruited a cross-section of the Church, students preparing for secular as well as church vocations. Midway through our hundred-year existence as a church, we founded a seminary. It was not until we were old enough to collect Social Security that we founded our first Bible college in the U.S. Curiously, until recently we have taken the opposite course in most of our educational enterprises outside the U.S.[3] Does this help explain why the intra-denominational ecumenism we call "internationalization" has been such a painful process?

Perhaps, only in our earliest decades as a denomination were we as heterogeneous as we are as we approach our centennial. Denominational statistics suggest that perhaps half the members of the Church of the Nazarene today have been members for fewer than ten years. This is not to say that we have grown by one-hundred percent during that period. We have a "big back door." Alumni surveys at Nazarene colleges indicate that the percentage of members of the Church of the Nazarene drops in proportion to the years since graduation. In other words, there is a higher percentage of Nazarenes attending our colleges than there are in our alumni associations. Perhaps, we have been repaying our debts to the denominations who earlier gave us some of their members.

Pragmatic Ecumenism

It is not my intent here either to lament or explain why so many Nazarenes now attend churches of other denominations. Evidence suggests that few Christians today share the denominational "brand-name loyalty" that was once a distinguishing feature of American Christianity. Some, perhaps correctly, bemoan our losses to other denominations as avoidable tragedies. But the resulting cross-fertilization of traditions may be "just what the doctor ordered." The infusion of "new blood" heads off the incestuous stagnation that develops when denominations become ingrown and parochial.

Few Nazarenes consider it tragic that a sizable proportion of our new members in the U.S. continue to come from the ranks of other denominations. The easy movement of "sheep" from one pasture to another is, of course, a mixed blessing. New Nazarenes have no memory of the opinions and practices that motivated the earliest Nazarenes to form a denomination. Practical realities have led pastors either to play down our denominational distinctives or to undertake the monumental task of reeducating their new members without unnecessarily alienating them. What has emerged in Nazarene congregations throughout the U.S. is what might be called a "pragmatic ecumenism."

Pragmatic ecumenism in Nazarene higher education has been a reality from the beginning. The percentages of Nazarenes on the faculties and in the student bodies of those early Nazarene-sponsored colleges may have been somewhat higher than they are in our colleges today. But the average number of accumulated years of membership in the denomination among the faculty and student body today is considerably higher than it was then. After all, we were a denomination in our infancy. Even college presidents had almost no seniority as members of the Church. Furthermore, our colleges continue to proselytize more new Nazarenes from their non-Nazarene students and faculty members than they lose during the college years.

I have not done the research necessary to determine the precise percentage of non-Nazarenes teaching on the faculties of Nazarene colleges. Anecdotal evidence suggests that a clear majority are (at least nominal) Nazarenes. Most of these are also graduates of Nazarene colleges. All our schools still presume that every faculty member will normally be a professing and practicing Christian. I have heard of some exceptional cases in which a Nazarene college has hired a full-time faculty member who was not. But this was because no qualified Christian, much less Nazarene, was available in some specialized field of study. The growth of graduate and other non-traditional programs in many of our Nazarene colleges has been accompanied by an increase in the number of part-time, temporary, adjunct faculty members. Most of these have been recruited from the pool of available, qualified candidates in the immediate area of the college and many have been non-Nazarenes. As a result, there are probably more non-Nazarenes on Nazarene college faculties today than ever. Such pragmatic ecumenism is less by design than by default. The underlying motive has been economic expediency, not ecumenical conviction.

The religion departments of Nazarene colleges have generally been the one exception to the practice of pragmatic "ecumenical" hiring. We seem to have preferred hiring underqualified Nazarenes to hiring candidates from some non-Wesleyan Christian tradition. Academically-minded pastors, without the customary advanced degrees were once a common fixture in many (if not all) of our schools. That day has largely passed, although most religion faculty members have spent some time pastoring before moving into the teaching ministry. Most religion faculty members are ordained Nazarene elders. The few non-Nazarenes who have served on our religion faculties have virtually all been members of sister Wesleyan-Holiness denominations, and most have eventually joined the Church of the Nazarene, or moved on (by choice or coercion) to another teaching assignment.

Troubling Questions

Do preferential hiring practices compel some professors to become—or remain—(at least nominal) Nazarenes in order to gain tenure on the faculty of a Nazarene college? How can we decide whether such convenient conversions are motivated by conviction or compromise? When is a willingness to abandon one's previous denominational affiliation a demonstration of changed loyalties and when a sign of fickleness? Has the institution sometimes created an atmosphere in which individuals feel coerced to give economic considerations greater weight than theological consistency? All else being equal, should Nazarene colleges hire the most qualified Christian applicant—whatever his or her denominational affiliation—for a faculty position, or prefer a less qualified Nazarene? If a qualifiable Christian candidate exists, should a Nazarene college ever hire a non-Christian applicant for any faculty position?

Is the ecumenicity of increasing denominational diversity in our denominational colleges a healthy development or a dangerous trend? Is there anything in our denominational heritage precious enough to preserve at all costs? Is it possible to sustain our distinctive Wesleyan-Holiness heritage and mission in the face of pragmatic ecumenicity? Is the solid Nazarene core of the religion departments cohesive enough to maintain our colleges' theological identity? Or, have we, on the contrary, been too parochial in staffing our religion departments? Does our reluctance to hire (say) a committed Calvinist or Roman Catholic to teach on our religion faculties suggest a subtle fear that such a person might expose some hidden weaknesses in our tradition and undermine the loyalty of our students?

Despite our increasingly academically qualified religion faculties, have we conceived of their mission to be to inform and educate or to serve as apologists for our tradition? Have we been guilty of confusing the religion department with the "piety department"? Although the religion faculty may be specialists in articulating Nazarene identity, to the extent that we are truly Wesleyan, is not the call to holiness of heart and life the task of every faculty member?

Should we pursue a more self-consciously ecumenical approach to Nazarene higher education? Or have we gone too far already? If pragmatic and economic considerations are inappropriate motivations for ecumenicity, what should motivate us? If we are to join hands with other Christians in fulfilling a common mission to be "salt and light" in an increasingly post-Christian age, what principles should govern our ecumenical cooperation?

Is ecumenicity in the mission of Nazarene higher education a compromise of our Wesleyan-Holiness heritage, or an authentic expression of it? Can we learn anything from our theological mentor, John Wesley, that will assist us on the perilous journey to an authentically Wesleyan ecumenism?

Principled Ecumenism

Wesley's sermon on the "Catholic Spirit"[4] offers some guiding principles that may protect us from the dangers of theological indifferentism, on the one hand, and dogmatic intolerance, on the other. Wesley identifies "the two grand, general hindrances" to ecumenical cooperation in mission as, first, that we "cannot all think alike and, in consequence of this, secondly, [we] cannot all walk alike" (39.0.3). Wesley envisions an ecumenicity that transcends such hindrances.

> Although a difference in opinions or modes of worship may prevent an entire external union, yet need it prevent our union in affection? Though we cannot think alike, may we not love alike? May we not be of one heart, though we are not of one opinion? Without all doubt, we may. Herein all the children of God may unite, notwithstanding these smaller differences (39.0.4).[5]

Wesley recognizes several pragmatic realities: That "opinions" unavoidably influence "practice" (39.I.1). That "good men . . . entertain peculiar opinions." That "a variety of opinion necessarily implies a variety of practice" (39.I.8). That "several men will be of several minds in religion as well as in common life" (39.I.3). "Although every man necessarily believes that every particular opinion which he holds is true . . . ; yet can no man be assured that all his own opinions, taken together, are true" (39.I.4).[6] In a world of diverse opinions and practices, Wesley rejects relativism, but recommends mutual tolerance.[7]

Today we would call Wesley's Methodist societies a parachurch organization. Membership was not conditioned on doctrinal opinions.

> Let them hold particular or general redemption, absolute or conditional decrees; let them be Churchmen or Dissenters, Presbyterians or Independents, it is no obstacle. Let them choose one mode of baptism or another, it is no bar to their admission. The Presbyterian may be a Presbyterian still; the Independent or Anabaptist use his own mode of worship. So may the Quaker; and none will contend with him about it. ("Thoughts" 266)

And yet, Wesley presumes that the Christian faith will and should assume institutional expression. "Every follower of Christ is obliged, by the very nature of the Christian institution, to be a member of some particular congregation or other, some Church, . . . (which implies a particular manner of worshipping God . . .)." He defends the Reformation principle of "private judgement," granting individuals the right to abandon the church of their birth and the manner of worship prescribed by that church (39.I.10). Although Wesley was clear in his own mind that his own Anglican "mode of worship" was scriptural, primitive, and apostolic, he refused to impose his beliefs on another. The Wesleyan "unity of love" did not insist upon denominational uniformity.[8]

Wesley refused to make membership in the same church or congregation a condition for Christian cooperation. He insisted, "my only question at present is this, 'Is thine heart right, as my heart is with thy heart?'" (39.I.11).[9] "'If it be, give me thy hand'" (39.II.1).[10] He was willing to "think, and let think." The only condition required of his Methodists was "a real desire to save their soul. Where this is, it is enough: They desire no more: They lay stress upon nothing else: They ask only, 'Is thy heart herein as my heart? If it be, give me thy hand'" ("Thoughts" 266).

The basis of Christian unity for Wesley was a "heart right with God." The supreme evidence of this was love for God and all humanity (39.II.2). The catholic spirit that enables Christians of different traditions to cooperate in mission arises from their mutual commitment to "universal love" (39.II.3; III.4, 6).[11] Such love does not depend on another's denominational affiliation, theological opinions, or "outward modes of worship." It embraces "neighbours and strangers, friends and enemies; . . . not only the good and gentle, but . . . the evil and unthankful." It includes "every soul that God has made . . . of whatever place or nation" ("Letter" 68). But it especially cherishes

> as friends, as brethren in the Lord, as members of Christ and children of God, as joint partakers now of the present kingdom of God, and fellow heirs of his eternal kingdom—all, of whatever opinion or worship, or congregation, who believe in the Lord Jesus Christ; who love God and man; who, rejoicing to please, and fearing to offend God, are careful to abstain from evil, and zealous of good works. (39.III.5)

Universal love is less an emotion or a disposition than a life-style marked by fervent prayer for one another's spiritual progress (39.II.5), mutual accountability (39.II.6), and other concrete expressions of love (39.II.7, 8).

For Wesley the possibility of cooperation in mission also involved a mutual commitment to classical Christian creeds and conduct. His list of "the main branches of Christian doctrine"—"the first elements of the gospel of Christ" (39.III.1)—was quite unlike those that emerged in nineteenth-century fundamentalism. Wesley's list of Christian fundamentals was both shorter and less preoccupied with doctrinaire orthodoxy than were those of most nineteenth century evangelicals. He was willing to make an issue only of those "important Christian doctrines" (Preface.3), which are "the essentials of true religion" (Preface.1).[12] First was faith in God as the creator and sustainer of the universe (39.I.12) Second was living faith in Jesus Christ as the divine and personal savior (39.I.13). Third was a faith "filled with the energy of love"—an ever increasing love for God that was undivided (39.I.14) and obedient (39.I.15, 16) and for "all mankind, without exception, ... even the enemies of God" (39.I.17, 18).

Wesley defines more fully what a catholic spirit is not than what it is. First, it "is not *speculative* latitudinarianism." That is, "it is not an indifference to all opinions" or an "unsettledness of thought." These are enemies, not friends, to "true catholicism." Though convinced in their own minds, people of catholic spirit are "always ready to hear and weigh" contrary opinions. They do "not halt between two opinions, nor vainly endeavour to blend them into one." A catholic spirit is not to be confused with muddled understanding or inconsistent principles (39.III.1). Second, a catholic spirit is not to be confused with "*practical* latitudinarianism. It is not indifference as to public worship, or as to the outward manner of performing it." On the contrary, those who possess it are convinced that their own "manner of worshipping God is both scriptural and rational" (39.III.2). Third, "a catholic spirit is not indifference to all congregations." Thus, those who share this spirit are active members of some local Christian fellowship (39.III.4).

Implications

What if conscious principles were more important than pragmatic constraints in Nazarene higher education? What if we asserted our distinctive Wesleyan identity rather than cultivated our generic similarities to other evangelical traditions? What if a clearly conceived mission, rather than market analysis, motivated our ecumenism? How would we be different? If Nazarene colleges were to adopt Wesley's catholic spirit as a fundamental operating principle, it probably would not significantly change faculty hiring practices. It might, however, bring our mission statements into greater prominence as the rationale for ecumenical cooperation. Although each college's mission statement has its unique features, most share some similarities with that of Northwest Nazarene College, where I serve as a member of the religion faculty. Its mission statement reads in part:

> Northwest Nazarene College is a Christian liberal arts college, fully committed to an educational process that pursues both intellectual and spiritual development. This pursuit is centered firmly in the Person of Jesus Christ, and is designed to instill a habit of mind that enables each student to become God's creative and redemptive agent in today's world.
>
> The essential mission of the College is the development of Christian character within the philosophy and framework of genuine scholarship....

All genuine Christians might in good conscience commit themselves to such a mission. But if "the task of the College" is also "to serve the church by providing an educated laity and ministry, loyal to Christ and emphasizing the Wesleyan doctrine of perfect love," a majority of the faculty, and probably all of the religion faculty must also be in full sympathy with the Wesleyan-Holiness tradition.

Every member of the faculty of every Nazarene college needs to be fully committed to its mission.[13] The Nazarene "Statement of Faith"[14] lists the theological opinions that we share with other religious traditions and that distinguish us from these other traditions. It is one thing to insist that these beliefs are at the core of our Wesleyan-Holiness identity as a denomination—to insist that we prefer a majority of the faculty wholeheartedly to espouse these beliefs. It is quite another thing to insist that all faculty members must share these opinions. If we sincerely believe that Wesleyans are not the only true Christians, why should we be reluctant to hire faculty members who are devout adherents of other Christian traditions? Or do we believe that our unique identity would be more threatened by conscientious Christians of other denominations on our faculties than by nominal Nazarenes in our ranks?

Too often we have hired non-Nazarenes by default rather than by self-conscious decisions. Isn't it high time for us to demonstrate our non-sectarian professions? If we really believe that we are not the only Christians, should we not actively recruit a core of committed Christians who are not Nazarenes, but who are willing to cooperate with us in the pursuit of our mission? To anyone whose heart is right with God we may extend the invitation: Give me your hand.

Diverse theological opinions among the faculty need not be divisive or detract from our colleges' mission. We should encourage faculty members to be as fervently committed to their personal Christian traditions as they are to the college's mission. But, every professor needs to be reminded that he or she serves on a Nazarene college faculty. Cooperation in achieving our mission allows us to relegate our personal opinions and practices appropriately to places of lesser importance. But it does not give us license to forget them.

The catholic spirit would call all faculty members who share the college's mission to solidarity with their colleagues in this mission. Petty differences cannot be allowed to become divisive. All who share a vital faith in Christ should be recognized as fully Christian, whether or not they are Nazarenes. It would not seem to be inconsistent with the catholic spirit, however, to insist that all prospective faculty members not only profess personal faith in Christ, but also accept the ecumenical Christian creeds. Nor would it seem inappropriate to expect that vital faith should evidence itself in the active pursuit of the life of holiness and the development of mature Christian character. Wesley would also presuppose that every faculty member should be a loyal member of a local Christian congregation.

In our effort to be appropriately ecumenical, we should remember that a part of our mission is to serve the Church of the Nazarene. Ecumenicity in faculty hiring should not compromise our denominational identity, lest we lose our reason for existence specifically as a Nazarene college. We must resist pressures from both the right and the left to betray our heritage.

It is here that the religion faculties of Nazarene colleges play a particularly crucial role. Typical college freshmen, even from Nazarene homes, bring with them almost no Nazarene memory, and little in the way of a classically Christian memory. Diagnostic tests suggest that few entering freshmen know even the most basic facts of the Bible. Required religion classes often serve as remedial instruction in the core beliefs and values of lost or never-known traditions. Non-Nazarene faculty members and inadequately indoctrinated Nazarene faculty members may need similar remedial instruction in the distinguishing beliefs and practices of the Church and its Wesleyan-Holiness tradition.

Competence in a professional field and personal piety in one's private life may not adequately equip a faculty member for the task of integrating faith and learning. Nazarene colleges owe it to their denominational constituency to assure that every faculty member adequately understands and appreciates Nazarene theology. This is not to say that all must accept it as their personal theology. On the contrary, Nazarene colleges should actively encourage their faculties and students to "think, and let think." This is the Wesleyan basis for ecumenism in Nazarene higher education.

NOTES

1. See Roy S. Nicholson's 1967 essay: "John Wesley and Ecumenicity," *Wesleyan Theological Journal* 2 (1967): 66-81. This is not to dismiss the denominational unions that emerged during this era as insignificant. Nor is it to suggest that such unions no longer occur. But a number of recent unions have been marriages of convenience, rather than conviction.

2. "Holistic evangelism" refers to the comprehensive scope of the gospel as it impacts every dimension of human life and society.

3. That is, we first founded Bible colleges and only recently have we started seminaries and a university outside the U.S. Do political and cultural factors better explain this phenomenon? After all, private, denominational liberal arts colleges are an almost uniquely American institution.

4. All Wesley quotations are from the 1872 edition of *Wesley's Works* edited by Thomas Jackson. "Catholic Spirit" is sermon 39, found in the first of the three sermon volumes, which is volume 5 of the *Works*. Quotations are excerpted from the 1995 digital version of these sermons, prepared by the Wesley Center for Applied Theology at Northwest Nazarene College, (available free of charge upon request). Section numbers, rather than pages, are cited throughout to make it easier to locate quotations in other Wesley editions, such as the Oxford-Abingdon bicentennial critical edition. "Catholic spirit" is the antithesis of religious "narrow[minded]ness" ("Letters to Miss Bishop" [November 22, 1769], 13: 18), "prejudice," or "bigotry" ("Of Attending Church" [February 13, 1782], 13: 247; and "Thoughts Upon a Late Phenomenon" [July 13, 1788], 13: 266; "Letter to Lloyd's 'Evening Post'" [February 26, 1771], 13: 402).

5. After a century as a denomination, differences in "modes of worship" exist within virtually every Nazarene congregation. Wesley's analysis of eighteenth century Christianity was that "the particular modes of worshipping God are almost as various as among the heathens" (53.I.8). Among contemporary Nazarenes, preferences of worship styles are probably more divisive than any other single issue.

6. Wesley reasons: "Every wise man, therefore, will allow others the same liberty of thinking which he desires they should allow him; and will no more insist on their embracing his opinions, than he would have them to insist on his embracing theirs. . . . 'Is thy heart right, as my heart is with thy heart?'" (39.I.6).

7. "And how shall we choose among so much variety? No man can choose for, or prescribe to, another. But every one must follow the dictates of his own conscience, in simplicity and godly sincerity. He must be fully persuaded in his own mind and then act according to the best light he has. Nor has any creature power to constrain another to walk by his own rule. . . ."

8. Wesley believed that his theological opinions and mode of worship were not a matter of personal choice. "I can no more think, than I can see or hear, as I will" (39.II.1).

9. Quoting the text of his sermon, 2 Kings 10:15.

10. Continuing the quotation from 2 Kings.

11. "Love me . . . with the love that is . . . patient,—if I am ignorant or out of the way, bearing and not increasing my burden;. . . . Love me with the love

that is not provoked, either at my follies or infirmities; or even at my acting (if it should sometimes so appear to thee) not according to the will of God. Love me so as to think no evil of me; to put away all jealousy and evil surmising. Love me with the love that covereth all things; that never reveals either my faults or infirmities,—that believeth all things; is always willing to think the best, to put the fairest construction on all my words and actions,—that hopeth all things;. . . . And hope to the end, that whatever is amiss will, by the grace of God, be corrected; and whatever is wanting, supplied, through the riches of his mercy in Christ Jesus" (39.II.4).

12. His focus was on "practical" or "experimental" (i.e., experiential) as opposed to "controversial" or "speculative divinity" (vol. 1, Preface, iii; vol. 2; Journal [Dec. 19, 1754], 247; vol. 8, "A Further Appeal to Men of Reason and Religion," III.10, 221; vol. 14, "List of Poetical Works," §7, 345).

13. Some people seem inclined to interpret mission statements in idiosyncratic ways. Does any one interpretation have greater authority than another? Who decides among competing interpretations? The president? the college board? The Board of General Superintendents? The historians? The religion faculty? Must mission statements be interpreted in a "strict constructionist" manner that is concerned only with their framers' original intent or, are culturally appropriate adaptations allowed?

14. The *Manual*'s "Agreed Statement of Belief" immediately follows the "Mission" statement in the Catalog of Northwest Nazarene College.

TRIBUTE

I owe Cecil Paul a great debt. He believed in me at a time when I am certain that I did not believe in myself. In so doing, he allowed himself to be a vehicle of God's grace and healing and provided me with a living apologetic of the Christian faith.

Donald A. Yerxa
Professor, Chair, Department of History
Eastern Nazarene College

CHAPTER ELEVEN

THE NAZARENE MIND: SUNLIGHT AND SCANDAL

Karl Giberson

The philosophy of main street America is written on its bumper stickers. Our bumper stickers announce that our children have made the honor roll (or, in a recent only-in-America case, have beaten up a kid on the honor roll!); that we care about the whales, that we did not evolve from monkeys, that we should not leave earth without Jesus, and that "abortions stop a beating heart." Americans love bumper stickers.

Christians also argue their causes on the bumpers of their cars. The trouble with bumper stickers, though, is that they have no small print. Their pithy "in your face" messages are never followed with a carefully reasoned argument. One would like to think however, that the driver of the car might be able to provide the "documentation" for the bumper sticker; alas, if the driver of the car is a member of any of the many American evangelical denominations, it may be unlikely that they could do little more than provide a biblical proof-text for the message on the bumper sticker.

The title of this essay alludes to Wheaton historian Mark Noll's recent remarkable analysis of the "evangelical mind" (86)—must reading for anyone involved in Christian higher education or concerned about the place of the Church at the beginning of the third millennium. Noll makes a tragic but compelling case that the evangelical mind at the end of the twentieth century is an atrophied, shrunken, shadow of its former self. Once upon a time evangelicals rode proudly in the vanguard of intellectual advance. Gone are the days when brilliant evangelical minds like that of John Wesley or Jonathan Edwards read and understood the leading thinkers of their time before they helped to "set the agenda."

What about the Nazarene Mind? Is it simply a microcosm of the larger evangelical mind? Or is it different? Do its differences make it more or less open to the criticisms that Noll levels at the evangelical mind?[1] In this essay I suggest that the Nazarene Mind[2] has indeed been largely scandalized in the way that Noll suggests. However, unlike the larger evangelical mind, the scandal of the Nazarene Mind is less structural and more a consequence of the Church of the Nazarene's emphasis on missions and church growth rather than the cultivation and nurturing of a universal and consistent understanding of its Wesleyan-Arminian intellectual heritage. This seeming imbalance is unfortunate since the Wesleyan-Arminian heritage that forms the intellectual wellspring of the Church of the Nazarene contains within itself an intellectual vitality uniquely capable of nursing that Mind back to health and making it the most vigorous within the larger evangelical sphere.

My optimism about the potential of the Nazarene Mind is based on my conviction that there is no reason why it *necessarily* must fall into the anti-intellectual quicksand in which so much of the evangelical church is currently flailing. Indeed the Church of the Nazarene, understood formally in terms of its doctrinal affirmations and particularly its view of Scripture, seems like it should be able to break free of the rigid biblical literalism that Noll blames for the "Scandal of the Evangelical Mind." The intellectual sources of the Wesleyan-Arminian tradition are much broader, supplementing and integrating Scripture with Reason, Tradition, and Experience. This intellectual quartet, when singing in harmony, goes by the name of the Wesleyan Quadrilateral; the quadrilateral, in marked contrast to the tradition of *sola scriptura* that informs many other evangelical traditions, allows, invites, and even demands, that the Nazarene Mind explore and embrace Truth wherever it may be found, without any *a priori* uneasiness about the necessary primacy in all areas of specific scriptural formulations.[3] As a geometric metaphor the quadrilateral suggests that Scripture, Reason, Tradition, and Experience[4] can legitimately be understood as distinct boundaries of a common truth, partners in a common conversation, co-authors of a common thesis. The *integral unity* of the quadrilateral is a vein of gold that I think the Church of the Nazarene has yet to mine; and we have missed this possibility because of the way that higher education in this country tends to divide knowledge into as many small pieces as administratively feasible and then to present each piece to the students in isolation from all the rest, as if knowledge—and not just our disciplines—were actually organized in this way. This, of course, is not a problem unique to Nazarene higher education; in fact, our colleges educate in a much more holistic manner than their secular counterparts and many educators have now begun to cry for some kind of large scale educational reforms that will restore some semblance of unity to the fragmented curriculum of higher education.[5]

To continue with the geometric metaphor of the Wesleyan Quadrilateral we might say that the Quadrilateral has been dismantled with Scripture going to the biblical studies department, Tradition going to the theology department, Reason heading off in the general direction of philosophy, and Experience migrating toward the sciences, social as well as natural. If Nazarene students are ever to appreciate the intellectual richness of their Wesleyan heritage it will be because they somehow discovered that the four one-dimensional straight lines that they encountered in four different parts of their undergraduate curriculum can be assembled into a curious geometrical figure that seems capable of shedding extraordinary light on those very intellectual problems that Mark Noll uses as examples of the "Scandal of the Evangelical Mind"—religious politics, art, scientific creationism, abortion, and so on. The problem, says Noll, is simple-minded biblical literalism. Evangelicals have developed a bad habit of thinking that anyone can respond to any issue—no matter how complex—by finding a few "self-interpreting" Bible verses that immediately lay the matter to rest. There is no need to consider the expertise of the biblical scholar in understanding the Scriptures; there is no need to consult the theologian to see whether or not one's personal interpretation is consistent with the historical understanding of the church; and there is certainly no need to consult the scientists to see whether they have anything relevant to add. The problem with biblical literalism, as I might put it in this context, is its failure to acknowledge that Tradition, Reason, and Experience should also be consulted.[6]

In this essay I will outline the nature and the consequences—both present and projected—of this failure and the extent to which it is the result of the structure of higher education. My perspective will be that of a science educator for that is my role in the Church of the Nazarene. I believe my concerns are the same as those that might be expressed by a social scientist, economist, or political theorist, were they to address the same problem as it appears in their disciplines.

The Mind of Christ

There are a number of specific problems I could use to spotlight the challenge of the fractured curriculum. I will choose two specific cases because they represent acute current problems for the Nazarene Mind. The specific problems to which I am referring have one thing in common—they are *intrinsically* interdisciplinary and simply cannot be discussed intelligently unless one is capable of integrating material that comes from all four sides of the Wesleyan Quadrilateral.

In what follows I am fully aware that I am departing from the way that the Wesleyan Quadrilateral has generally been interpreted in the past. But, I should add in my own defense, it is certainly true that the "quadrilateral" is not understood in the same way by all who claim to structure their rhetoric under its rubric. Some of my fundamentalist critics inform me that Reason, Tradition, and Experience serve no other purpose than to explicate the literal meaning of Scripture. On the other hand, many theologians use the quadrilateral to make the point that the Wesleyan Tradition is not one of biblical literalism. In any event I think the quadrilateral is a powerful rhetorical symbol that can be used to argue that the Wesleyan Tradition can accommodate and integrate ideas from science.

It is probably important to acknowledge here that it is not clear exactly *how* science is to enter the Wesleyan theological conversation. Certainly most current models of the Wesleyan Quadrilateral offer no suggestion as to how this is to be accomplished. A very recent book on John Wesley's theology (Maddox), for example, offers no suggestion that science might have anything to do with Wesleyan theology. The index of subjects includes no scientific topics; the index of persons includes no scientists. The discussion of the Quadrilateral offers no suggestions on how scientific insights might be incorporated. And yet Wesley himself was deeply and profoundly interested in science.[7]

My concern about the discipline-oriented, fragmented, piecemeal mode of delivery of undergraduate education in our colleges is the near impossibility of this format to enable students to think intelligently about some of the great moral and theological questions of our time. While it is important—even essential—that students receive a firm grounding in the discipline of their choice, especially if their undergraduate program is to be a preparation for graduate school, it is also the case that a discipline- oriented approach to education compromises one's ability to address many "real-world" interdisciplinary questions in a meaningful, productive, and ultimately redemptive way. Furthermore some problems are simply left unaddressed because they do not lie comfortably in the middle of a discipline where it is clear just who is in charge.

The kinds of social issues that concern me include such questions as abortion, creationism, therapeutic counseling, medical ethics, environmentalism, multi-culturalism, euthanasia, censorship, contraception, children's rights, the arts, public versus private education, pornography, and so on. Every one of these issues is important and will confront the graduates of our colleges when they enter the so-called "real world." They will have to make decisions about electing officials, signing petitions, participating in protests, supporting causes, choosing pastors, and that all important task of passing on the accumulated wisdom of their generation to that of their children.

To think clearly, critically, and (most importantly) *redemptively* about multi-faceted, "interdisciplinary," social issues demands that one successfully integrate insights from independent perspectives that would have been provided in different undergraduate courses. Typical undergraduates at our Nazarene colleges will have taken a Bible course that might help them bring scriptural insights to bear on a problem; they will have taken a theology course that might help them appreciate how the Christian tradition has approached such problems in the past; they may have taken a biology/anthropology course that provides some insight into the nature of human life and culture. And so on.

I think this point is best made by considering specific examples. Any of the above issues would suffice to make the point, but I will focus on abortion and creationism because they have an explicitly scientific dimension.

Two Examples: Abortion and Scientific Creationism

Abortion is certainly the most controversial of social issues[8] and it is not my purpose here to defend a position on abortion; nor do I feel that I even have a position I am prepared to defend. And I am sure that everyone who reads this is as dismayed as I am over the unproductive and useless way this question is addressed in public discourse; but I think we also need to be concerned about the inarticulate, although certainly less emotional, way that this question is discussed in our denomination; I am regularly appalled at how uninformed even our "well-educated" constituency is. Recently, for example, an anti-abortion petition from a conservative Christian organization appeared on the hospitality desk in the foyer of a local Nazarene church. At the top of the petition was the slogan "Abortion stops a beating heart." As the signatures on the petition accumulated I became concerned that many of my fellow church members—most of whom have a college education—who signed that petition were unaware of the fact that by far the majority of abortions do not "stop a beating heart."[9] It is an elementary fact of biology that a developing embryo does not have a beating heart—or any heart for that matter—until three or four weeks after conception. Any procedure which acts early enough—such as an IUD, for example—halts the reproductive process before there are any heartbeats, or brain waves, or any of the other activities normally associated with "life." In fact it is the absence of these very activities which is often considered to signify death in critically ill patients.

Whether or not the "stopping of a beating heart" is morally relevant to the abortion question is *not the point*; it may in fact be completely irrelevant. But we make an avoidable *factual* error when we oppose all abortions on those grounds. Christians should not be signing a petition on the mistaken assumption that all abortions "stop beating hearts."

In another common example of confusion on this question a well-educated Nazarene with an advanced degree recently shook a finger at a Sunday School classmate and stated with great authority "The only difference between you and a one-day old embryo is *size!*"[10] This statement was made with the best of intentions and was not driven by any knee-jerk political agenda; however this statement is simply false; it is only possible to make a statement like this (or the one mentioned in the previous paragraph) if one is completely ignorant of the elementary biology that explains how a fertilized egg develops into a fetus. A one-day old embryo is not a "tiny person" that, if enlarged a thousandfold, would look like a child. There was a time when this idea was commonly embraced by biologists,[11] but that time is long past and people who choose to involve themselves in the abortion debate of today need to know this.

Let me repeat here that the above considerations are not *necessarily* relevant to the question of the morality of abortion and are in no way intended to be a defense of any particular position on this volatile issue. But if Christians wish for their perspective to be heard and appreciated they must at least get their facts straight. Fifteen-hundred years ago St. Augustine suggested we should take all means to prevent such an embarrassing situation, in which people reveal vast ignorance in a Christian and laugh it to scorn. When Christians take strong stands on issues that they do not understand and speak much nonsense about these issues, it certainly makes it appear that the positions—no matter how well intentioned or justifiable in other ways—are embraced out of ignorance. This is a scandal.

Using the Wesleyan Quadrilateral (expanded to include traditionally "non-theological" material) as a framework for the discussion of this question might involve the following interdisciplinary investigation:

1. Scripture—what does the Bible say? Does it discuss the unborn in the same language that it uses to refer to people in general?

2. Tradition—what has the Church believed historically about the rights of the unborn? How have the terms "human" and "life" been understood? Has it ever been a "front burner" issue?

3. Reason—what are the natural processes by which human beings acquire their physical existence? Are there relevant differences that emerge at birth? Are there relevant differences that emerge prior to birth? How does science define the terms "human" and "life"?

4. Experience—how do people who have had abortions view their decisions? How do those who contemplated it and decided against it view their decisions?

And so on.

I would like to think that graduates of Nazarene schools—especially those that will be entering the pastorate and exercising important leadership roles—will be able to enter into the public discussion of abortion in a meaningful way; I would like to think that our graduates might be able to do more than simply scream epithets in front of abortion clinics; I would hope that the voices of our graduates will be informed voices of reason, compassion, integrity, and balance; and I sincerely hope that our message is not "laughed to scorn" because it emerges out of a context of what St. Augustine called "vast ignorance." But I do not know if those students will be able to simultaneously integrate the various perspectives that are relevant to a complex issue like this one.

In *The Scandal of the Evangelical Mind* Mark Noll identifies "scientific creationism" as the leading evangelical social issue of our time after abortion. It has become, even in the Church of the Nazarene, an increasingly divisive topic on which the denomination, like some in the larger evangelical community, struggles to find an accommodating "middle ground" while the two poles of the debate get further apart. At the present time a very unstable equilibrium exists[12] in the Church of the Nazarene with many embracing some form of theistic evolution and others retaining a strong commitment to an essentially fundamentalist scientific creationism. In his marvelous book *The Creationists*, premier historian of science, Ronald Numbers quotes a study that indicates that Nazarene support of scientific creationism at the birth of the modern movement was exceeded only by the Assemblies of God and Seventh Day Adventists. The survey, done in 1963, prior to the modern creationist revival, indicated that about 80% of the polled membership of the Church of the Nazarene supported creationism (300). It is hard to see how such a tension can persist indefinitely without the conflict coming to a head; when that occurs the voices of our educated laity will need to be raised.

The question of origins is another enormously important volatile issue. Treated in such piecemeal fashion in our undergraduate curricula, it is almost miraculous that anyone ever graduates with a clearheaded perspective. Science majors often graduate with a reasonably clear understanding of natural history but remain totally confused about how one might reconcile this with their rather primitive understanding of the religious dimensions of the question. Religion majors often graduate with a reasonably clear understanding of the religious dimensions of the question but remain uncertain about how one might reconcile this with their primitive understanding of natural history. There exists a "cultural divide" here with very little communication across the divide. In many cases the two sides seem oblivious to the relevance of the insights from the other side, and it is not uncommon to find narrowly educated "specialists" who take a certain satisfaction in their one-side-of-the-Wesleyan-Quadrilateral perspective, confident that whatever they do not know must somehow, by definition, be irrelevant to this particular question. The result is a devastating inability for Nazarenes to talk intelligently about origins because there are so few graduates of our educational institutions that know enough about the interdisciplinary complexities of the question. It would be pointless here, of course, to criticize our graduates; we must instead (1) encourage our colleges to take the lead in breaking out of the disjointed way that undergraduate education is delivered in this country; and (2) encourage our denomination to create a "climate of theological humility" that will encourage Christian college faculty to freely explore the many dimensions of faith and scholarship. I will address each of these concerns individually below.

The question of origins, like that of abortion, is one that demands both a scientific and a biblical/theological understanding. On the biblical and theological side, I wish that all of our science majors had a detailed grasp of the exegetical issues surrounding the first few chapters of Genesis. I wish that they knew that Genesis 1 is structured very much like a poem and has been viewed by many historically important Nazarenes like H. Orton Wiley as a sort of "hymn of the dawn," with minimal scientific content (449). I wish that they knew that the name of the first person created by God is the generic Hebrew word for "Man"; I wish they knew that the two creation accounts in Genesis cannot be reasonably harmonized with one another and that the historical chronology of the first few chapters of Genesis cannot possibly be taken literally (e.g., what was the origin of the "city" that Seth encountered in Genesis?) I wish that they knew that very few of the major historical figures in the church, including thinkers as diverse as Augustine and Wesley, interpreted Genesis in a way that even remotely resembles what the fundamentalists are promoting today. I wish that they knew that "scientific creationism" originated in a bizarre prophetic pronouncement of Ellen White, nineteenth-century guru of the Seventh-Day Adventists. And I wish they knew that very few of the leading theologians and biblical scholars in the Church of the Nazarene hold this fundamentalist view of creation.[13] Alas, most of our science graduates know none of this and often leave our colleges with the seriously mistaken notion that their "liberal" scientific understanding of creation cannot be reconciled with the "conservative" notions that are their (mis)perceived legacy of the the Wesleyan-Arminian tradition.

In the case of creationism, "tradition" is sadly overlooked as many Christians labor under the mistaken impression that their literalistic reading of Genesis is the "plain truth of the Scriptures" and that all Christians until very recently shared this view. It would be very helpful if Nazarenes knew that Wesley himself was an important eighteenth century champion of science who, rather than insisting that all scientific insights must come from the Scriptures, was very informed about the (secular) science of his day and strove to find ways to integrate scientific insights with his religious views.[14] It is hard to imagine, though, where such a discussion might emerge. Courses in religion departments are not going to take time away from their disciplinary interests to teach students enough about science and its history to recognize, much less appreciate, the implications of Wesley's science; courses in science departments are certainly not going to spend much time looking at Wesley. If the students are going to "put it all together" it will be on their own, or perhaps over coffee outside of the classroom, with a professor who is comfortable straddling the boundaries of their discipline to help them with the difficult task of integration.

After more than a decade in Nazarene higher education I am increasingly convinced that one of the large scale pedagogical problems we face is the mismatch between the narrow disciplinary way that we deliver the material and the broad integrative way that the students attempt to process it. (Let me hasten to add that I have no problems with disciplines; certainly knowledge at the end of the twentieth century has become so advanced that scholars cannot progress to the "cutting edge" of that knowledge base unless they pursue a very specialized course of study. And there is probably no education any more narrow than that of the physicist; my doctoral research in "Laser Induced

Optical Pumping" did not even educate me to speak competently on many issues within physics, much less within science in general, and certainly not outside of science.[15])

I am afraid that I am often guilty of making the assumption in my freshman astronomy class that the students will accept the canon of material that constitutes modern astronomy without insisting that all that material "fit" with their other "non-astronomical" beliefs. For example, I must struggle when presenting the "Big Bang" theory with the fact that all the members of my class believe firmly, even fervently, that "In the Beginning God Created the Heavens and the Earth." My lecture thus must address the profound rhetorical challenge of not *sounding* like it is incompatible with the scriptural affirmation. This is difficult.

I asked my astronomy class this past semester to comment on any ideas from the course that seemed problematical or difficult to reconcile with their religious beliefs. Here are some examples of what they said:

"I do not understand how our bodies are made of stardust.... I was always taught that we were made of dirt, never stardust."

"Scientists tell us that rocks, trees, water, and our planet plus the whole universe was once an ultra dense concentration of matter and energy much smaller than the head of a pin. For some odd reason I cannot grasp that unless one can say that is how God began His 'let there be light' situation."

"Looking back onto my astronomy class, I can't help but wonder how everything that I learned in this class may contradict my beliefs."

"I would rather a million times choose the biblical account for the existence of everything that is in the universe being the result of the omnipotent wisdom of the almighty God, than that of the mere figment of an astronomer's imagination."

These statements are representative of different but very common perspectives. If I may generalize from my experiences at Eastern Nazarene College, the typical college freshman makes at least some attempt to "integrate" new material from their college courses with whatever body of knowledge they bring to college with them. This body of knowledge has been synthesized from a variety of sources, one of the most important of which was their religious education. This is not a novel or remarkable insight—it is rather a description of how human beings learn. When we teach our students as if their minds contain a collection of "blank slates"—one for each of the disciplines they will study and no connections drawn between them, we fail to accomplish our task.

This difficulty in understanding new ideas that do not fit the existing framework is not a "student" problem that goes away when you "grow up." (At least it did not go away when I grew up!) I am now a professor of science; I am convinced of the truth of the modern scientific picture of the world, including its origins. This is my "framework" into which I "fit" new ideas. I thus have great difficulty making sense of theological or biblical insights that appear to contradict that scientific picture. For example, I once took a theology course where the professor stated that "all the creation was fallen." In response to a question he went on to say that this means that "all aspects of the creation, including the physical universe studied by science are fallen; this fall extends to and includes the particles in the universe." When I questioned what it could possibly mean to say that "electrons are fallen" there was no answer; in fact I still think that there can be no answer to this question and I remain confused, years later, as to what could possibly be meant by the statement—that the physical universe is fallen.[16]

In my personal struggles to make sense of the significance of the fall for the physical sciences I believe that I am engaged in the same attempt to integrate new (for me) theological understandings with my prior scientific beliefs[17] that is reflected in the quotes above from my astronomy students. I do not see how we can expect students to integrate material from different courses into the kind of coherent synthesis so essential for meaningful dialogue *if the teachers of these students have no idea how this is to be accomplished.* How can we expect professors with zealous commitments to their disciplines to make room in their courses for related material from other disciplines? And how can we expect an academic professional to take the time to become sufficiently educated in other fields—which they may already perceive as irrelevant to their discipline—to accomplish this task? Or perhaps the question is even more fundamental—why should professors even *care* about that portion of their students' education that is outside their field?

This seeming lack of interest in the integration of religious and scientific understandings of the world is one of the causes of the muddled and unproductive way that origins are discussed today. I am continually amazed at how many well-educated Nazarenes think that the *imago dei* theological concept rules out biological evolution because "God does not look like a monkey!" Or that evolution is easily reconciled with a literal reading of Genesis by simply making the days in Genesis into long periods of indefinite duration. And so on.

The second challenge in developing a coherent denominational conversation on origins is the intellectual restraint that many college faculty—especially religion faculty—must work with; this is especially true for those that struggle to be sensitive to the concerns of a conservative constituency, even though they may be tenured and do not fear for their jobs. The fact that a vibrant "climate of theological humility" does not yet exist creates countless problems, constraining open and honest discourse, tolerating confusion, and even sanctioning misunderstanding. With very few exceptions the faculty in our colleges who deal with sensitive religious and theological issues in their courses choose to place a "filter" between them and their students so that the students will hear nothing sufficiently dangerous to merit a report to their parents who will report to their district superintendent who will call the president who will call in the faculty member and make it clear that the survival of their institution depends on keeping such "subversive" notions to oneself.

This problem is most discouraging when it results in a scenario where an ill-informed wing of the constituency is able to minimize the best intentions of our denominational scholars and academics to mitigate the "Scandal of the Nazarene Mind." This is most acute in our general education courses in biblical studies and theology, and in those courses that deal with scientific perspectives of origins. Any powerful pedagogical attempt to inform entering freshman that their fundamentalist biblical literalism[18] is only one way to approach the Scriptures may result in all kinds of political grief for the instructor. So the instructor must employ a "language of ambiguity" to minimize controversy.

Here are some examples of how this "language of ambiguity" is used to sanitize potentially controversial information:

A biblical studies instructor once told me that he would like to feel free to say the following about Genesis: "The first chapter of Genesis is a theological affirmation of God as the creator of all that is. The account reflects a primitive view of the universe that is almost completely inaccurate from a scientific point of view and should not be read for scientific content."

What the instructor feels free to say: "It is not the goal of the first chapter of Genesis to teach science but rather to make the theological point that God is the creator of all that is."

The result: the students retain their fundamentalist belief that Genesis is scientifically accurate, perhaps mitigated slightly by an awareness that the main point is theological rather than scientific.

A science instructor once told me he would like to feel free to say the following about evolution: "Human beings emerged from the same natural processes that gave rise to the rest of the natural world. . . ."

What the instructor actually says: "Human beings did not come from monkeys."

The result: the students are happy that their professor is not an "evolutionist."

These examples can be multiplied endlessly. Any of the readers of this essay who have spent significant time in Nazarene college classrooms can probably identify with the "language of ambiguity" mentioned above and may even have their own personal examples.

How can the Church of the Nazarene develop a clear theology of origins if we cannot even discuss the issue openly? Some years back an administrator at Nazarene Theological Seminary and I planned a "Consultation on Science and Theology" to be held at the seminary. To organize the conference we assembled a planning committee, intending to meet at one of the Nazarene colleges. We obtained approval from the administration of the college to use their facilities for the planning meeting and made the relevant travel plans. The administration of the college, however, canceled our meeting at their institution at the last minute because they knew that we might discuss "evolution," of which some of their constituents disapproved.[19] We then spent denominational funds renting facilities at a nearby Howard Johnson, the manager of which seemed unconcerned about the topic of our meetings.

What can be done about this "climate of fear"? How can we replace it with a *"climate of theological humility"*? Is it possible to hire Christian scholars to pursue the "Truth" and then teach it to our students while simultaneously appeasing a constituency that may not want any of their sacred cows altered? This "climate of fear" is very real and works to sustain the "Scandal of the Nazarene Mind." Sunlight breaks through as humility and openness replace uneasiness and dogmatism.

The institutions of higher learning in the Church of the Nazarene are filled with dedicated, bright scholars who are capable and more than willing to help the denomination develop an adequate understanding of origins—one that does justice to the theological insights of the Wesleyan-Arminian Tradition[20] without forcing the church to embrace the pseudo-scientific creationism that makes American Evangelicalism the laughing stock of the worldwide scientific community.[21]

Conclusion

In this essay I have dealt only with abortion and creationism as topics which provide some insight into the challenges confronting Nazarene educators, and I have also attempted to move beyond mere critique to offer some constructive suggestions as to how the "Nazarene Mind" might be rejuvenated. But I fear that our denominational problem grows out of a much larger American problem—an ignorant and strongly anti-intellectual culture being educated in increasingly specialized system of higher education. It is not exactly clear how to proceed.

However, several points are clear—

1. As long as the Church of the Nazarene is willing to ordain pastors without a broad and truly *integrated* education it will be difficult for the Church to break free of the anti-intellectual fundamentalism that is scandalizing the larger evangelical mind and exerting pressure on leadership to embrace increasingly less Wesleyan perspectives.

2. As long as the general education of those students who are able to acquire a quality education, and especially those pastors receiving the considerable benefits of graduate study, is done exclusively in the piecemeal, discipline-oriented way that we are doing it now, we can never expect the majority of our students to "put it all together."

What can we do about this style of education? American higher education has a certain structure, and it is not feasible, or perhaps even possible, to abandon that structure in our denomination colleges. I teach two general education courses at Eastern Nazarene College. Because of my concern for the issue of creationism in our denomination's I have modified these courses to include some of the material mentioned above. The response of most of the students has been favorable. The only lecture that actually elicits comments of appreciation in astronomy is my lecture on "Astronomy and the Doctrine of Creation." Students regularly comment that "I found that class very interesting; I had no idea that it was possible to integrate those different ideas." My colleagues however, are not uniformly appreciative of my efforts; some of them perceive me as a rank amateur who presumes to teach in areas where I have no competence. Some fellow science faculty see me as having "abandoned physics for philosophy." There is, no doubt, some validity to these criticisms; certainly American higher education has little room for professors without a strong commitment to the narrow canons of their field of specialization. I think that this tendency towards excessive disciplinary specialization at the undergraduate level will make it difficult for us to break out of our current mold.

I am confident, however, that the Church of the Nazarene, with its broad rich Wesleyan tradition has the resources to accomplish its task.

Given the proper encouragement our network of colleges could play a major role in mitigating the "Scandal of the Evangelical Mind."

Epilogue

My relationship with Cecil Paul was based to a large degree on our mutual interest in interdisciplinary integrative education. My first conversation with Cecil—on the phone before we had been introduced—was one in which he encouraged me to submit an article to the *Herald of Holiness* addressing the issue of scientific creationism. He anticipated correctly that such an article would be controversial, but he was prepared to support the endeavor, believing strongly in the value of dialogue. He later encouraged me to write *Worlds Apart* and was very disturbed when its publication met with so much political resistance. He mentioned several times about helping me find another publisher.

Much of Cecil's own work involved the integration of psychology and religion, another very controversial area but one that sorely needs such wholeness. He recognized that pastors spend much of their professional time counseling and that training in theology and biblical studies did not equip them very well for that task. While on the faculty at Eastern Nazarene College he labored long and hard to establish a graduate program in pastoral counseling, overcoming objections from faculty who felt that pastors would be better served by additional grounding in theology and biblical studies. When one considers that powerful opposition to psychology still exists among conservative evangelicals, it is all the more remarkable that Cecil was breaking ground in this area two decades ago.

Cecil Paul was an integrative, interdisciplinary, holistic, thinker; and he was capable of inspiring others to this vision. His influence on the Church that he loved was profound and positive. His brief tenure as the president of ENC established a legacy that continues to inspire those who caught his vision. I would like to think that there is some small part of him in this essay, for his inspiration to me as a young faculty member at Eastern Nazarene College was significant; I would like to think that Cecil's vision is perhaps present in all of these essays, for he influenced many people during his all too short time among us.

NOTES

1. For a spirited response to Noll's charge that the holiness tradition bears significant responsibility for the "Scandal of the Evangelical Mind" see Donald A. D. Thorsen, "The Future of Biblical Studies in the Wesleyan Tradition: A Theological Perspective," *Wesleyan Theological Journal*, (1995), 182—202.

2. By "Nazarene Mind" I am referring to the way that the denomination conducts its internal intellectual discourse: how it deals with controversial issues, how it responds to intellectual challenges, how it trains its youth, what it values in its college and seminary faculty and how it appears to a secular community. It goes without saying (but I will say it anyway) that there are many *individual* minds within the church that are exemplary. I have been blessed by an extensive association with chemistry professor Lowell Hall at Eastern Nazarene College and physics professor Keith Walker at Point Loma. Hall and Walker, however, both restrict their scholarly work to standard contributions within their disciplines; they publish in recognized secular journals and make little effort to relate their science to anything characteristically "Nazarene."

3. It is instructive to contrast the response of the Church of the Nazarene to my book *Worlds Apart* (Kansas City, Beacon Hill, 1994) with the response of the Christian Reformed Church to Howard Van Til's *The Fourth Day* (Grand Rapids, MI: Eerdmans, 1986), a similar venture into the controversial science-religion arena. Van Til, a professor of physics at Calvin College, created such a storm of controversy in the Reformed Church that he was formally investigated by ecclesiastical authorities who made it clear that their tradition had boundaries that constrained the range of discourse on this topic. In contrast, the Nazarene response to *Worlds Apart*, while upsetting many individual Nazarenes, including some in high places, probably could not give rise to any form of serious "inquisition," such as that convened to investigate Van Til. (At least that is my optimistic interpretation of the Nazarene *Manual*!)

4. I realize, of course, that these four elements have never been understood to be on anything resembling an "equal footing." The Christian Tradition has always drawn its primary inspiration from Scripture but the mere acknowledgement of Reason and Experience in the conversation makes it possible for the Tradition to reconsider the respective roles of the members of the quadrilateral. This essay is really suggesting that the Wesleyan Quadrilateral serve as a rhetorical platform on which to build a more interdisciplinary theology—one that might incorporate some of the insights from contemporary science.

5. In a development that I have found personally interesting there are now a few "big league" schools that offer graduate programs in "Science and Religion." It is actually possible to obtain a Ph.D in this highly interdisci-

plinary area at Berkeley, University of Chicago, and Princeton. There are also a number of journals now in this field. It is also encouraging to note that two of our leading Nazarene theologians—Mike Lodahl of Northwest Nazarene College and Al Truesdale of Nazarene Theological Seminary—are doing work in this area and developing courses at their respective institutions that further the science-religion conversation.

6. It is also worth emphasizing at this point that biblical literalism emerges much more naturally and confidently out of the tradition of *sola scriptura* than the more broadly based Wesleyan tradition.

7. Without claiming even an introductory familiarity with the vast literature on Wesley, I wonder if there is work to be done in identifying and perhaps even "recovering" the role and influence of science in Wesley's theology. It is certainly the case that science and theology did not have the chasm separating them in the eighteenth century that exists today. (See also note 13).

8. As I write these words the controversial trial of John Salvi is going on just a few miles away. Salvi is on trial for forcing his way into an abortion clinic and shooting several people who worked there. His lawyers are arguing that he is insane; like-minded zealots are hailing him as a hero.

9. The most common type of abortion is the failure of the newly fertilized egg to implant itself properly in the womb. This happens spontaneously about half of the time; it can also be induced by certain contraceptives. Later term abortions performed before the heart has developed at about week four also do not "stop a beating heart."

10. It is curious that much of the religious objection to abortion assumes a purely scientific (biological) definition of human as if the *definition* of human is determined by science rather than by theology or philosophy.

11. The belief was known, surprisingly, as *creationism* and was based on the assumption that a sperm was a little tiny person that had only to grow in size to become a mature adult human. The modern study of embryology has shed considerable light on the process of embryonic development and we now understand that there is a *qualitative* as well as a *quantitative* difference between a newly fertilized egg and and a baby ready to be born.

12. It would be very useful for the church to conduct a survey and put some numbers with this question.

13. I am often amazed and dismayed at how widespread is the perception that the religion faculty in the Church of the Nazarene are far more conservative than the science faculty on the question of origins. This point was brought home forcefully at the "Consultation on Science and Theology" held at Nazarene Theological Seminary in 1989. During an informal discussion where the participants felt free to speak openly it became clear

that the religion professors in the room had far more "progressive" views on Genesis and origins than did many of the science faculty. I personally recall being very impressed and even somewhat relieved at many of the comments made by Nazarene religion faculty. I cannot overemphasize the importance of religion faculty engaging in regular dialogue with their scientific colleagues.

14. See, for example, John W. Haas, Jr., "Eighteenth Century Evangelical Responses to Science: John Wesley's Enduring Legacy," *Science and Christian Belief*, v. 6, no. 2, October 1994, 83-102.

15. One might legitimately ask the question here whether or not I have any relevant competence to write about the subject of this essay. (I sometimes ask myself this question!)

16. Not all Nazarene theologians understand the Fall in this way, of course. In fact there is an interesting diversity of perspectives, some of which fit quite nicely with contemporary science and some which do not.

17. While my "prior" framework is scientific, a non-scientist who attempts to become scientifically literate will have a different "prior" framework and would confront analogous, although different, epistemological challenges. ("Prior" here is used only in the sense of "temporally previous," not logically more foundational.)

18. Of course, sound pedagogy would dictate that freshman courses not be confrontational and emotionally upsetting for students. The reality is that the content of such courses is often compromised to minimize the chances of negative reactions. The result is that certain obsolete notions about Scripture and theology seem to persist indefinitely.

19. A few years later the president of this college later sent me a very warm letter expressing his appreciation for my book *Worlds Apart* and praising me for the helpful way that I had integrated evolution with Wesleyan theology.

20. Of course it is essential that the science and religion faculty in our colleges engage each other in some serious preliminary dialogue to ensure that everyone gets on the same page, or at least into the same book.

21. So called "Scientific Creationism" is now so well known in this country that science texts often include an analysis of it under the heading of "pseudo-science." It is considered to be at the same level of credibility as astrology, spoon bending, and geocentrism. *What an insult to the gospel—to be attached to the intellectual equivalent of spoon bending*!

CHAPTER TWELVE

EXCELLENCE IN EDUCATION: PARROT OR LEARNER

Mary E. Conklin

Cecil Paul was an educator. The classroom was his arena—he excelled both as a student and a teacher. Later, he moved on to give direction to an educational institution as its president. Thus as we reflect on the professional life of Cecil Paul, it is appropriate that we reflect on the topic of education, education at small Christian colleges.

The small Christian college is the introduction to the world of higher education for many students from evangelical groups. Some students return as faculty who seek to hone their teaching skills in the classrooms of such institutions; some get a taste of administration. Other faculty seek affiliation with Christian colleges either out of concern to join the effort to integrate faith and learning or because such an environment is tolerable until a "real" job develops. Regardless of how students and faculty come to a small Christian college, two fundamental questions apply: "Why are we here, and what do we want to achieve?" *If* we think about such questions, I assert that as we get involved in the program whether as a student, a faculty member or an administrator, *we assume* that what we are doing represents the reasons for our presence and that it will enable us to achieve what we want.

Frequently as we become accustomed to a setting our sensitivity to its ways diminish. Campus practices assume the mantle of tradition, whether they are the scheduling of Homecoming or library regulations or the definition of what is a good student. However, if we are going to continue to exist and hopefully grow as an institution, we must at times pull back the mantle and see what we have created; we must not assume that our best hopes and wishes for Christian higher education are reality.

Peter Berger in *Invitation to Sociology* alludes to this peeling process as he defines sociology as a perspective that transforms the familiar, so we see the commonplace in a new way. One way to transform the familiar is to scrutinize our assumptions. Berger provides a most useful term for this scrutiny—"debunking." Debunking is the *process* of unmasking the pretensions to see what is really there: Does the official interpretation truly reflect what is really done? (29-42) One way of debunking is to compare the stated practice with the actual practice. So let us "look at" the small Christian college.

To consider the small liberal arts Christian *college* suggests that the orientation selected for the institution is that of a college and not a Bible school. Consistent with this distinction, there is concern to prepare students for a variety of occupations other than ministry. These two choices do not exhaust the options, for a technical college would be another possibility; yet many denominations have chosen either the liberal arts college or Bible school to educate their students. More specifically, given the breadth of courses offered from fine arts to sciences to literature and languages to education, many small Christian institutions not only call themselves colleges, but have defined themselves as "liberal arts colleges." But is the basis for the label of "liberal arts" the breadth of required exposure or is it because of its distinctive goals?

For many people "liberal arts" is synonymous with the requirement to take a few courses in a variety of disciplines to broaden students' awareness. Students take a literature course in which they may read one of Toni Morrison's novels, take a mathematics course that exposes them to logic and basic mathematical processes and some fine arts courses to help them appreciate Rodin's sculpture, Monet or Chopin. Students left to their own preferences might well not select these courses. What many students, parents, and faculty often lose sight of in this smorgasbord approach is *why* these particular courses are required. It is not just for breadth of exposure, but that literature, philosophy, history, fine arts, mathematics teach the students something beyond the factual data. What makes these courses distinctive is that they help "to train the whole person to be at once intellectually discerning and humanly flexible, tough-minded and openhearted; to be responsive to the new and responsible for values that make us civilized. It is to teach us to meet what is new and different with reasoned judgment and humanity" (Giamatti 109-110). Giametti further defines liberal arts with its focus on intellectual discernment, tough-mindedness, and responsiveness to the new. This definition constitutes a daunting standard and one that might be perceived as dangerous, when the institution has a long-standing commitment to Christian values that are held as goals for students. Yet how willing are we for "the liberty of the mind free to explore itself, to draw itself out, to connect with other minds and spirits in the quest for truth" (Giamatti 109)?

Many faculty members and administrators argue that the moving force behind *their* college is to teach students to think. However, before we accept this self-identification we need to consider the actual practices found, for the type of institution should determine the content of the educational experiences and the approach used in providing the learning opportunities. Thus when we assert we are "liberal arts" institutions, is the content of the educational experience and the approach used consistent with our claim? I suggest that many colleges may aspire to be liberal arts institutions but may fall short of the ideal.

If we want to lay claim to the label of being a liberal arts institution, we need to consider the orientation towards learning found on the campus. I contend that a liberal arts institution is characterized by a focus on learning that permeates the campus. As students enter the institution, it is clear that learning occurs—where one goes from "not knowing" to "knowing," where learning is valued by administration, faculty and students. We need to consider how decisively the message is imparted to students that this is a campus dedicated to intellectual pursuits. As we engage in the complicated issues of student enrollment, we have perhaps unwittingly diluted the message that this is an institution of higher learning. We need to

> make a city of green thoughts, an ingathering of achievement ennobled by aspiration, of ideals tempered by application, a civilized life lived not alone but in concert. All this is what you engage, as your life is now the life of the University, and the University existence begins to animate yours. (Giamatti 128)

Does the academic life of the college begin to animate the life of our students?

Rosovsky, who served for eleven years as the dean of the Faculty of Arts and Sciences at Harvard University, helps us as we think about learning. The first characteristic he associated with a "liberally educated person" is the ability to think critically. Although "critical thinking" has become commonplace in academic settings, it refers to an *essential* ability. Students need to be able to explore and examine ideas with precision as well as to select and apply relevant ideas. They need to test ideas against what else they have learned.

In developing the point about critical thinking, Rosovsky notes the importance of being "able to think and write clearly and effectively" (105). Many students have not discovered the value of writing as a way to clarify thought. In general little value is seen in an ability to write, let alone see it as an art. Unfortunately, many faculty under the burden of large classes construct exams that have no written sections and require few papers. Thus the students' tendency to denigrate writing is reinforced by faculty, faculty that ironically may be some of the "best" teachers but have limited time to mark the number of essays required for reinforcing good writing.

Also, fundamental to clear thinking and writing is the search and ownership of ideas and information. In an age where entertainment dominates our culture, increasingly college students do not possess much information that makes them minimally educated citizens. Not only they do not know the capital of Idaho, do not recognize the value of mood in writing or know how to calculate bowling scores without a computer, in many cases they also do not know how or where to go for such information nor do they desire to know. Students want to study the specific issues to be covered on the exam (and many faculty accommodate them by listing specific issues to be tested).

Rosovsky continues to describe a liberal education by asserting that it should produce a person who has a "*critical appreciation* of the ways in which we gain knowledge and understanding" (105). To develop critical appreciation of the ways of knowing, a student needs courses that span from mathematics and science to history and philosophy. A student needs to discover how we know what we know. That discovery should fuel the desire to know more. Thus in the process basic information needs to be acquired. What should then be emerging in the student is something quite fundamental—a persisting orientation that the student be a lifetime learner (Rosovsky 106). There is no way any institution of higher learning can impart to its students all the information they will need to know for their first job, or their second job, or their third. Given the pace of technological advancement, this is particularly true. Learning does not, cannot and should not stop when one leaves the classroom. The next step needs to be coupling learning with the ability to evaluate critically the ideas acquired and to use the information cogently. This fundamental orientation of being a lifetime learner and thinker becomes an essential orientation as we head for the twenty-first century, besides being a hallmark of a liberal arts education.

As we consider what the dominant learning orientation is on a campus, one important venue to evaluate is the classroom. Is the concern to have students who merely feed back the material covered in lecture, complete with appropriate punctuation, or to have students who understand ideas but also wrestle with implications and applications? In the quest for understanding ideas and applying them, students need to be helped to understand that multiple "right" answers exist. Additionally, do we seek to cultivate students who question and challenge even the sacred [Durkheim defined "sacred" as anything to which we accord awe and respect (27)], and do we accept students who, in the process, may come down on the side of values that appear contrary to our own? Is emphasis on thinking evident daily in the classroom and in the extra-curricular activities? What should be the criteria for determining if there are intellectual struggles in the classroom?

As we think about the curriculum and the attitude towards learning found on the campus, we have discussed aspects external to the student. There is an internal element—the student's attitude towards learning. Too many students enter the collegiate scene without the conscious awareness that they make a decision about the type of student they will be—parrot or learner. This is a critical decision for a good portion of the learning depends on the student and her effort. Both parrots and learners acquire information and feed it back, one with thought and reflection and hopefully personal ownership; the other responds with no thought. Parrots are not able to explain the meaning of what they are saying nor are they able to apply the knowledge. Lastly, and somewhat humorously, parrots frequently use the information inappropriately!

What complicates making the choice between parrot and learner is the existence of a culture James Coleman, the noted sociologist, discovered when he studied high schools. The culture of the high school did not place value on academics, particularly being an excellent student. You could be a good student and be positively evaluated by your peers *if* you were also a "jock" and socially active. That standard seems to have entered the collegiate world. True learners exist on campus, but seem to be marginalized. Which type of student are we trying to produce?

Too often we find students who do not read the required text (and complain if multiple texts are used) let alone other supplemental resource books. For research papers there is inquiry about the minimum number of sources to be used. Students who assert opinions are often chagrined when we require reasons to support the contention. The request to structure a logical argument and to perform with excellence is difficult, a difficulty perhaps fueled by a society with a growing affinity for video and passive entertainment.

What may contribute to this parroting norm are structural issues of the college. One issue is a heavy teaching load, where there are four courses to teach and sometimes as many preparations each semester. Additionally, large freshmen classes do not provide adequate opportunity for discussion or much feedback on papers. This occurrence delays the exposure to learning that encourages the student to test her intellectual mettle. Inadequate development of new faculty may also contribute to "parroting" since the new teacher needs seasoning to approach the material from her own multiple critical perspectives.

Regardless of the source, this insufficient approximation of liberal arts is a concern, for the church needs laity with a liberal arts preparation. While there may be need for institutions to prepare clergy [the author feels that a good liberal arts foundation would enhance the ministry of most clergy] and institutions to dispense technical skills, it does not negate the need for the liberal arts. Full-fledged liberal arts is not a choice but a necessity; for such preparation, I would argue, should enable students to develop all of their potential so to honor God and be faithful stewards (Holmes 29). Arthur Holmes, author of *The Idea of a Christian College*, writes of a need "to become more fully a human person in the image of God, to see life whole rather than fragmented, to transcend the provincialism of our place in history, our geographic location or our job" (44). While this process of becoming all that we can could occur anywhere in theory, how much more incumbent is it for a Christian institution to create an environment which exudes a liberal arts orientation. We have a responsibility as we enroll students to then maintain a setting that fosters intellectual and personal growth in the image of God.

With the recurring emphasis on thinking that should occur in a liberal arts setting, Holmes and others help us to understand the special nature of this thinking—thinking "Christianly" where we "accept all things with the mind as related, directly or indirectly, to man's eternal destiny as the redeemed and chosen child of God" (Blamires 44). Harry Blamires recognizing the secular characteristics of the dominant culture within which we live wrote:

> [B]ut as a *thinking* being, the modern Christian has succumbed to secularization. He accepts religion—its morality, its worship, its spiritual culture; but he rejects the religious view of life, the view which sets all earthly issues within the context of the eternal, the view which relates all human problems—social, political, cultural—to the doctrinal foundations of the Christian Faith, the view which sees all things here below in terms of God's supremacy and earth's transitoriness, in terms of Heaven and Hell. (3-4)

Thus we need to help students develop the capacity of examining issues from an eternal perspective, i.e., to think "Christianly." The development of this kind of thinking is the hallmark of a true follower of Christ.

Blamires points us to the critical issue, i.e., the need to recognize fully the extent of secularization in our thinking, and in turn in our actions and our goals. I am confronted with this secularization nearly every semester in Introduction to Sociology when we discuss what is valued in our society and what do the students in the class value. Too few times in eighteen years of teaching have students made a statement about pleasing the Lord as being the ultimate goal or value in life. Students frequently evaluate jobs in terms of the salaries attached to them, not what job would please the Lord.

What should set apart Christian liberal arts institutions is our awareness of the extent to which secularization has penetrated our culture, even our religion; too often the Christian college is not cognizant of such an orientation. From our lack of emphasis on justice and righteousness, to our lack of emphasis of Sunday as a holy day to be set apart, to defining unwed pregnant girls as having "a problem," to the emphasis on material success as life's goal, we have bowed to the dominant culture. Thus as Colson notes in *Against the Night* we find ourselves no longer possessing a transcendent standard, but one seemingly governed by opinions and preference (57). The Christian liberal arts college—and I would add the church—appears to have acceded to the view that absolutes are impediments to self-realization (Colson 41). Granted, such a secular stance was not the intended goal of the small Christian colleges, but it is there.

As the author of this paper I can offer my assessment of Christian liberal arts institutions, but what makes it difficult to tackle and remedy these deficiencies is that all the concerned constituencies do not agree on the problems, or the solutions. Several constituencies shape what a given college is and does: the sponsoring denomination (if one), trustees, parents and students. Part of the difficulty in deciding what we are and what we want to be as an institution is their perspectives.

The denomination's religious leaders originally wanted an institution that properly socialized members' offspring in the beliefs of the group. The focus on what and how the religious ideals are communicated may fail to acknowledge a fundamental issue of liberal arts education—the primacy of teaching over the promulgating of certain religious beliefs. If there is a single-minded attention to religious ideals, little regard may be given to ways that incorporate diversity in the faculty and among students in terms of social class, ethnicity/race and gender. Without intentional emphasis on general curriculum and social diversity, students may not learn what ideas responsible Christians need to know in order to be salt and light in the world.

In the formative years of institutions there were usually cries for excellence as understood then; the longer the institution exists, however, less attention seems to be paid to reviewing the institution's definition of excellence. Educational excellence seems to be defined in the common denominator of keeping close to what has always been thought and done. Graduates who leave with questions about their faith and the practices of the church are often chalked up as failures—not as appropriate products of a Christian liberal arts colleges who are working out their faith.

Trustees of a college with denominational affiliation are frequently selected because they reside in a designated geographical area and are "known to be good Christians and loyal church persons"—worthy characteristics undoubtedly. However, if qualifications for service are primarily these two factors without care taken about educational background and experience in the liberal arts, I wonder how such individuals can wisely and usefully make educational policy decisions for the institution. Philosophical issues of education and Christian education must be significant issues for the selection and ensuing discussion among the trustees.

An additional concern is generated by the trustee selection process. If a stated number are elected per geographic region where do considerations for gender ratio, ethnic diversity and social class variations get factored in? Trustees who represent these concerns are essential for holding the institution accountable in areas of governance, student life and academics where these exact variables may be overlooked. I am aware that trustees who do not personally possess one or another of these characteristics can still advocate these issues, but what is the implicit message sent to students and faculty by a predominantly male WASP group who are distinctly middle class?

The other tendency in trustee selection that most disturbs me is the insularity—the requirement that each trustee must be a member of the sponsoring group. While the purpose of the institution may be to teach students the cardinal beliefs of the faith and of the church, does this require that all trustees be of the sponsoring denomination? Such a requirement limits the linkages to the larger Christian community that might occur if trustees were selected at large. It would help foster significant awareness among other organizations at the board level about what the college has to offer. Most importantly the practice builds bridges. As models for the rest of the institution, recognition of what other Christian educators can contribute sets an example for students and faculty.

The inclusion of representatives from other groups can enrich the pool of ideas from which the institution may operate. Strategies and practices that work well elsewhere can be evaluated. Outsiders may also function to foster a more inclusive perspective as issues are put into a broader context. The suggestion here is for leavening, not total saturation by outsiders. Trustees can play a key role in the vitality of an institution for they have perspective on the academic, spiritual and social aspects of the college that come with distance. We must garner the full measure of what trustees can contribute.

Parents have different concerns. Often parents want a safe place for their daughters to secure a college degree. Parents are concerned about graduation rates and costs and often assume that the education offered is "satisfactory" if the institution is accredited and graduates are finding jobs. Few parents have (or take) the opportunity to visit classrooms or talk with faculty. Fewer still look at the books in the bookstore as a guide to quality. Many parents seem to want their offspring to acquire the skills that will make them employable, an understandable view. Yet, while many are concerned about the economic aspects associated with the preparation the college provides, it seems infrequent that parents are as concerned about the critical thinking abilities their child is developing or the values and ideals their offspring reveal. Some are quite concerned if their child returns home at vacation or in the summer questioning family practices or issues, not recognizing that questions come with true education.

Students frequently are seen as consumers of whatever information is dispensed. Students are concerned that the courses they take be the ones employers are going to value. Few students ever think about what *the ideas* of a course will do to them as people; increasingly as the competition stiffens in the labor market, ideas are only evaluated in terms of their alleged dollar value. Understandably financial sacrifice by parents and the students themselves promote attention to employment. Additionally, too few students consider the value of being contributors to their own or to others' education. The realization escapes most students that education is an interactive process.

The other aspect of students as consumers is that the consumer strongly influences what the market offers. The result is a variety of majors without significant attention to constructing the major courses within the context of a liberal arts setting (e.g., Business, Accounting, Computer Science, Interior Design, Child Care and Engineering). These majors attract students and fill classrooms, but can thwart the intent and goals of a liberal arts institution with their heavy emphasis on skill acquisition. On the other hand, I took a year-long accounting class that was thoroughly liberal arts in its orientation. These professional skills courses must continue to incorporate ways to think "Christianly."

The consumer motif appears in student admissions. Colleges compete for the consumers of their "product." One way to guarantee full enrollment is to treat admission standards as "negotiable." Students with grades and SAT scores that would hardly qualify them to play NCAA Division I sports or those slightly above that cut off may be admitted to some Christian colleges. Remediation work may be necessary in order to prepare these students for courses such as literature, philosophy, or history; otherwise, the courses may be reduced to a collection of mere facts to enable less academically able students to pass. How tragic if they never get to the exciting questions associated with the development of the mind. Less prepared students usually benefit from four years of college, but *if* they rarely catch a glimmer of what liberal arts is about, have we done them a disservice by accepting them. Nothing is quite as discouraging as having access to a great journey but having little or no success.

Peter Berger in his classic, *Invitation to Sociology,* likens us to puppets, where social expectations pull our strings and we respond with little thought about what we are doing (176). The culture we are in, then, provides the norms we respond to. This basic point when coupled with the culture of the 1990s has provided students who are into being entertained, vacuums that suck in stuff that amuses. It permits passivity and consumption. This orientation is fine if one sees students as consumers—taking in the information dispensed, hopefully dispensed in as diverting a manner as possible. However it bears little resemblance to the hallmarks of liberal arts education.

To what extent has the small Christian college bought into these labels, however schizophrenic the result may be. Has the college then tried to be all things to all constituencies? The concerns of denominational leaders, trustees, parents and students are valid to a degree, but put too much emphasis on the context and not enough on the process and content. The church college becomes a safe haven for offspring for parents and the church leaders where we do not question accepted practices and lifestyle issues are assumed to meet a scriptural standard. Does the church body responsible for its existence then hamper its development with requirements for trustee membership and faculty selection that may foster isolationism? To what extent has the small Christian college then accepted what it has become in terms of racial and ethnic composition and gender?

No one questions the motivation of those involved in Christian higher education, whether we are talking about trustees or students or church leaders. Yet we cannot lose sight of what we allege we want to achieve—an excellent Christian liberal arts education. We must *all* strive for excellence. If the church fathers and mothers years ago thought an educated laity was important, and it is, we cannot afford to fail the church by turning out counterfeits. Our graduates need to be the best of Christian liberal arts institutions.

What I have endeavored to present is another view of the familiar. It is hard to change perspective; at times it is threatening. But growth may require change. Perpetuation of tradition for the sake of tradition is an indulgence we cannot afford. Students are too valuable. Students that graduate from small Christian liberal arts colleges are too valuable; we must be good stewards of those whom the Lord has entrusted to us.

The New Testament account does not tell us how the good and faithful steward achieved the five-fold return, but it is safe to assume it was with effort. May we be as full of effort.

TRIBUTE

Growing up in the Church of the Nazarene I had many adult role models for Christian discipleship and pastoral ministry, but no one who embodied a commitment to higher education as central to their faith. I found in Cecil this kind of person. As God's call on my life directed me to interdisciplinary study, teaching, and living, he became a true mentor in his example and encouragement to me in my chosen field.

Douglas S. Hardy
Assistant Professor of Psychology
Eastern Nazarene College

SECTION THREE

LIVING THE VISION

Without a vision, we become self-absorbed and preoccupied with our own comfort and security. The community and the cause become secondary and we risk losing it all.

Cecil Paul, from *Choices*

TRIBUTE

"Look with me at the marks of a godly life...."

Integrity: "We are not as Moses was with veiled face covering the fading glory, but with unveiled face we behold the glory of the Lord." Cecil cared deeply what people thought of him, but he cared even more deeply what God knew of him and he lived accordingly.

Honesty: "We do not distort God's Word, we are not clever." Every minister knows the tension between what people want to hear and what the simple sense of God's word demands. Cecil lived in that tension with grace.

Humility: "We do not preach ourselves, but Christ Jesus as Lord and ourselves as your bondservants for Jesus' sake." Cecil could have sought the way of personal ambition, but he sought to be the servant of God's people.

Mission: "Christ's love compels us." On Cecil Paul's desk when he died, a last, great word from our friend who stepped into the Presence of God last week: "Not sold out to the world ... sold out to mission!"
—*from Funeral Sermon, August 5, 1992, 2 Corinthians 2:5*

Russell Metcalfe
Pastor, Wollaston Church of the Nazarene
Wollaston, MA

CHAPTER THIRTEEN

PROPHET AND PRIEST: PIONEER AND PRESERVER IN PARTNERSHIP

David P. Whitelaw

Cecil Paul identified the challenge of the contemporary church as that of overcoming "creeping [institutional] inflexibility" in order to counter institutional sclerosis, or the loss of ability to change or adapt. The gain would be "to improve the present moment" without the illusion that one can take the kingdom out of God's hands. His life and work suggest both risk-taking and life-nurturing dynamics in his philosophy. Was he both indefatigable pioneer of the human spirit as well as responsible preserver of a churchly tradition? His journey in leadership in Christian liberal arts education and in churchmanship provides reference coordinates for examining the administrative mission and method of a religious institution.

This essay will attempt to clarify (in the light of Dr Paul's life) the role of a department of philosophy and religion by examining the histories of two contrasting schools of theological education on two continents over the past one hundred years. The thesis is this: a liberal, humane vision and a responsible, theological discernment and commitment in the department of philosophy and religion leads to a creative "re-traditioning" of a heritage.

This inquiry begins by describing Cecil Paul's tradition defining the perceived roles of educator and churchman in terms of "prophetic" and "priestly" functions. Next, the windows of two worlds contemporary with his life and work are opened: that of the University of Chicago Divinity School, with the motto "Creatively Out of Step," and that of the Theological Faculty, Universiteit Stellenbosch, with its denominational commitment to the Dutch Reformed Church in South Africa. Priestly (preserving) and prophetic (risk-taking) styles and strategies are discovered. Finally, comparisons and conclusions are drawn which suggest that the roles of "pioneer" and "preserver" may function in partnership when both are transcended by the dialectic of a renewing symbiosis. This symbiosis makes it possible to go beyond the limits of each contributor, so that each is balanced, renewed, and empowered by the other.

The Role of a Department of Philosophy and Religion

H. Orton Wiley was one of the first Nazarene educators to write a defense of a Christian liberal arts college, emphasizing its roles as custodian of the heart and spiritual intensity, as cherisher and unfolder of a quiet and searching intellect, and as developer of a wise and cultured character (Kirkemo 22-23). Under the siege of early difficulties he struggled with increasing tensions between a commitment to liberal education (prophetic role) and a conservative demand for denominational loyalty (priestly function). He therefore supported the movement towards a closer identification of Pasadena College with the Church of the Nazarene but firmly resisted any attempt to professionalize the Department of Philosophy and Religion into a "Department of Ministry."

The culture of the school and the department for him was "holiness defined in terms of service and humility" (qtd. in Kirkemo 79). He was not the person to vigorously withstand a growing introversion and cultural isolation, but he did resist the philosophy of E. P. Ellyson and others (Kirkemo 31, 74) who stood for education as indoctrination—"come to us and we will instruct you in what the church teaches" (qtd. in Wilkes 59-88).[1] There were limits beyond which Wiley would not go. There was a spirit and a vision which he would not surrender.

> The study of Christianity was to remain an intellectual study as well as a preparation for the ministry; and that tradition, the trade-off of increased Nazarene symbolism for preservation of academic integrity, became the tradition associated with the name Pasadena College.

Wiley would therefore never allow the Department of Religion to become merely a Department of Ministry (qtd. in Kirkemo 75).

Observations from the "Breckinridge Clergy Consultation Documents" on clergy preparation for the twenty-first century appear to endorse the Nazarene commitment to preparation for ministry within a liberal arts context, while recognizing the need for complementing this by both professional theological seminary and Bible college routes to ministry. This suggests forward movement on the trajectory plotted by Wiley.

The role of a department of philosophy and religion in a liberal arts college requires clear focus on its primary subject, *theology,* and its primary context, the sponsoring denomination and contemporary society. With respect to these, one pair of related offices—that of prophet and priest—serves to illumine its function. The department's distinctive nature is qualified more accurately by the word *theology* than *religion*. It functions more as the shaper of critical, reflective theological thought than as a department of phenomenological religious studies. This description does not minimize the place of biblical studies but recognizes their implicit theological importance. The department's responsibility is to teach theology in a manner which is accountable to three "publics": society, academy and church (Tracy 3, Marty "Modes"). The roles of prophet and priest are better (mis-)understood in church than in society but can serve usefully in relation to all three publics. Cecil Paul's analysis of "mission and messages vs. methods and systems" is suggestive of a helpful correlation of the roles of prophet (mission and message) and of priest (method and system) in institutional response to change and risk.*

Within Cecil Paul's tradition the use of the formula for the three offices of Christ as Prophet, Priest, and King is prominent. John Wesley seems to have used these as shorthand for a complex code of ideas. For Wesley, these offices provided a "grammar" for norming practical-theological activities aimed at forming the beliefs, affections, and practices of his people (Maddox 109-114). For our purposes it is sufficient to note that all activity which contributes to shaping Christian character bears this mark of balance.

The prophet in biblical history is one who stands as mediator and representative for God before the people; the priest is one who stands as mediator and representative of the people before God (Young 28). The prophet or spokesperson (Hebrew, *nabi*) was also visionary or seer (Hebrew, *ro-eh*). They were the receivers and recorders of inspiration and message (Sternberg 79) while the priests (Latin, *pontifex* = bridge-builder) were interpreters and translators of that message/writing (text) into cultic practices. The adjective "prophetic" derives from various sources. It is the description of one who speaks by divine inspiration or in a manner to reveal the divine will; it is the predictive nature of a statement, or it may be the "vanishing of material sense to give way to the conscious facts of spiritual truth." Prophetic role in this essay will focus more on its function in the present than on future, predictive functions (that is, on prophet as forthteller, rather than as foreteller).[2] In other words, how may present courses of action be shaped and critiqued by expectations which lie in the future?

Herbert Schneidau proposes a more radical function for the prophet in society, "The prophets denounce the culture and probe its ideology to the foundations." They offer society the gift of "unceasing critique of itself" (10).[3] Within Israel, this took shape as a "hostile symbiosis between kings and prophets," these institutions emerging almost simultaneously. The opposition between priest (derived from Old English *proest*, presbyter = one ordained as mediator between people and God) and prophet is frequently overdrawn, but "cultic" prophets did not exist in Israel (Schneidau 55, 208). Meir Sternberg heightens this dissonance between prophet and priest another decibel when he claims, "the viewpoints of God and prophet are always distinct in principle and often dissonant in practice"(94). The prophets are themselves subject to critique. Perhaps the most effective prophets, Sternberg would imply, are those who are themselves most powerfully aware of being critiqued.

For our purposes, a department of philosophy and religion, as well as an individual, may be understood as fulfilling the roles of prophet and presbyter, probers and preservers of relationships between people and God. Such a department therefore cannot escape the realities of being accountable to church and society, to academic disciplines and to public service. Neither can it escape the implicit tensions and contradictions which exist between functions which call for prophetic vision as well as priestly system. Historic examples of educators in various institutions provide models for interpretation in this essay. Two institutional models are examined, located in Chicago (United States of America), and Stellenbosch (Republic of South Africa).

Divinity School, Chicago: Prophetic Probers—"Creatively out of step"

The University of Chicago played a major role in enabling the church to come to terms with "the modern mind" and indeed to shape it, at a time when both Roman Catholicism and Protestantism were embroiled in the fundamentalist-modernist controversy in the early twentieth century. A student from those years describes his impressions in retrospect:

> The theologians of Chicago . . . were often prophetic seismographs detecting deep subterranean tremors of creative ideas. They were like sensitive barometers recording the coming winds of doubt; they often had theological telescopes trained . . . on new constellations of philosophical thinkers, and they spent much time at the critical microscopes peering intensively at texts and contexts seeking to "disimprison" fact (in the phrase of Coleridge) into larger interpretations of reality. (Arnold 8)

Charles Harvey Arnold has written a short history of the Divinity School and the "Chicago School of Theology" (1866-1966) under the title, *Near the Edge of Battle*, chapter 1 is titled, "Pioneers and Prophets." Arnold, nurtured in Southern conservatism and personalistic idealism, did not have great sympathy for this divinity school, which he described as "a sinkhole of Hell" infested by theological and other gangsters (vii). He quotes Ernest DeWitt Burton, however, who always claimed that the place that was "nearest the edge of battle" provided the strongest evidence of being the "one to which Providence called" (1). Although Rockefeller's "Oil King" money provided material resources, "it was the toil and heartbreaking labor of a whole generation of prophets and pioneers" that made possible the phoenix-like rise of the University of Chicago out of the ruins of the old university and the Baptist Union Theological Seminary of Morgan Park.

The school, founded in 1860, grew in the decade of 1866-1876 as the Baptists became the leading denomination in Chicago. Among the first students was a young shoe salesman named Dwight L Moody, who, as "the greatest American lay evangelist" inspired the ecumenical movement through the conversions of young John R. Mott and Robert Speer in the 1880s (Arnold 4). In 1878 the decisive event that shaped the future of the institution also occurred when the president, Dr Northrup, presented the name of William Rainey Harper, the "young man in a hurry" who worked as if "he wished to teach everyone in the world Hebrew," to fill a vacancy in the Seminary. He became president twelve years later, at the age of thirty-four!

This was the era of shock following publication of Charles Darwin's *Origin of Species* (1859). "Higher criticism" of the Bible was emerging as a challenge to the "Bible-toting, Bible-quoting Protestantism" founded on the inspiration and inerrancy of the text. Rockefeller and Harper became connected in the merging of the Seminary with the founding of the University of Chicago (1892) later to become one of the great research universities of the nation and the world. The Baptist Morgan Park Seminary had been conservative, Puritan-pietist, evangelical, evangelistic and Calvinistic. Later, Nazarene students such as Stephen S. White (1946), Carl S. Bangs (1959) and Troy W. Martin (1990) were to complete doctorates there. Now Chicago was to attract persons "creatively out of step" with that tradition as conservatism became everywhere embattled or in retreat. Creighton Peder writes: The scholars who came to teach at the Divinity School at the University of Chicago attempted to adapt the scientific method in order to advance the critical study of the Bible and of religious history (10).

The stated aims and purposes of the Divinity School originally were "to fit men to become preachers of the Gospel"—that is, simply a continuation of the goal to "produce good, solid Baptist ministers for the work of the churches and the missions" (Arnold 14-15). The first concern was to turn out "practitioners" and not "investigators" (researchers). But the rapid growth of specialized knowledge changed this. Soon Harper was to say that it was questionable whether both scientific investigation and professional competence could be "accomplished in the same school." "The line between scientific Divinity . . . and practical Divinity must be more sharply drawn" (Arnold 16). One may discern in these statements evidence of the increasing tension developing in the Divinity School, tensions which may be characterized as scientific/practical or prophetic/priestly.

How did the Divinity School resolve this problem? Dean Shailer Mathews became one of the foremost exponents of the radically empirical, "modernist" method of the Chicago School, which sought to move beyond "cloister" to "clinic" (in the sense of pragmatic, critical, experimental, functional method). Arnold writes that "the distinctive unifying factor in the early Chicago School was the Socio-Historical methodology of its members. . . . At Chicago it became the *seminal* method for investigating religion and the Christian faith" (34-25). From his vantage point in 1936, Mathews answers like this: "It chose to do both." Mathews had no great tolerance for detached, ivory (or ivy) tower academics. He was the typical "progressive, aggressive, pragmatic, instrumentalist, Deweyan spirit" who stood as a prototype of so much of the education and culture of those times. For him, the roles of prophet and priest were symbiotic.

As the school developed in recognizing the growing needs of the churches for a diversified ministry, however, this statement was formulated in 1930:

> Whoever is to enter the ministry or any other religious vocation should be an expert in the field of religion. That is the field he can properly call his own. Religion is not to be scientifically understood by amateurs. (*Divinity Student* 3)

In the shift from the evangelical aim of fitting persons to preach the Gospel to the equally important task of fitting the churches in the modern world to receive the Gospel, one could argue that an intentional prophetic self-critique of the institution in its world was emerging.

Dr. Bernard Loomer became the theoretician who articulated this new approach and method: the nature of theological education as critical, incisive reflection. In "The Aim of Divinity Education," he projected in no uncertain terms what the new single-minded aim would be:

> ... the best justification for divinity education (and) for a seminary in these days is not professional in nature.... The aim of divinity education is the disciplined development of heart and mind toward the integrity of faith and intellectual inquiry for the sake of the cultivation of the human spirit in relation to and service to God. (*Announcements of the Divinity School.* October 1950)

Arnold comments: "It was in essence a *vision* and not a working proposal, ... a radical statement of Protestant theological education, and to many, the only solution." He wanted to correct and transcend the earlier socio-historical method. He articulated this desire in the statement: "One of the Faculty's greatest concerns is to discover a Protestant conception of authority which is constructive, democratic, disciplined and adequate (*The Divinity School News* November 1, 1946). Loomer wanted to restore the theologian in the community of faith as a component pole in Protestant authority. By disciplined mind, heart and spirit, he was to be the prophetic leader in his church and community. "In Loomer's vision of this leader there is something of Amos at Bethel, Christ on the cross, the Genevan Reformer, and the Baptist 'seeker'" (Arnold 20-1).

This was the Chicago School's distinct and singular contribution to theology in America: a *spirit and a method* (critical reflection; experiential, empirical method) which attempted to meet modernity on its own terms and to equip church and society to do so. Observe the interesting correlation of *spirit* (prophetic function) and *method* (priestly task) in symbiotic partnership towards creative transcendence of polarized parties in church and society. However it must be said that the Chicago School became known as prophetically *avant garde* rather than priestly in its nurturing of churchly life and faith. It "took on the more extreme forms of the positivism of the empirical sciences of the time, tending towards 'historicism', itself a kind of philosophy." More and more, Chicago became known as the "hotbed of radical theology" (Arnold, 34).

Theological Seminary, Stellenbosch: "Priestly Self-Preservation"

The role of visionary and steward were equally important in Cecil Paul's life and work. Where Chicago (University and Divinity School) embodied the role of visionary in its context, Stellenbosch (University and Teologiese Seminarium) in South Africa provides a model of a particular kind of stewardship of churchly tradition for comparison.[4] Neither one presents an example directly comparable with that of a Christian liberal arts college in North America; however both offer illuminating insights.

Dwight L. Moody founded the Moody Memorial Church and Moody Bible Institute in Chicago during his lifetime. The father of Dwight Lyman Snyman, a candidate minister in the Western Cape Synod of the Dutch Reformed Church, had been enamored of Moody Bible Institute's vigorous evangelical response to the fundamentalist-modernist controversies of the early decades of this century. This is captured in the name of his son, who later became pastor of the University Church in Stellenbosch, Cape. In South Africa, Dwight L. Snyman embodied the priestly antidote to the prophetic modernism of the Chicago School in the minds of one strand of the Reformed tradition.

The Rector (President in North American terms) of the Teologiese Seminarium was Johannes du Plessis, leader in the evangelical missions movement in southern Africa at the time, close friend of evangelist and churchman Andrew Murray, and author of his biography (1918). He was also, however, a foremost scholar and articulator of historical-critical method in his work as a theologian and biblical student. The fundamentalist-inclined dominee (minister) Snyman laid charges of heresy against him to the presiding Synod (dominance of the Kuyperian school within the Reformed tradition was being asserted). The complaint, not sustained, was referred back to his local presbytery.

Ben J. Marais, later Dean of the Divinity School of the University of Pretoria, and one of South Africa's leading church historians, was a student at Stellenbosch at this time. He skipped classes on occasion with other students to follow the trial of his theology professor. This dragged on for years, even to the point of hearings by the Privy Council in England. Finally, no verdict of guilty being handed down, du Plessis offered to take early retirement in order to resolve the deadlock between himself and Snyman, his own pastor.[5]

Astute observers of church and society in South Africa claim that this extended trial resulted in the narrowing confinement of the rich Dutch Reformed heritage within one of the streams of that tradition. It stifled the church theologically for the generation to come and, in fact, permitted uncritical endorsement of the theological justification of *apartheid* which resulted in a program of institutionalized segregation and racism (Deist, Hofmeyr, le Roux, Marais, Saayman discussed in Whitelaw "Heading Towards" 176-192). Marais, arguably the foremost church historian in South Africa in his day, saw this constriction of the Reformed tradition into a reductionistic, unidimensional, compartmentalized form, as devastating in its consequences.[6] Political segregation as a pragmatic, utilitarian policy became theologically justified through attempts to ground it biblically during the years 1935-1985.

Finally, the Dutch Reformed Church itself condemned the policy as unbiblical and confessed that the practice of *apartheid* was sinful (Cloete 1984).

My conclusion is that the priests of this tradition functioned as preservers of a cherished cultural pattern of living, provided theological justification for the system, and elevated it to the status of a creation of the Gospel itself. Church and kingdom, nation and culture, message and method were uncritically equated, for all practical purposes. The role of prophetic critique was stifled in fulfilling the function of priestly preservation of the *status quo*. It took leaders like Ben J. Marais, Beyers Naude, and others to fulfil the prophetic role within that tradition.

Contrasts, Comparisons, Conclusions

Cecil Paul proposed what he called "the servant solution" where we learn to "collaborate, cooperate and communicate on our shared mission."* This suggests that prophets and priests, for him, were in a joint venture requiring the symbiotic engagement of both functions. He might add, from his Wesleyan tradition, the role of king to that of priest and prophet (Christ as king/healer: Maddox 110, 309, n95).

From the study conducted, Chicago offers the option of being prophetically *avant garde* and "creatively out of step" with one's culture and tradition. Stellenbosch presents the example of conservative preservation to a fault, where the richness and diversity of a tradition is reduced to a monolithic and mechanical adherence to one strand in that tradition. These models provide a distorted picture, since it is possible to view Chicago positively and Stellenbosch negatively. Paul's tradition offers a way of transcending both. But for this to occur, he himself would want to be subject to critique.

There are clearly dangers in both models, in my view. Equally, there are valuable and valid elements in each, which, if owned, would avert the collapse of creative dialectic envisioned by someone like Jacques Ellul. Martin Marty has called him the "quintessential Protestant of our time," and recommended him as the "one person from the Protestant orbit" to be introduced to "let the church know what its agenda should be (1981, 1970: 17-8). Ellul warns that any institution or society which avoids the dialectic tension of self-critique is condemned to reproducing itself in its own image. This is exactly the program of conservatism—self-preservation. Its enemy is the iconoclastic prophet, tearer-down of images.

Cecil Paul was a leader drawn irresistibly toward the future. He emigrated there ahead of his peers. His premature death may symbolize this. Institutional priests were sometimes threatened by his innovative zest for progress. Iconoclastic prophets were restrained by his embracing of the historical roots of his tradition with deep rooted integrity.

Proposal

The role of a department of philosophy and religion in a Christian liberal arts institution is continually lived out in a creative tension between priestly (preserving) and prophetic (innovative) strategies. If the primary commitment of the prophet is fearless (self-)critique and that of the priest is selfless loyalty to a corporate enterprise, then Cecil Paul points to a strategy which expects and fosters a dialectical tension between these. Practical steps towards implementation need to be identified for consideration.

I suggest that two words guide this discussion: "limits" and "beyond." The word "limits" provides a means of considering the boundaries of task and the restraints of cultic convention. The priest's task is to recognize these and to responsibly and efficiently order successful accomplishment of mission goals that are recognizably an embodiment of the community's identity, through methods and systems. The priest is a (bridge-)builder and a guardian of the community.

The prophet's function is to provide vision from "beyond," a sense of mission and an inspiring message which will energize the community and galvanize it into authentic living. Her function is to test and critique the structures and strategies which the priest protects and preserves. The prophet is called to be a "seer" whose vision goes beyond custom, cult and convention. His most critical task is to function self-critically, not just to be a prober of the *persona* of the community.

How may "limits" and "beyond" be translated into radical, realistic, yet responsible courses of action? There are almost inexhaustible resources within the wellsprings of institutional being of a liberal arts college like Point Loma Nazarene College. Here is a programmatic proposal in this context. What options are open to the Department of Philosophy and Religion?

1. "Limits": The words "limits" and "systems" belong together. There are geographic, demographic, historical, economic and denominational boundaries and parameters which call for plotting on an institutional map. Coordinates of rational self-understanding enable us to corporately recognize our current position on the educational landscape. The institution is a "College" with the descriptor "Nazarene" and it is located not so much on the "Pacific rim" as on the "edge" of San Diego near the border with Mexico, in

Southern California. By 2050 the state will be more than 50% Hispanic and non-Anglo American. The Board of Trustees of the College is by constitutional definition and prescription constituted of members of the Church of the Nazarene. PLNC is located near the city and congregation of origin of the denomination, Los Angeles First Church of the Nazarene. The college is led by a president who has completed twelve years in which spiritual development has been the priority. Now it has a new Vice-President for Academic Affairs and leadership has proclaimed "excellence in academics" as the primary objective. The student body is about 40%, staff and faculty 65% Nazarene. So, what are the limits?

2. "Beyond": The words "vision" and "beyond" belong together. The religion and philosophy department can reach beyond itself and its time (forward and backward) into unexplored depths from which resources may be brought to energize a new vision. For example, Phineas F. Bresee (the founder of the sponsoring denomination and co-founder of Pasadena College) embodied the power of vision that transcended boxed-in limits (truth in a book, mission in a denomination, education in a secular environment). H. Orton Wiley would not allow a reductionistic vision of a "Department of Ministry," nor a truncated vision of a church with amnesia, whose memory could only reach back to 1908 or 1517. "Pasadena College" was the great symbol that the institution would not become dogmatic nor sectarian. Wesleyan interpretations of Scripture always called for going beyond the text to living truth, never allowing limits of fundamentalist inerrancy of a text to be determiners of orthodoxy. John Wesley offered the vision of "practical divinity" that was an alternative to elitist theorists taking precedence over entrepreneurial pragmatists. The word "beyond" suggests we are not confined to wooden reimposition of "the way things are."

I have recently put forward the view that society and religion in North America are characterized by the dynamic embracing of change in contrast with Europe which was marked by structured coherence and order (Wilson qtd. in Whitelaw 1996). Marsden and Dayton put this in terms of two contrasting stances, described as *presbyterian* and *pentecostal* "paradigms." These may also be expressed as *Christological* and *pneumatological* ways of ordering religious life and social change. My proposal is that persons and institutions within the Wesleyan/Holiness tradition have, within their corporate heritage, the memory of a way of going beyond their present limits, with elements of both the presbyterian and pentecostal in their history.

This is to reach towards a symbiotic partnership in a *Trinitarian spirit* and *method*. It would be expressed in more supple and simple liturgical orderings of community than those of the Anglican tradition in which Wesleyan identity is rooted (early Methodist love feasts, class meetings and societies attempted this without displacing or replacing the Anglican eucharist). It would produce an appropriate equivalent of the *Book of Common Prayer*. It should be more ready to accept a marginal position than to insist on denominational controls. It should concentrate more on the *process* which cultivates Christian community with distinctive Wesleyan/Holiness (Nazarene) *ethos* and understanding than on quantitative identifiers of Nazarene boundaries. It should design a *method* which gives distinctive expression to its unique competencies and composition as a community.

John A. T. Robinson, the Anglican churchman and New Testament scholar, has written about this same problem of reaching beyond limits without surrendering Anglican identity (viii,3-6). He (and other Anglicans like Trevor Verryn) see the primary carrier of their tradition in Benedictine liturgy, rather than in doctrinal orthodoxies of a particular stripe or ecclesiastical practices or congregational lifestyles of quantifiable specificity. The claim is that one has two options: either be held at the center of the tradition by an empowering spirit, or control and define the boundaries and edges of the community so that it is distinguishable and distinct from the world around it. Either one has to live with a shifting center (not discovered until too late) or with blurred and fuzzy edges (causing frustration to purists or legalists).

The proposal of this essay is that the stories of Chicago and Stellenbosch (read with a [Cecil] "Paul"ine interpretation) give us two words as a start to consider "limits" and "beyond." These are *spirit* and *method*. The spirit of a prophet and the method of a priest, if joined, enable us to respect limits and go beyond them with confidence that we are being held true at the center to our defining identity. What is that identity? It lies in the concept of *community*.

A community is cultivated by a process which embodies a vision. It is hardly carried and preserved by quantifiable external measurements and descriptors such as the word "Nazarene" or "classical tradition" applied to faculty, students or programs. (How many Nazarene faculty, students? Is the name written into the title of the school? etc.) What is important is the vision which is corporately owned and articulated in continual translation into daily life and terms for the uninitiated. What is essential is the practice and process of community whereby the classical traditions (of Christian faith, of academic philosophy and practice) are re-traditioned in ways that are *radical* (returning to their roots of identity), *realistic* (robust and relevant in contemporary strategies) and *responsible* (accountability in community).

What practical steps may the Department of Philosophy and Religion take?

1. Fearlessly and confidently adopt a *spirit and vision* that are embodied in a mission statement offered to the probing test of the best practicing exponents of various traditions and professions outside of but not alien to the department;

2. Carefully implement a *process in community* which will carry the spirit of the mission with integrity of Christian identity;

3. Experiment with and develop a distinctive *method* which gives unique expression to the strengths and competencies of the department. In the Wesleyan context, this could be an embodiment of its unique historical *practical theology* (neither a consecutive theory-plus-practice model, nor an expressivist, experiential model, but a public, practical theological method and pedagogy).

Wesley has shown us something of what it means to bring theological reflection into the service of nurturing Christian life and witness in community (Maddox 14). Like Bonhoeffer, whose life called for a "revitalization of discipleship learned and lived in Christian community" (Fowl and Jones 142), institutions need to learn to read the Scriptures in communion and translate them into embodied life.

A Christian institution which alienates the prophet condemns itself to a reproduction of its own life in its own image collapsing into entrapment in the culture of its past or its present. An institution which retrenches the priest may destroy the basis for the recovery of its roots in renewal of that image in a manner which moves beyond the present towards the lost memory of the reign of God in the future. Does Cecil Paul, imperfect priest and prophet, stand today in the presence of the king-healer, who transcends both, his advocate and ours?

NOTES

1. "At NU, under Ellyson, knowledge was content, education was indoctrination, and academic freedom was unnecessary." A contemporary study by Paul Wilkes (59-88) suggests two dominant educational philosophies in North American theological schools: 1. "Come to us, we will empower you to find the energy to change the future" versus 2. "Come to us, and we will instruct you in what the Church teaches."

2. P. Kyle McCarter, Jr. (99): "a prophet of Yahweh" Samuel is now recognized by his contemporaries as having been engaged by Yahweh to do his bidding. The term that designates his office is *nabi* (rendered *prophetes* by the Greek translators, hence our term "prophet"), a noun probably . . . denoting "one summoned (for a specific assignment or office)." Hebrew *nabi* may thus connote "one called to duty by a god." This explanation was . . . most vigorously argued by W. F. Albright; *From the Stone Age to Christianity*, 2nd ed. (Baltimore: Johns Hopkins, 1946): 231-2. The prophetic history presents the office as all-embracing. Samuel the prophet is also priest, warrior, judge and governor.

3. Herbert N. Schneidau warns, "only a few of the prophets can long sustain (this prophetic vision) . . . and then only because their experience of Yahweh is so intense that it overbears the depression they feel in looking at their society (7). Again, ". . . what the Bible offers culture is neither an ecclesiastical structure nor a moral code, but an unceasing critique of itself." This is a "deliberately chosen and painfully intense experience of alienation . . ." (16).

4. I have examined the role of Johannes du Plessis (1868-1935) at some length in *A Crisis of Credibility: Contemporary Dialogue with Colenso and du Plessis*, 1987 (12-27).

5. Ben Marais was an esteemed colleague at the University of South Africa in the Department of Church History during my tenure there (1980-1988). He related this history in detail and on numerous occasions, as requested, recalling how he had been powerfully impressed by the example of the du Plessis family, who sat in the front pews of the church pastored by Dwight L. Snyman, and listened to his sermons, all the years the trial lasted, into the early 1930s, when he took retirement.

6. Ben J. Marais and 12 colleagues protested the attempt to ground the political policy of *Apartheid* in the Scriptures and withstood the removal of Colored (mixed race) voters from the Voters' Roll in the 1950s. He, along with Beyers Naude, became the primary lone voices in dissent in the tragic years of institutionalization of *Apartheid* from 1948 onwards. Personal conversations with both of them confirm my judgement that this absence of dissent was the most serious legacy of the du Plessis controversy.

CHAPTER FOURTEEN

A TRINITARIAN PARADIGM OF THEOSIS: A CONTEXT FOR THE EMERGENCE OF A WESLEYAN NOTION OF CHRIST TRANSFIGURING CULTURE

K. Steve McCormick

The *context* out of which an authentic Wesleyan notion of culture can begin to emerge arises from Wesley's vision of the Christian life that drank deep of the Eastern fathers of Byzantium. Wesley's vision of Christian reality had "recovered" from the East, a paradigm *of theosis* (divine-human participation) that was grounded in the divine purpose of the Holy Trinity. This Eastern (Cappadocian) understanding of the Trinity models a unity of Persons that establishes a freely given capacity for divine-human participation. The Triune God is a community of Persons, a Being who is communion, who has created the world and humankind to grow in the image (*imago*) and likeness (*imaginis*) of God. This same divine-human participation was revealed by the energy of incarnate love (Zizioulas). It is in this Trinitarian context and from humanity's special relationship with the Holy Trinity that Wesley asks, *"Is thy faith filled with the energy of love?"* It becomes strikingly clear, that Wesley's vision of the Christian life, in his recurrent paradigm of *faith filled with the energy of love* (Outler 97,n.4),[1] arises out of the divine purpose of the Holy Trinity as the structure, pattern, and order of the Christian life.

This paper begins with a brief overview of various theological underpinnings of Wesley's Trinitarian paradigm of theosis. Further, the salvific, cosmic, and cultural dimensions of Wesley's Trinitarian paradigm is explored as it leads to his vision of *Christ transfiguring culture* by way of *theosis*. Finally, I will briefly compare Wesley's paradigm of theosis, grounded in the image of unitive love, to Niebuhr's "types" of

Christ and culture, in order to elevate salient features of Wesley's Trinitarian paradigm. This paradigm of Christ transfiguring culture seems to offer a better *way* and *goal* of the kingdom of the world "becoming" the kingdom of God than Niebuhr's type of Christ transforming culture. Moreover, although Wesley's vision to reform the Church and the nation uses the language of "transformation," its imagery is more akin to the imagery of transfiguration, since it arises out of his Trinitarian paradigm of theosis.[2]

Niebuhr's model seems too interventionist in an Augustinian (Burns 598-619) and Calvinistic framework, at the expense of divine-human participation transfiguring culture. Further, I note that a very different perspective on the "purpose" of the incarnation is expressed in Niebuhr's five variant types; i.e., each type shares one common motif: *apotheosis*.[3] Expressed in terms of Wesley's Trinitarian paradigm of theosis, any "type" of Christ and culture that is not grounded in the divine purpose of unitive love results in either a "world affirming" in the *Christ of culture* and *Christ above culture* to the point of a monolithic identification and accommodation of Christ with culture or a "world denying" in the *Christ against culture* and *Christ and culture in paradox* to the point of an isolationism, separationism, irresolvable dualism, and even an interventionism. By contrast, I will argue for a *perichoresis*[4] of Christ and culture, thereby, a shared participation which is at the heart and meaning of transfiguration.

A Trinitarian Paradigm: Faith Filled with the Energy of Love

The clearest and most significant example of Wesley's paradigm for understanding the nature of the Christian life is found in his sermon on "Catholic Spirit," when he asks the question: "Is thine heart right, as my heart is with thy heart?" Wesley demonstrated vividly with penetrating insight, the purpose and goal of this Trinitarian pattern not only established but also images an order and structure for the Christian life that is best expressed in his pivotal paradigm of *faith filled with the energy of love*. This Trinitarian unity of persons establishes the free capacity of all human and non-human creation for participation in the life of the Holy Trinity.[5]

> *Is thy faith (enepgoumene di agapes)—filled with the energy of love?* [Italics mine] Dost thou love God? I do not say "above all things," for it is both an unscriptural and an ambiguous expression, but "'with all thy heart, and with all thy mind, and with all thy soul, and with all thy strength?'...." (Outler Bicentennial 87-88)

Wesley saw plainly that this Trinitarian pattern reflects the divine purpose of the Holy Trinity for all, because in that same image of the Trinity as a unity of persons in community, we have been created. In the incarnation (*hypostasis of ousia—Logos* becoming flesh) that humankind finds its purpose, meaning and destiny (*teleos*) modeled by the divine energy of love. This purpose of condescending love was best captured in one of Irenaeus' most profound expressions: God became what we are so that we might become what He is (Roberts and Donaldson 1:256).[6]

The incarnation liberates humankind from its own bondage created by struggling to live outside of unitive love. This liberation of condescending love recreates, restores, and renews into the image and likeness of God—the Holy Trinity—for divine-human participation. Wesley clearly understood in his *Explanatory Notes Upon the New Testament* on 2 Peter 1:4 the divine energy of love that makes humankind "partakers of the divine nature": . . . Being renewed in the image of God, and having communion with him, so as to dwell in God and God in you.

Charles Wesley's hymns on the Trinity resonate with the same paradigmatic tune of faith filled with the energy of love, invoking the persons of the Holy Trinity to transfigure human nature, renewing humanity into the image and likeness of the Father, Son, and Spirit.

> *Heavenly Adam, Life divine,* / Change my nature into Thine; / Move and spread throughout my soul, / Actuate and fill the whole; / Be it I no longer now / Living in the flesh, but Thou.
>
> *Holy Ghost, no more delay;* / Come, and in Thy temple stay; / Now Thine inward witness bear, / Strong, and permanent, and clear; / Spring of life, Thyself impart, / Rise eternal in my heart. (568 [Italics mine])

In the coming of Emmanuel, Wesley made it clear that God the Son and God the Spirit in the "economy" of salvation is at the center of his Trinitarianism. In his "Letter to a Roman Catholic" of 1749, Wesley offered an "olive branch" (Outler *John Wesley* 492) to his Roman Catholic friends. Wesley's "olive branch" was offered because of this "involvement" of the Son, the one hypostasis of the Trinity, as unitive love rooted in the Trinity that makes everyone capable of theosis. "I think you deserve the tenderest regard I can show, were it only because the same God hath raised you and me from the dust of the earth, and has made us both capable of loving. . ." (*Works* 10:80-81).

The energy of incarnate love in God the Son reveals humankind's authentic nature—both inner-human and inter-human—as persons in communion without determination. And yet, Wesley makes it explicitly clear, the personal presence of the "Three-One God," as a unity of persons and not offices (*Letters* 266).[7] Thus, by the energy of the Spirit, humanity might continue to grow forever in the likeness of God:

> I believe the infinite and eternal *Spirit of God*, equal with the *Father* and the *Son*, to be not only perfectly holy in himself, but the *immediate cause of all holiness in us; enlightening our understandings, rectifying our wills and affections, renewing our natures, uniting our persons to Christ, assuring us of the adoption of sons, leading us in our actions; purifying and sanctifying our souls and bodies, to a full and eternal enjoyment of God.* [Italics mine] (*Works* 10:82)

Moreover, Wesley's Trinitarian structure was centered on the incarnation, because of his constant insistence on the soteriological dimensions of theosis patterned and structured in the Trinity.

This divine purpose of the Trinity, enabled Wesley to describe in his sermon of 1785 on "The New Creation," the *final goal* of a faith filled with the energy of love. Wesley envisions an eternal divine-human participation as a consequence of the *way* of faith filled with the energy of the Spirit that has cosmic, cultural, and soteriological implications. In this sermon, Wesley affirms that the way of unitive love affects not only humanity but the whole of the creation: "Hence will arise an unmixed state of holiness and happiness far superior to that which Adam enjoyed in paradise . . . a continual enjoyment of the Three-One God, and of all the creatures in him!" (Bicentennial 2:500-510)

The "Three-One God" came to us in our world not only to redeem the whole creation, but also to show the whole creation its ultimate end—joyous unbroken communion with the Triune God. The whole creation was created for divine-human participation. And now, by the energy of the Spirit, as co-heirs, and co-creators in this new life in Christ, we are to participate in the transfiguration of the world and its culture, until the kingdom of this world has become the Kingdom of heaven. Stanley Harakas in his article "The Integrity of Creation and Ethics" has concluded his thesis on this very note:

> . . . humanity must come to see itself as intimately related to the non-human creation, to see itself as one with it in deep and profound community with it. In fact, humanity must come to see itself for what it really is, both king and priest of God's creation with the profound sense of our sacred calling to minister to the creation, to offer it as a sacrament to God, to serve its legitimate needs, to protect its purity and wholesomeness, to present it like a liturgical *anaphora* to its Lord. (42)

Trinitarian Dimensions: Salvific-Cosmic-Cultural

What then are those specific theological underpinnings of theosis that establish a Christian vision and context to move us "toward a Wesleyan theology of culture," one decidedly Eastern in focus but not at the expense of Western overtones?

The salient doctrines of soteriology in Wesley's *ordo-salutis* arise out of this Trinitarian pattern of divine-human perichoresis. How could God dwell in humanity if humanity could not dwell in God? A brief synopsis of his doctrines of justification and sanctification will suffice to highlight a mystery of redemption that is congruent with the mysterious purpose of the incarnation. Wesley carefully sketches out an *ordo-salutis* patterned after the same image of perichoresis mysteriously present in the "Three-One God."

> ... Salvation begins with what is usually termed (and very properly) *preventing grace;* ... the first dawn of light concerning his will. ... Salvation is carried on by convincing grace, usually in Scripture termed *repentance;* which brings a larger measure of self-knowledge, and a farther deliverance from the heart of stone. ... [w]e "are saved by faith;" consisting of those two grand branches, *justification* and *sanctification*. *By justification we are saved from the guilt of sin, and restored to the favour of God; by sanctification we are saved from the power and root of sin, and restored to the image of God.* [Italics mine] (Bicentennial 3:203)

Wesley's penchant for "third alternatives" demonstrates such an organizing principle of theosis. This was most apparent in his driving passion to settle the dilemma of Pelagian optimism and Augustinian pessimism(Outler *Theology* 23-43). Wesley first glimpsed that "third alternative" in his own Anglican tradition, a tradition of *via media*. The constant problematic of the Church of England's middle way between Protestantism and Roman Catholicism was lodged in the faith-work debate that was still vexed with the old axial question of divine grace and human freedom. Anglicanism found in the Eastern fathers of the "golden age" a paradigm of theosis that balanced the demands of both evangelical and catholic traditions. Wesley would take that forgotten strand of theosis in his own Church of England's synthesis (Allchin) and anchor it to his own Trinitarian paradigm.

The image of the Trinity as a unity of persons in communion modeling the very structure, pattern and order of divine-human participation would become the very image of the *way* and *goal* of the Christian life. Hence, Wesley would find in this Trinitarian paradigm a tremendous mystery of condescending love that images the way of salvation as *"Pardoned in order to Participate"* (Outler "Place" 31).

The Augustinian-Pelagian dilemma centered on the pivotal question of divine grace and human freedom from the two traditions that were synthesized in the *via media* of Wesley's Church of England. Wesley had pinpointed the heart of that dilemma, expressed in the faith-work debate, in his sermon on "Catholic Spirit." Wesley asked: "Is thy faith filled with the energy of love?" This was ardently answered in his tripartite essay: "The Original Nature, Property and Use of the Law;" "The Law Established by Faith, I;" and "The Law Established by Faith, II" (Bicentennial 2:1-43). This tripartite essay is not only helpful in retracing the tracks that helped Wesley forge his own "third alternative" between the evangelical and catholic notions of *faith and love*, but it also offers a clear vista into Wesley's Trinitarian paradigm of theosis that establishes a context for the emergence of a Wesleyan notion of Christ transfiguring culture.

This Trinitarian paradigm of theosis helped Wesley redefine the relation of faith and love with the concomitant doctrines of justification and sanctification. Wesley's resultant soteriology could be explained as follows: the *relative* change in justification was not without the *real* change in sanctification, because both the "guilt of sin" and the "power of sin" must be atoned for if one is to participate with the Great Physician and be healed and restored into the image of the Holy Trinity (Bicentennial 11:106).[8]

What then, are the cosmic and cultural dimensions of a Trinitarian paradigm of theosis? From the previous synopsis of Western soteriology, saddled with the axial question of Augustinian pessimism and a Pelagian optimism, we will be able to observe the same dominant motif of apotheosis in its cosmic and cultural expressions. Niebuhr's classic work, *Christ and Culture*, profoundly expresses, and perhaps unwittingly, fails to overcome this motif.

The Enduring Problem: The Mystery of Perichoresis

Niebuhr contends that if culture is the "way of life" that humankind creates for itself, then Christian culture is the way of life derived from the words, life, death and resurrection of Christ (1-44, esp. 29-39). The ontological nature of the "Three-One God" (Bicentennial 2:510)[9] for Wesley is paradoxical, antinimous, and forever mysterious, while the uncreated and unmerited Presence of the "Three-One God" is personally and intimately known in condescending love. Because of this unknowable mystery in the Holy Trinity, the "Three-One God" is not the True, the Good, and the Beautiful. And yet, the presence of the "Three-One God" as unitive love is personally known with the True, the Good, and the Beautiful. This apophatic (known) and kataphatic (unknown) nature of the Trinity must constantly remind humankind of the "mystery" of Christ transfiguring culture. Such a mystery is at the heart of what Niebuhr has diagnosed as the "enduring problem" of Christ and culture (1-44).

The "enduring problem" of Christ and culture is displayed in the mysterious perichoresis of the Divine in the human and the human in the Divine without either losing their identity. In other words, when God in Christ became what we are, He did not lose His identity, consequently, we shall not lose our identity in becoming what He is (Nellas 23-43).[10] This is the mystery of the incarnation that is basic to understanding the mystery of Christ transfiguring culture.

The mystery of perichoresis as it relates to the problem of Christ and culture struggles with both the *mystery* and the *presence* of the "Three-One God." There is a need to allow God to be God, and an equal need to personally know that the God who is, is the God who is present in all. The constant temptation, however, is to deny God's mystery by identifying Christ's presence with the True, the Good, and the Beautiful in culture. Or, to deny God's presence with the True, the Good, and the Beautiful of culture by emphasizing God's mystery. Both the mystery and the presence of the "Three-One God" must be acknowledged if there is to be a transfiguration of the world and its culture into the *imago imaginis* of unitive love, by the renewing, restoring, and recreating energy of Christ by the energy of the Spirit (*Select* 9:409).[11] This explains why a Wesleyan type of Christ transfiguring culture cannot be squeezed into the variant "types" of Christ and culture, not even into Niebuhr's fifth type of Christ transforming culture (Niebuhr 190-229).

Wesley's Trinitarian paradigm, evident in his sermon, "The Circumcision of the Heart," argues for a different slant on the incarnation showing exactly why his paradigm would not fit into any of Niebuhr's types. That sermon proposes a uniquely insightful eudaemonism that pairs happiness and holiness (Outler, *Theology* 81-84). Only in joyous communion with God does one find true happiness and holiness or vice-versa. Thus, rather than fixating a fallen world and its culture, Wesley gazes on the solution (*goal*) of unitive love that has already given the power or energy of the *way* as shared participation.

> One happiness shall ye propose to your souls, even an union with him that made them, the having 'fellowship with the Father and the Son,' the being 'joined to the Lord in one Spirit. . . .' [w]hatever ye think, speak, or do, be it in order to your *happiness in God, the sole end as well as source of your being.*

Have no end, no ultimate end, but God. Thus our Lord: "One thing needful." [Italics mine] (Bicentennial 1:408)[12]

The *purpose* of the incarnation, according to this Trinitarian paradigm, is for Christ to become what we are so that we might become what He is. Not only does the energy of condescending love renew and restore the image and likeness of humankind for shared participation, but also that very act of love in the words, deeds, and destiny of Christ shows the *way* of unitive love.

The *way* and *goal* of this participation has been concretely, tangibly, and visibly modeled in condescending love. It is precisely at this point of understanding the words, life, and destiny of Christ for the way of life—the way of Christian culture—that the divergent perspectives of East and West concerning the purpose of incarnation begin to emerge. This, of course, is where the divergent perspectives of Christian culture expressed in the Western world have resulted in a "cultural relativism," because ultimately this world and its "way of life" is not a place where full divine-human participation can take place.

In Niebuhr's *Christ of Culture* one side of the spectrum is a monolithic identification or accommodation of Christ *with* culture (45-82). This type works within an endocosmic and endocultural context; the way of culture is the way of Christ. The other side of the spectrum expressed in the type of *Christ against culture separates* Christ from culture and awaits the eschaton for transformation (83-115).[13] This was classically expressed in Tertullian's question: "What does Jerusalem have to do with Athens?" This type works within an acosmic, acultural, and ahistorical context.

Two other variant "types" that seek to modify or soften the extreme types of a "culture affirming" or "culture denying" type can be found in the *Christ above culture* and the *Christ and culture in paradox* type. The attitude of *Christ above culture* seeks to adjust the extremes of the Christ of culture with what could be seen in Aquinas' concept of super-added grace (Niebuhr 116-148). Nature and grace are mutually inclusive and not exclusive so that by this super-added infusion of grace one is able to identify the way of Christ with the finest way of culture. This is most clear in the outworking of Aquinas' soteriological formulation of "faith formed by love" (*Nature and Grace*). Gabriel Biel's synthesis of this Catholic formula was best expressed in his axial phrase, "to do one's very best" (qtd. in Oberman *Forerunners* 123-141). Biel was grossly perverted in the later Scholastic period in a Pelagian optimism that is expressive of a "culture affirming" type. Both types of *Christ above culture* and *Christ of culture* eventuate in the same conclusion of apotheosis.

In other words, there can be no fully shared participation because the Divine cannot be the Divine if it is nothing more than the best culture has to offer. The Holy Trinity is not the True, the Good, the Beautiful. Where is the sense of mystery in the *way* of Christian culture if it is simply the finest of culture? Moreover, how can the culture be filled with Christ if it is filled with itself?

The other side of the spectrum—Christ against culture—rejects those two "culture and self affirming" types and somewhat modifies in the type of *Christ and culture in paradox* (Niebuhr 149-189). A separationism or isolationism of Christ against culture would eventuate in total chaos. Luther, therefore, suggested an irresolvable dualism between the "two kingdoms" as an alternative. The kingdom of the world and the Kingdom of God must exist side by side, paradoxically, with the Christian participating in the worldly kingdom, albeit never intending to transform the kingdom of the world. This was most evident in Luther's soteriological formulation of "faith formed by Christ." Luther's pessimistic view of human nature and optimistic view of grace created an irresolvable paradox in his doctrine of the "two kingdoms" that is consistent with his forensic view of salvation. Once again, both variants of the Christ against culture and the Christ and culture in paradox eventuate in an apotheosis since they admit an irresolvable dualism or separation of Christ and culture.

Niebuhr's fifth type of *Christ transforming culture* is a mediating position of the two extremes of Christ against culture and Christ of culture (190-229). This motif of transformation rests on a teleological and eschatological frame that aims toward an operative and co-operative understanding of transforming grace from a cosmological and incarnational perspective. In an Augustinian and Calvinistic context that waits for the eschaton, the intervention of Christ transforms the world and its culture, its "*way of life*." Moreover, the accent on the Holy Spirit in this transformative motif is minimal at best. Where is the emphasis on the energy of the Spirit that is "already" transfiguring this material world and its culture? Where is the focus on the eschaton transfiguring in the here and now of this material world and its culture (way of life) by the energy of the Spirit? If the world and its culture have been shown the way of unitive love by the words, deeds, and destiny of Christ then where is the shared participation by the energy of the Spirit that realizes the Kingdom of God in the kingdom of the world?

Whether Augustine's view of God has been rightly or wrongly interpreted (McKenna and *Nicene* 17-228), it has still resulted in a determinism (Gunton 33-58) that either blatantly denies shared participation or subtly subverts divine-human participation because it rests acquiescently on the eschatological intervention of transformation. In the final analysis, this seems to lack the ontology of perichoresis (Zizioulas), of Christ filling the culture so that the culture can be transfigured into Christ. Once again, the transformation motif understood outside of the Trinitarian paradigm of unitive love admits no perichoresis of Christ and culture because this world with its culture is not a place where divine-human participation can exist (Meyendorff 129-137). And finally, it must be said that the eventual impasse of all five types essentially bypass the intended purpose (Eastern) of the incarnation: God became what we are so that we might become what He is. Christ has filled the culture so that the world and its culture can be transfigured into joyous communion of unitive love by shared participation.

The *way* and *goal* of divine-human participation grounded in the Trinitarian energy of unitive love, suggests an alternative "type" of *Christ transfiguring culture*, instead of Niebuhr's type of Christ transforming culture. A transformative motif that is finally anchored in an interventionist model, albeit with operative and co-operative grace, does not admit to a fully shared participation. Thus, the structure, order, and pattern of condescending love images the *way* as self-emptying rather than self-affirming. This models a different *way* and *goal* of transformation than Niebuhr's types. Christ can only transfigure culture by filling culture with the energy of love by the energy of the Spirit. The "way of culture" is transfigured only when it is filled with the "way of unitive love."

The mysterious process of transfiguration, as being emptied in order to be filled with the energy of condescending love by the energy of the Spirit, places the accent on the gift of unitive love which is the *gift of* the "Three-One God" who is forever present by the energy of the Spirit. The filling is not so much a *gift from* God as it is a *gift of* God (Langford 24-48). This is clearly not the meaning of transfiguration grounded in the "Three-One God." Stated more simply, one is only filled with the gift of unitive love as one is emptied of oneself, and only when one is emptied does one discover the *way* of unitive love.

The way of unitive love mysteriously transfigures culture because it is emptied of a self-affirming participation in culture that crudely breaks the unity of love by identifying or accommodating the Christ of culture. Likewise, the way of unitive love mysteriously transfigures culture because it has been emptied not only of its self-affirming culture but has been filled with the mystic presence of unitive love. Christ is not against culture because Christ has filled culture in order to transfigure culture.

Conclusion: The Mystic Presence of Christ Transfiguring Culture

Christ transfiguring culture is a tremendous mystery of the divine filling the human so that the human can fill the divine. Paul boldly sketches this out in Eph. 1:9-10, 22, 2:18-22:

> For he has made known to us in all wisdom and insight the mystery of his will, according to his purpose which he set forth in Christ, as a plan for the fullness of time, things in heaven and things on earth.... So then you are no longer strangers and sojourners, but you are fellow citizens with the saints and members of the household of God, built upon the foundation of the apostles and the prophets, Christ Jesus himself being the cornerstone, in whom the whole structure is joined together and grows into a holy temple in the Lord; in whom you are also built into it for a dwelling place of God in the Spirit. (RSV)

If *Christ transfiguring culture* is analyzed on a rational plane that has been dominant in Western thinking since the ascendency of Aristotle, then the complex set of paradoxes that have been played out in Niebuhr's types seem to end up in *apotheosis*. The mystery of unitive love, however, was demonstrated in the recapitulation of condescending love, the summing up of *all* in Christ.[14] Condescending love has shown us that *all creation*, both human and non-human comes from God in the *Logos* Who empties Himself and becomes human not only to reveal God to *all* but also to reveal the true image of unitive love in *all* by gathering *all* to Himself, and thus, restoring *all* into the image of the Father in the Holy Trinity. The mystery of divine-human participation happens only in the same modeled way of self-emptying that comes as a gift of God who is forever present filling *all* with the energy of the Spirit. To be renewed into the image of unitive love is to be filled with the energy of God that raised Christ from the dead and continues to transfigure *all* into the image of unitive love by the energy of the Spirit. The kingdom of this world is being transfigured into the Kingdom of heaven by the energy of the Spirit. This is why Charles Wesley could sing:

> Stand amazed, ye heavens, at this:/ See the Lord of earth and skies; / Humbled to the dust He is,/ And in a manger lies. . . . / *Of our flesh and of our bone,/ Jesus is our Brother now,/ And God is all our own.* [Italics mine] (134)

At the risk of misunderstanding, allow me a final prophetic note from our former musings on the mystic presence of the Three-One God. If "the fear of the Lord" really is the beginning of wisdom, then where is our sense of dread, the absurd, our sense of sin and even novelty in the *way* of our shared participation with Christ transfiguring culture? Have we so docetized the *way* of the Christian life by narrowly identifying our own Church-culture (Traditionalism) with the *way* that we no longer participate in the mystic presence of unitive love, but wallow in our own narcissistic piety? Have we become so insulated in our coward complacency because we have substituted our own Church-culture for a "dead faith of the living" (traditionalism) (Pelikan)? The docetizing of the way is nothing short of idolatry because the way is no longer the way of condescending love filled with the energy of the Spirit but is rather the dead faith of the living that filled with the energy of self-affirming love. Has our traditionalism become a substitute for the way of the mystic presence of unitive love?

Be reminded once again of Christ who is the one Head of all things in heaven and on earth. Since all creation, both human and nonhuman has been "summed up in Christ," the only end (*goal*) of creation is joyous unbroken communion with God. The *goal* of all creation as it is summed up in Christ, was transfigured in all of its glory by the mystic Presence of the "Three-One God." Christ, therefore, has shown us not only who we are in that transfiguration, but has shown us the *way* of "becoming who we are."

In that transfiguration, Christ has shown creation His vision for all, by showing creation who it is, in all of His glory, and thus, reveals the way of all creation becoming who it is, by the energy of the Spirit. As creation sees its end of "happiness and holiness" it becomes that end—happy and holy—by the transfiguring power and energy of divine-human participation. The future of the Kingdom of God is being transfigured "already" in the material kingdom of the world, by the energy of the Spirit in divine-human participation. "*Is thy faith filled with the energy of love?*"

NOTES

1. Outler notes how Wesley had reversed the order of energy and love in the Greek to accent love.

2. See *Wesley's Explanatory Notes on the New Testament* 2 Cor. 3:18.

3. I have chosen Niebuhr's work over Paul Tillich's *Theology of Culture*, (London: Oxford UP, 1978) because his type of Christ transforming culture rests on a much more solid understanding of incarnation and salvation, creation and eschatology than does Tillich's. Tillich's ontology still

reflects much of Schelling's idealism and results in a "self-affirming" motif that is not as helpful as Niebuhr in lifting out Wesley's type of Christ transfiguring culture in a Trinitarian paradigm of theosis. Moreover, it will be argued that although Niebuhr's type of transformation contains many profound and insightful directions for understanding the problem of Christ and culture, it is finally a synthesis of the other variant types, which are essentially types of apotheosis; i.e., types that do no purport a full divine-human participation. For a good overview of Niebuhr's work consult, Geoffrey Wainwright's *Doxology: The Praise of God in Worship, Doctrine and Life.* (New York: Oxford UP, 1980); also Charles Scriven. *Christian Social Ethics After H. Richard Niebuhr: The Transformation of Culture.* (Scottdale, PA: Herald P, 1988).

4. I am using "perichoresis" in the sense of mutual-interpenetration and unbroken communion as is imaged in the Persons of unitive love—the Holy Trinity. The image of the Holy Trinity is an icon of perichoresis for understanding Christ and culture.

5. Although this particular focus on the Trinity in Wesley is my own, I am grateful to Fr. Stanley Harakas for his insight in past conversation, as well as from a private copy of his paper presented to the American Academy of Religion at the Eastern Orthodox Studies Consultation November 1991, "The Doctrine of the Trinity in Eastern Orthodox Ethics."

6. Irenaeus speaks quite vividly of the incarnation accomplishing the will of the Father in making humankind into the image and likeness of God (Roberts and Donaldson 1:567).

7. Wesley's letter to Miss Jane Catherine March on August 3, 1771 clearly shows his opposition to speaking of the Holy Spirit as an office in a depersonalized way. The mystery does not lie in the fact 'These Three are One,' but in the manner accounting how they are one. But with this I have nothing to do. I believe the fact. *As to the manner (wherein the whole mystery lies) I believe nothing about it. The quaint device of styling them three offices rather than persons gives up the whole doctrine.*" 5:270. (*Italics* mine).

8. In Wesley's "Farther Appeal," salvation is considered from an Eastern perspective with the therapeutic metaphors controlling the forensic ones: "By salvation, I mean, not barely (according to the vulgar notion) deliverance from sin, a restoration of the soul to its primitive health, its original purity; a recovery of the divine nature; the renewal of our souls after the image of God in righteousness and true holiness, in justice, mercy, and truth." See Albert C. Outler in "The Place of Wesley in the Christian Tradition," 25, 29-32; and "John Wesley's Interest in the Early Fathers of the Church," 10.

9. See also Wesley's sermon "On the Trinity", Bicentennial 2:385 and his *Explanatory Notes Upon the New Testament* with the insistence that the Trinity is interwoven with the text of Luke 4:18.

10. See. John Meyendorff. *Christ in Eastern Christian Thought.* (Crestwood, New York: St. Vladimir's Seminary P, 1987); Georgios I. Mantzaridis. *The Deification of Man.* (Crestwood, New York: St. Vladimiar's Seminary P, 1984); Vladimir Lossky. *The Mystical Theology of the Eastern Church.* (Crestwood, New York: St. Vladimir's Seminary P, 1976)

11. Listen to the eloquence of the "golden tongue" of John Chrysostom as he speaks of the energy of the Spirit as the energy of condescending love: " . . . For just as the earthen vessel is formed from clay and fire, so also the body of these saints being clay, and *receiving the energy of the spiritual fire,* becomes an earthen vessel. . . . For when thou seest the Apostles raising the dead, yet themselves sick, and unable to remove their own infirmities, thou mayest clearly perceive that the resurrection of the dead man was not effected by the power of him who raised him, but by the *energy of the Spirit.*" (Italics mine)

12. Wesley repeatedly argues that our createdness is for participation and thus that is our only end and happiness. cf. also Bicentennial Ed. 11:62. In an "Earnest Appeal to Men of Reason and Religion" Wesley writes: ". . . thou was made in the image of God, . . . For what end then did he create thee but to dwell with him above this perishable world, to know him, to love him, to do his will, to enjoy him for ever and ever!" *Explanatory Notes on the New Testament,* John 1:4, Ephesians 5:14, Luke 1:33. For Wesley, one's happiness and holiness or vice-versa is not a happiness for the sake of oneself. Happiness is not self-affirmation in the Greek sense of wholeness. Happiness or holiness in Wesley's mind, seems to carry more of the idea of healing (the therapeutic metaphors dominate the forensic ones in Wesley) in the sense of having been disinfected from oneself.

13. See Tertullian, "The Prescription Against Heretics," *The Ante-Nicene Fathers.* vol. 3, (Grand Rapids, MI: Wm. B. Eerdmans, 1978), 243-269.

14. Although I am using the recapitulation of all things summed up in Christ from Irenaeus' *purpose* of the incarnation, I have been greatly helped by Craig Keen's *excellent* article "(The) Church and (The) Culture: A Little Reflection on the Assumptio Carnis" *Wesleyan Theological Journal,* 24, (1989):91-102.

CHAPTER FIFTEEN

GIFTS FROM A VISIONARY: CONTINUING THE WESLEYAN TRADITION OF THE DEVELOPMENT OF ALL PERSONS

Jan Simonson Lanham

It is a gift of unparalled treasure to be able to look into the life and mind of another and find qualities, insights, dreams and potential that need to be coaxed or nurtured into blossom. This activity requires not only a keen insight into people but also a graciousness that does not fear encouraging others to a new level of empowerment and service. This was a grace and a gift that Cecil Paul possessed, and I was only one of many beneficiaries. Because he had such a strongly rooted sense of who he was in Christ and in the kingdom, he could reach out to so many, even to people like myself who feel so ordinary.

His unwavering faith in people pulled efforts out of them that were sometimes pleasantly surprising. He always held out more hope for others than they seemed to grasp for themselves. Yet in this process something wonderfully transforming and energizing would take place. Cecil stood firmly in the Wesleyan tradition that emphasizes the development of the gifts of all believers and the encouragement to utilize those gifts in service to God. Like John Wesley, Cecil Paul labored to mentor, encourage, inspire and instruct.

Cecil Paul was a visionary who had an ability through intelligence, creativity, and perseverance to breathe life and structure into his vision. I have never met anyone who had so deep an understanding of the importance of a vision that propels us beyond self-absorption and stagnation and provides the energy for creative community and identity anchored in our pursuit of the mind of Christ coupled with an outward vision toward the world.

Cecil would point to the work of Viktor Frankl, who out of the horror and despair of a concentration camp, came to understand the importance of the will-to-meaning in our lives. "What man actually needs is not a tensionless state but rather the striving and struggling for some goal worthy of him" (166). Frankl went on to state:

> By declaring that man is a responsible creature and must actualize the potential meaning of his life, I wish to stress that the true meaning of life is to be found in the world rather than within man or his own psyche, as though it were a closed system. . . . Human existence is essentially self-transcendence rather than self-actualization. (175)

From his earliest days on the Canadian prairie as he would recount, he was compelled by a sense of vision that kept him focused on pursuing education. His vision took on a new dimension in his adolescence as he was exposed to the challenge of a faith commitment, and he expanded his vision to incorporate God's direction and purposes in his life. Even during times when outside support was limited, he had a driving force within that kept him steady and committed to values and goals that were reflective of his love for God and God's love for him.

One of the serendipities that came my way because of Cecil Paul was the opportunity to co-author the book, *Choices: In Pursuit of Wholeness*. Day after day we would meet to talk and write about choices facing college students concerning identity, intimacy, values, meaning and vision. In those discussions, I had the enormous privilege of listening to one who was not afraid to engage his mind and struggle with issues. I also experienced the grace of being listened to, affirmed, encouraged and challenged.

In the last chapter of *Choices*, we discussed the importance of finding a vision in our lives which seems even more relevant today than we first thought. In Amos 8:11, is an interesting depiction of the prospects of famine. "'The days are coming,' declares the Sovereign Lord, 'when I will send a famine through the land—not a famine of food, nor a thirst for water, but a famine of hearing the words of the Lord'" (NIV). This kind of famine results when we try to exist without an overarching vision informed by the word of God. Why is vision so important to us individually and corporately, spiritually and emotionally? What areas of concern does our vision call us into? Without a vision, what do we face?

"Without a vision we may survive, but we cannot love life" (Paul and Lanham 74). Our sense of vision can enable us to discern the really important from the seemingly important. We need a sense of vision to lift us beyond the increasingly hectic routines of our everyday schedules and help us gain the broader perspective. Our exhaustion even from "good things" can rob us of our ability to really experience joy in our present moments.

"Without a vision we become self-absorbed and stagnant, like dead water having no inlet or outlet. We become narcissistic, with all its elements of anxiety and guilt" (Paul and Lanham 75). Tragically, we seem to be reaping a whirlwind from those whose narcissistic needs demand immediate gratification. It takes a larger vision to see ourselves as part of a greater community to which we both give and receive and thus create life-sustaining inlets and outlets. It takes a vision to understand how our lives are enriched by those around us, particularly those who represent different backgrounds, cultures, and perspectives. One of Cecil Paul's oft-spoken aspects to his vision was his appreciation and understanding of the enrichment that is possible in our diversity.

In *Choices*, we also suggested that "without a vision we lose our sense of identity and make choices that destroy our intimacies. The significant rise in marital and family problems within church-related homes raises some profound questions. Why has such devastation visited our land? Without a vision for service, we focus on ourselves and settle for limited answers to the questions of identity, intimacy, and values" (75).

This area seems to be even more critical today. Our world and our churches are experiencing an alarming incidence of family problems, particularly in the area of family violence and abuse. In the tradition of Wesley whose interests included social concerns and later evangelicals who were at the forefront of the social concerns of their day such as abolition, temperance and suffrage (Dayton; Hassey), our vision of the kingdom of God and right relationships within it should compel us all to be concerned about these areas of sexual abuse and domestic violence.

One area that has been both a source of great joy and great pain has been my counseling work with victims of sexual abuse and domestic violence. Cecil's encouragement not to shrink from hard things was instrumental in my continuing work with victims both inside and outside of the community of faith. My work in this area, particularly with those who have been abused within the community of faith, has underscored the need to remind all of us of the possibilities of right relationships within the kingdom and within families.

Cecil Paul would often describe his understanding of leadership as an inverted triangle where servanthood, mutual submission and right relationships were the order rather than the distortions of power which lead to domination and oppression. This has become a source of enormous concern for me as I sit with those who have been abused. In the fertile soil of power and powerlessness, sexual, racial and economic violence can blossom. The church has the privilege and the responsibility to challenge societal notions of power distribution which allow some to experience power and others to know only the deprivation of opportunity.

Genesis 1:27 notes that both male and female were created in God's image. Acts of sexual violence and abuse are abhorrent in view of the sacredness of human beings as God's creation. Jesus consistently challenged the societal notions of power and spoke to lift relationships to a new level of respect and mutuality. His admonitions to James and John who wanted positions of power next to Christ reminded them that power was not the focus of his kingdom. Jesus welcomed children, healed those shunned by others, spoke to women who were outcasts, and finally allowed himself to be ignominiously crucified on a cross.

This is not the pattern of dominance or holding tightly to power or position. Marriages within the body of Christ have been likened to the relationship between the church and Christ himself. This relationship is a covenantal one that is characterized by sacrificial love, servanthood, mutual respect, and mutual submission. There is a disturbing trend in some areas of the church that seeks to limit power and authority to one gender. In so doing, we miss the extraordinary opportunity that we have to proclaim relationships that affirm equal partnership.

While it is not a terribly popular thing to say in some circles, I have seen too many situations where rigid patriarchal hierarchy in Christian homes has set a fertile stage for sexual abuse or domestic violence. The clinical work of James and Phyllis Alsdurf described in *Battered Into Submission* echoes my own observations. They suggested:

> The connection which many battered women make between their ability to suffer violence from their husbands and their Christian commitment reflects, we believe, what is widely taught within evangelical churches about the submission of women in marriage. It is a perspective which makes women more susceptible to violence and heightens the likelihood that battered women will remain in abusive relationships. (82)

In a disturbing study by Neal and Mangis "Unwanted Sexual Experiences Among Christian College Women: Saying No on the Inside," the authors reported on the correlation between the women who had given in to unwanted sexual pressures and the traditional sex stereotypes of their homes. It was suggested that submission theology which depicts men as superior and women as inferior may breed passivity and dependence in women and take away their voice when it comes to asserting themselves in sexual situations.

Carol Holderread Heggen in making suggestions to the church on the prevention of sexual abuse in Christian churches and homes has commented:

Gifts from a Visionary

> The church must creatively challenge the assumption that patriarchy represents the best and only way to live in relationship. It must fight the belief that God intended for men to dominate women and children. Congregations should be places where people experience shared power, where they learn new models of partnership. The church should provide settings in which women, men, children together discuss ideas and make plans. The church should be a place where respect and position are not determined by worldly measures of gender and power but by kingdom standards of love, spirituality, and giftedness. (176)

Victims of abuse have also challenged me in the area of addressing some of the distorted images of God that can emerge. Since our earliest images of God tend to be formed in the crucible of our relationships with our earthly parents, it is understandable why victims of abuse often envision God as distant or uncaring, aloof or judgmental. It is a wonderful privilege to be able to share with victims the good news of God's unconditional love for them despite their own feelings of self-hatred or blame or low self-esteem. Unconditional love that pours out of the very heart of God towards God's creation is a wonderfully transforming experience when it is truly experienced and affirmed. As a community of faith, all of us have the privilege of being grace-givers and bearers of hope to those in our midst whose hope has dimmed.

When our vision incorporates the values that Jesus taught we have solid moorings to keep us steady. In Matthew 23, in an interesting encounter with the Pharisees and teachers of the law, Jesus outlined the values of the new order of his kingdom. They are no less important today. In contrast to the prevailing ways of the Pharisees and teachers, Jesus challenged them and us to lives of consistency, reciprocity, humility, equality, servanthood, justice, mercy, faithfulness, accountability and integrity. When our lives are bereft of these anchors, it is too easy to make poor choices that destroy our relationships, our witness, our work, and ultimately our hope.

Our sense of vision can also compel us toward Christian community and fellowship and then beyond to service to our world. When Jesus commanded us to love our neighbors as ourselves, he wisely incorporated the two most basic aspects of our life in community. We must have a vision of ourselves as loved by God so that we can reach out in love towards ourselves as well as our neighbors. While "self-esteem" is considered to be a suspect word by some because they have attached it to an inappropriate, overweening sense of self-pride, Jesus calls us to an appropriate love of ourselves as God's child. It is only from that basis that we can consistently and appropriately love each other.

Jurgen Moltmann suggested:

> A closed human being no longer has any hope. Such a person is full of anxiety. A closed society no longer has any future. It kills the hope for life of those who stand on its periphery, and then finally destroys itself. Hope is lived and it comes alive, when we go outside of ourselves and, in joy and pain, take part in the lives of others. It becomes concrete in open community with others. God has accepted us. He has hopes for us. In spite of all the intimidations of our lives, he keeps us alive and gives us courage to be. Therefore, let us impartially accept one another and hope for one another so that we mutually keep each other alive and invested with the courage to live. (35)

In working on *Choices*, one of the scriptural passages that I particularly enjoyed was the life-affirming story of the encounter of the Samaritan woman with Jesus. The story of the woman at the well remains for me a pivotal story which not only speaks to Jesus' ability to break through barriers but also to the Lord's desire to communicate his good news and life-transforming grace and mission even to a woman of questionable past who by all societal and legal standards was an outcast to everyone. The disciples certainly reflected the standards of the day when they registered shock and dismay as they returned from the village to find Jesus talking to this woman. Yet, Jesus revealed to her the truth of the living water and of his messiahship and turned not only her life but also the whole village's life upside down. Breaking through these barriers allowed this Samaritan woman to discover not only a new identity in Christ but also a new hope as well. Now, having received the gift of grace and the good news, she responded by becoming a bearer of grace to others.

Jesus' compassionate and affirming treatment of a woman in this instance and in encounter after encounter heralded the breaking-through of many cultural, social, economic and religious barriers. This movement perhaps can be said to culminate in Paul's declaration in Galatians 3:28, "There is neither Jew nor Greek, slave nor free, male nor female, for you are all one in Christ Jesus" (NIV).

The encounter of Jesus with the Samaritan woman has been important for me on many levels. It depicts the pattern of liberation and freedom that Christ offers to those who would accept his transforming grace. It heralds that a Christian's sense of identity can be firmly rooted in our daughtership and sonship with God despite our paths. It also lays out for the community of faith the glorious acknowledgement that salvation is not only individual but also it reaches to the corporate community.

For me this story is not only a depiction of Jesus' relationship with others, but it is also a pattern that Cecil Paul intentionally and conscientiously sought to live out for others. In the many, many hours that he devoted to counseling others and in his professional academic career, he challenged himself and others to ground their sense of identity in Christ and to reach out to others breaking barriers of all kinds in order to let the compassion and grace of Christ be visible in our imperfect human actions.

Cecil Paul's encouragement of women as equally-gifted, equally-sent and equally-filled with the Spirit has had lifelong ramifications. I will always be grateful for his willingness to put women in positions of leadership that have not often been tried. The encouragement of women in areas of leadership, public ministry and service are important to creating an environment that is less conducive to the abuse of power by equalizing the distribution of power to some extent and by demonstrating a leadership model in which both men and women are servant leaders.

His confidence in both his men and women colleagues brought out their best efforts. His encouragement of me throughout my graduate program in pastoral psychology and in the development of my counseling work helped me to have a vision for a small role that perhaps I could play within God's kingdom on earth. I have discovered that it takes women and men of strength to be able to reach out to affirm the other gender so that we all can be self-respecting, strong and loving. In this action, Cecil demonstrated one of the practical ways that we can continue the Wesleyan tradition that emphasized the development of all people, male and female.

It has been an interesting experience for me to read some of the letters that Wesley wrote to a number of women preachers. Women figured prominently in the leadership of the class societies that Wesley organized wherever he went. In the last decade of his life, Wesley broke new ground by officially recognizing a number of women preachers and encouraged them through letters, books and mentoring. In response to a question concerning why Wesley encouraged women to preach, Chilcote ascribes this answer to him, "Because God owns them in the conversion of sinners, and who am I that I should withstand God" (182). One example of this was in a letter written on August 2, 1788 to Sarah Mallet in which he states:

> It is a pleasure to me if I can show in anything the regard which I have for you, as I am firmly persuaded that you have a conscience void of offense toward God and toward man. I do not doubt but you have given God your

heart, and do in all things wish to do His holy and acceptable will. But if so, it is no wonder that you should meet with crosses, both from the devil and his children, especially as you believe you are called of God to bear a public testimony against him. . . . But I trust you will never be weary of well doing. In due time you shall reap if you faint not. Whoever praises or dispraises, it is your part to go steadily on, speaking the truth in love. . . . Go on, therefore, and fear nothing but sin. (Telford 77-78)

Cecil Paul, too, was a bearer of hope. He did not shrink from the tough problems of life but desired to bring a vision of God's healing and reconciliation into the midst of those situations. Philippians 2:14-16 reminds us that as children of God we can shine like stars in the universe as we hold out the words of life to our hurting generation. Cecil Paul was indeed a shining star. In the last chapter of *Choices*, we suggested that:

> Everyone's life becomes the instrument of someone or something. Whose instrument are we and what songs are we playing with our lives? Are we shining like stars? We cannot cloister ourselves if we want a world to see the reflected light of Christ. We must take the challenge to combine our vision for service with our power to serve. Only then will our pursuit of wholeness make us instruments of God. (84)

CHAPTER SIXTEEN

RETRACING THE VISION: THE IMAGINATIVE MIND IN A NAZARENE COLLEGE

Margaret "Peg" Bowen

Who can find an imaginative mind? Its price may not command a bonus in six digits. It may not make good in the marketplace. Even so, unethical practices are far from it. It fashions an idea, helps others see it; they achieve it together. It is not afraid to go outside the envelope, to lift the lid, to color outside the lines—to bring others in. Its success stretches, enlarges, and exhilarates all who are touched by it. Continually it seeks creative solutions to the most difficult of problems. Night and day the possibilities of positive change drive it on. For example, it looks at a rundown building, buys it, and in its hands it is renewed for service. Overtime is no stranger to the imaginative mind. Well into the night it is never idle. Its students respond in awe and respect. Its achievements are the talk of town and gown. Many with excellent minds have excelled, but an imaginative mind surpasses them all.

Just what is an imaginative mind? Its presence attracts. Its absence bores. While it is unclear how the process works; there is no grid or formula to produce an imaginative mind. When it is present, *everyone knows*, and when it is absent, *everyone knows*. In its presence is wonder and play—not play for the sake of exercise in pursuit of health, fitness, or vanity, or for the purpose of escape, but play that informs and energizes the dream of the gifted and giftless who, as Madeleine L'Engle says, "must retrace the vision which includes angels and dragons and unicorns, and all the lovely creatures which our world would put in a box marked *Children Only*" (21). Christians seem both fascinated and fearful of angels, dragons, and unicorns. All but children and romantics unceremoniously dump unicorns on the scrap heap of mythology. Dragons belong to the exotic East or pre-Christian Europe. While

Christians read the Bible as though it ended with Jude, John reveals phantasmagorical creatures in his Revelation vision that frighten as well as intrigue:

> In the center, around the throne, were four living creatures, and they were covered with eyes, in front and in back. The first living creature was like a lion, the second was like an ox, the third had a face like a man, the fourth was like a flying eagle. Each of the four living creatures had six wings and was covered with eyes all around, even under his wings. . . . The locusts looked like horses prepared for battle. On their heads they wore something like crowns of gold, and their faces resembled human faces. Their hair was like women's hair, and their teeth were like lions' teeth. They had breastplates like breastplates of iron, and the sound of their wings was like the thundering of many horses and chariots rushing into battle. They had tails and stings like scorpions. (4:6b-8a; 9: 7-10a)

Whether understood or misunderstood, interpreted or charted, the images evoke chilling and fascinating possibilities for the lay and clerical reader alike who in every generation must retrace John's vision. Even though the experience of reading Revelation for many readers is like reading, C.S. Lewis or a gripping mystery novel that will not let go, most readers do not wish to meet John's creatures in the dark.

The struggle between the panorama of good and evil plays itself out in the power of the image to inform the reader of events infinitely larger in scope than the words. Every reader must find a place in John's vision. In the end the reader becomes a little child, chin poised on the apron of the stage, looking at the metaphysical battle of good and evil dramatized in word pictures that adult logic and comprehension cannot fathom; faith accepts the vision, believes, and rests in the knowledge that good triumphs.

But Revelation seems more like virtual reality than anything relating to the solid, conservative lifestyle of *most* at Nazarene colleges and universities, and as the twenty-first century approaches, unicorns seem to serve no legitimate purpose but fantasy and subjects of New Age baubles. Angels, on the other hand, present a more attractive alternative—pretty, predictable, childlike, and good—as familiar as a Christmas card or a toddlers' pageant. In them is the promise of personal safety and protection from evil, a significant appeal to Christians in today's society where evil and the threat of evil intrude daily in TV images and the shocking words of the printed page. In the swirl of this uncertainty, what person has not gratefully experienced the touch of an angel in a mother, a mentor, or a friend who came at the moment of deep need—uncalled and unbidden by any human intervention?

These images capture and hold our attention like glossy pictures in a child's first storybook. Likewise the power of God's image in mankind revealed from Genesis to Revelation captures and holds. Humanity is drawn to fellowship with God through the many representations of God in mankind in both the Old and New Testaments that culminate in the birth of Christ. The power of the Gospel is expressed in the good news that "the Word became flesh and made his dwelling among us" (John 1:14). God in the flesh. The Good News of the Babe of Bethlehem—God with us—lived out in the lives of faculty, staff and students. Each person, God's picture. Each person, a snapshot of what God is like. It is in these images that the imaginative mind is best expressed.

For the educator, whatever the topic of instruction, images leave impressions that remain longer than the contents of the words alone. Biblical warnings about false images—trying to put the God of gods, the Most Holy One, into wood and stone—remind us of this principle's power. On the other hand, religious symbols, art, and biblical heroes powerfully point the believer to God and usher the believer into His presence.

In the fall of 1995 my husband, John, had the opportunity to preach at Korea Nazarene Theological College in an English language chapel. He struggled with how to present the Good News to students who are novices at listening to native American speakers. He decided to tell the story of Mary and Martha and their brother, Lazarus, who had died despite their pleas for Jesus to come. Using Mary's complaint, "'Lord, . . . if you had been here'" (John 11:21a), he challenged students to be healed of the "If Disease." If I were wealthy . . . , If I were smart . . . , If I had been accepted at a more prestigious school. . . . As he concluded his main points, a drum rolled. He fairly bellowed the words, "*Lazarus come out,*" and a fully-bandaged figure staggered from behind a whitened garden tomb. As two coeds unwrapped the grave cloths from Lazarus' face and head, whether or not students understood many words that were spoken that morning, they got the picture.

Realizing the impact that an image makes, it is not unrealistic to expect that the product of an imaginative mind is an image—a visual picture: a painting, a sculpture, a musical score, an invention, a discovery, a poem, a story, film—a tangible embodiment of the imaginative process. If this is true, there must be some Michelangelos or John the Divines sitting in Nazarene college and university classrooms. Where are the imaginative minds of the more than seventy-five years of Nazarene higher education? From a child's earliest days in Sunday school is learned: "In the beginning God created the heavens and the earth" (Gen. 1:1). Children have the eyes to see the earth and the heavens—the sun, the moon, the stars. They stop to look at bugs and pick a flower. All around them they see the product of God's creativity. Most everyone marvels at the interpretation of a dandelion, an animal, or a village drawn by the uneven hand of a child. Somewhere between childhood and adolescence the looking and creating stop, replaced by bombardments from TV, the silver screen, and pulp prose. Part of the task of Nazarene higher educators, through science courses, arts and music, theology and Christian doctrine, literature and other diverse disciplines, is to retrace the vision of God for the learners—for them to see that their lives are the image.

Where can this be realized in Nazarene higher education? Through the administration? In the facilities, the classrooms, the laboratories? In the faculty, staff, and students? In the programs of study, course offerings? And just what is the purpose of an imaginative mind in the context of Nazarene higher education? Would Nazarene educators, students, and constituency recognize its presence—applaud it—or fear it? At Nazarene schools it is still pretty much meat and potatoes—solid, foundational undergraduate education, despite the lure of the 1980s for courses to proliferate in response to the explosion of information, technology, and ephemeral cultural trends. Despite the establishment of non-traditional programs and institutes, Nazarene schools have reconfirmed their commitment to traditional liberal arts as the best way to develop the minds and hearts of their charges. In light of this, how do Nazarene educators address the development of the imaginative mind within the context of a Christian college—tradition, orthodoxy, limited financial resources amid the subtle fear, fascination, and misunderstanding of imagination itself? I asked myself these and many other questions as I struggled to write this essay.

In thinking about this, I have been guilty of equating Nazarene higher education with a stripped down, bare bones version of higher education. I focused on the negatives—the lack of facilities, finances, and resources for the types of exciting educational experiences that might foster the genius of a Michelangelo or a John. But even the heroes of Nazarene education had their bouts with doubt as Bertha Munro writes: "A crumpled bit of yellow paper which I came across reminded me of the spirit with which we welcomed our new leader [Rev. G.B. Williamson]. It was headed, '1936-37 Means Opportunity to Create.' It went on, 'In the clutter we can criticize or create. God saw chaos and made it cosmos'" (151).

Perhaps as educators we take our roles in the process of nurturing the imaginative mind too seriously. John wrote on an island without even a computer! Maybe we need more angels and dragons and unicorns. Provincial blinders hindered me from seeing the good, innovative, exciting and excellent work of faculty and students despite limitations we all have noted on our wish lists for our institutions. I felt defeated, aware of my own limitations and lack of creativity, and I was indicting myself and my alma mater as well since I am a product and part of Nazarene higher education. I began to realize that I was using popular, secular thinking where things and a "Who's Who of Success" determine value rather than the Christian focus on the worth and uniqueness of every individual. I judged in terms of what a Nazarene college can offer in comparison to the "big girls" and the "big boys." It was like deciding where to study based on the best dorms. Then I had the audacity to ask (and the ignorance not to know the answer), "Where are the graduates who have achieved the prizes and the fame?" I was not looking simply for the product of the imaginative mind, but I was defining it by its acclaim. I had neglected the heart and core of Christian education: *developing the person in the image of God.* In the end, education is really about people and their influence. Cecil Paul knew and demonstrated this throughout his all too short life: his focus was on people and their futures—their possibilities.

Psychologists are trained to define and solve people problems. Cecil was intimately aware of the problems that plague humanity, but his approach to solving those problems as a psychologist and a Christian had an added dimension: from his Christian perspective he was able to redefine a person's potential and raise hopes and expectations far beyond the limitations of the perceived problems. This Christian perspective made central the value of redemption to an already people-centered discipline. He did not simply believe that people could reach their potential by solving their problems or trying harder. Instead, he worked on the principle that an individual's potential—the ability to imagine and attain far more than is apparent—is reached through the power of redemption and resurrection. The power to be more than possible on his or her own, to imagine and see the possibilities for a fulfilling life accompany the redemptive work of Christ within the human psyche. For the redeemed, reality is redefined into something that was not seen or imagined prior to experiencing the grace of Christ to open the eyes of those focused on the littleness of a limited existence. Where others saw ordinary people, Cecil, through the eyes of Christ, saw beyond that ordinariness to lives of service and opportunity. Like Michelangelo, where others saw a rock, he saw David and Mary and me. This is the mission of all institutions of Nazarene higher education—to see and articulate for our students and each other the image of God in our lives—the possibilities of God's grace that ever-present limitations crowd from our view.

What must be present for the imaginative mind to discover its potential and to flourish? *Time.* "Art," says Calvin Miller, "is never hurried" (20). The word "time" says it all. There is none. Or there seems to be none. Or it is all prioritized in chaotic order. The reverie of dandelion picking and buttercup sniffing hours—the child—is passed. Time is money. There is so little time; it is a quality not a quantity.

Couples and families communicate more with each other on the telephone and through the daily planner than they do face to face. Friends cannot share a cup of coffee without an eye on the clock. What Nazarene educator, unless innately endowed by the Creator with just the right genetic make-up (that of a long-distance endurance athlete who runs each marathon mile in under four minutes) has the time to manage, with a modicum of creativity, family and home concerns, personal piety, church attendance, church activities, a full teaching load (plus), class preparation, grading, office hours, committee work, performance review, further study, research and writing, advising, and still have time to embrace an imaginative mind? These essential parts of the typical educator's personal and professional life day by day leech away the moments for reflection and creative thought.

Despite the TV drain many students are as highly scheduled by their "daytimers" as their elders. If a student actually does it all—classes, labs, copious reading, research, papers, practicums, part-time jobs (some as much as 30 hours), spiritual disciplines, family obligations, and extra curricular activities, little time remains for thinking, creating or inventing. Imagination does not flourish on such a timetable, neither do people. We cannot expect our students to be creative when every semester we "up the ante" for an A ostensibly to fight grade inflation and prove how good our students are—or we are.

The imaginative mind cannot fear the wastebasket or the cutting board. Failure is a part of the journey of the imaginative mind. We know that the pressure can end in tragedy: the lure of an easy solution—plagiarism—is strong. We have all seen it, agonized over it, and addressed it, sometimes effectively, sometimes not. While maintaining high and demanding standards, all experienced academicians would agree that a flawed paper is much better than a flawless *copy*, but we usually reward flawless products. I also see one pattern that concerns me: the failure of a promising student. These students write better than the average student. They hand in nothing. They are perfectionists. They are not free to fail, yet they do, in a larger measure because the internal pressure to get it right the first time is so great that they are caught judging their product before it is shown in the arena. Students must be free to experiment and try their wings, despite rigorous academic criteria and standards. Instructors must learn to allow failure that is not failure. The answer lies in the delicate balance where freedom, grace, and the legitimate need to follow rules and structure collide! For the imaginative mind to flourish, judgment must be withheld. Judgment, both positive and negative, stops the mind. No need for further thinking or more creating exists. Educators must develop techniques for corrective surgery that heals and encourages. Because it is easy to perfect an academic brand of Phariseeism, the critic without and the critics within must be faced and stared down. The great accuser himself would whittle away our students' confidence.

A part of imagining and creating is a tolerance for ambiguity. Arthur Koestler says that "the creative act . . . always operates on more than one plane . . . a double-minded, transitory state of unstable equilibrium where the balance of both emotion and thought is disturbed" (35-36). For academics, and for Christians too, this can be an uncomfortable state. Sometimes our disciplines seem to demand that all ducks be in a row, everything logged in pen and ink. However, in the creative process the imaginative mind reaches stages where everything does not fit. New and even outlandish possibilities are proposed and explored. This should not undermine the person of faith. If students have been instructed and nurtured in a maturing faith where profession of faith and integrity meet, from that secure place, they can freely explore. The Christian imaginative mind is not on a fantasy trip for the sake of fantasy. It is not on an exploration that leads to the untrue. It is not an abandonment of Christian principles. Warren Wiersbe makes the following distinction: "Fancy helps me escape reality, while imagination helps me penetrate reality and understand it better. Fancy wrote 'Mary Had a Little Lamb,' but inspired imagination wrote Psalm 23" (23). The imaginative mind may be child*like*, but it is not defined as child*ish*, and while in the Christian context its goal is a truthful image, the process is not without "dis-ease."

"Internal discomforts" drive the creative mind, according to Anthony Starr (268). A dissatisfaction with what is, raises the possibilities of something more, something better, something new. Are conflictual situations unfamiliar to Christian thinking and living? Did not Jesus bring discomfort to the legitimate heirs when he said, "Do not suppose that I have come to bring peace to the earth. I did not come to bring peace, but a sword (Matt. 10:34). Christians wrestle with this uncharacteristic statement spoken by the One who brought an unprecedented level of concern for the ordinary, the common, who often lifted them to the extraordinary. What if . . . mud can bring sight? What if . . . a touch brings healing? What if . . . a decaying body can live again?

These thoughts are intriguing thoughts, not unfamiliar to the imaginative minds' enjoyment in wrestling with questions, mystery, and challenges. How is the biblical account of creation reconciled with information from recent scientific developments? How was water changed to wine? And the ultimate question, is Christ who He says He is and was He raised from the dead? Everything hinges on that. Imaginative minds want to believe in Good News that is worth risking their minds, lives, money, and status. Nazarene educators can do that. Their challenge is to introduce students to the Word, to the thinking of great minds, and to be fearless amid the swirl of academic debate. Spiritual formation occurs in this open examination of the Word. While tradition may stifle, the opportunity for fresh, and pertinent exploration of the faith should be the experience of all students who enroll in our colleges and universities. Orthodoxy instructs the mind to think in certain paths. The imaginative mind thinks in new ways and uncharted paths. If "two roads diverge in a wood," the imaginative mind may go straight through the bush, which at the time may not look too intelligent. Why make a new road when two already exist? Does going straight mean a different wood will be explored or a different destination reached?

A person who goes straight where no road exists sees what the rest of us do not see. Imaginative thinkers possess this vision. They, in fact, can envision for the rest of us when we cannot see anything. Cecil Paul could envision what we could be, what we could become. He helped the communities he touched to see in themselves what they could be when they could not see it themselves. If Nazarene higher education is to meet the needs of the present generation of students, Nazarene educators must do this for students and for each other—to believe that through Christ-centered education the possibilities of the individual can be unlocked. To this end, the entire college experience focuses on nurturing the spiritual development of each student and the unique talents and gifts that sometimes come to college buried under debris. It is exploring with that student, the possibilities of individual potential as they fit into the life of the Christian community, whether in the arts, humanities, science, business, religion or the professions. This focus on envisioning the future for each student, does not negate the importance of approaching subject matter uniquely, or using current, captivating teaching techniques, or solving problems creatively, but it places the value where Christ would place it—on the individual.

In Cecil's presence each person was an individual, not a role, not a number. Cecil touched people individually like Jesus who healed individual persons, called individual men, and legitimized individual women. People are the most important part of an education, and Cecil knew that. The education of the whole person as stated in the educational catalogs of Nazarene institutions of higher education must remain central. Nazarene educators must continually assess what and whom they value. Students are precious, our sacred trust. Who is successful in the institution's eyes? Is it the poet and her use of language or the lawyer and her language? Is it the artist or the doctor? Does one discipline aid humanity more than another? Is one discipline queen? What power is valued? Financial, political, spiritual?

Limitations are not a hindrance to creative people. For Cecil, growing up on a farm in rural Canada his first eighteen years—unchurched, unevangelized—was not a limitation. His genius was nurtured in the solitude of mountain and field. Those farming days gave him ample time and space to think and reflect on life and its central questions. It was not an accident that Moses came out of the wilderness. A wilderness experience provides a basis from which to distinguish the real from the false. He understood the essential difference between the person and the deed. He could differentiate, but withhold judgment. He was patient and accepting of all kinds of human beings. His life was informed by the cares and problems of ordinary people. Cecil was for everybody. The blinders were not present.

Cecil was able to chart a course—to see how things could be and make them happen in concrete form. In 1971 he founded the Wollaston Counseling Associates which later became the Beechwood Counseling Center in Quincy, Massachusetts. As President of ENC, the Leadership Education for Adults (LEAD), a non-traditional degree completion program took shape to fulfill the dreams of those whose business education had been interrupted. Also a much needed, beautiful library was built and dedicated in the spring of 1992. Cecil did not establish programs or build alone. He had the ability to bring people on board. His vision was an empowering one in which he could pass along his ideas to other people. He got people talking, dialoguing, coming to consensus in a Task Force, even though we may have rolled our eyes when he suggested yet another one! Just as G. K. Chesterton describes the life of the mind, "Thinking means connecting things, and stops if they cannot be connected" (61), Cecil knew the value of people working together to bring all of their ideas to bear on a particular problem. He was able to pull together diverse people to talk. He made time for their imagination to work, even though Cecil was driven by what he envisioned could be accomplished in us. Madeleine L'Engle says that "the artist yearns for 'success,' because that means there has been a communication of the vision: that all the struggle has not been invalid" (34). As Nazarene educators, we continue today to retrace the vision of the mission before us to validate Cecil's struggle, to validate our own struggle, and the struggle of the heritage left by the women and men whom we follow.

Cecil developed a sense of direction for Eastern Nazarene College, and it was always outward, bringing the outside in. His leadership in the establishment of the LEAD program reflects this. Eugene Peterson reminds us that "the important theologians have done their thinking and writing about God in the middle of the world, in the thick of the action: Paul urgently dictating letters from his prison cell" (40). If Nazarene higher education —even as its mission is defined within the Church of the Nazarene—is to reflect the image of God, that education will have to give students a very real sense of what the world is. An accurate vision is essential because it is precisely there that the work and mission of the Christian lies. Like Cecil, who was unthreatened by the world around him, we must learn from it—its needs, heartthrob, joys, and sorrows to equip ourselves for a more powerful and inclusive ministry of reconciliation. The Christian educator needs to narrowly define Christian values in terms of New Testament theology, but then move out from there as a student of the world. Then a ministry of wholeness can commence.

Central to Cecil's vision for all of the educational constituency was wholeness. He envisioned a place where the imaginative mind flourishes best—a community of seekers, scholars, servers, givers, and lovers who are given grace to fail and try again, to explore, to imagine "what if . . . " and time to listen for the voice of God. It is time to retrace the vision once more for each student. The need of young adults who attend Nazarene institutions of higher education is not only for a liberal arts education but also for a hope and a future. Like Allan Bloom, Cecil would say to us, "Examine [your] life and survey the potential" (50). That potential is as present and empowering in each of us as the image of God.

CHAPTER SEVENTEEN

EDUCATION AS RECONCILIATION

Gerard A. Reed

In some ways Christian professors resemble highway crews, trying to post road markers at busy entry ramps where faith joins reason, where Christ infuses culture. Though at times isolated in "ivory towers" of semi-monastic sub-cultures, scholars cannot ignore the squealing tires, the grating sounds of horns and engines, the driven world of motorists speeding too rapidly to study life's maps—if indeed there are maps to be found.

Life's tensions trouble us. As always, faith-full teachers seek to rightly relate the realms of revelation and reason, of faith and learning. On the other hand, they engage in the intense contemporary struggle, within the academic amphitheater, to establish the scope and focus (indeed the value and viability) of the traditional liberal arts in higher education. To make sense of—and then to even tentatively reconcile—some of these tensions establishes the agenda and tests the mettle of Christian thinkers and educators.

The task, of course, is hardly new. Rooted in Hebraism, with its educational commitment fleshed out in synagogues scattered throughout the ancient world, primitive Christians stressed the need for nurturing converts. St Paul advised parents to wisely rear their children, and as early as 96 A.D. St. Clement of Rome used the phrase *"en Christo paideia"*—"Christian education."

Across the centuries believers have proposed and followed diverse approaches in dealing with the realms of "Christ and Culture." Some, like Tertullian, *separated* from the world—especially the realm of pagan philosophy or secular learning—so as to rigorously follow a narrowly biblical path. Others, such as Valentinius, followed varieties of Gnosticism and sought to *accommodate* Christian faith to alluring strains of Hellenistic philosophy.

Yet in the Ancient Church other thinkers charted a *via media* between the separatism of Tertullian and the secularizing accommodationism of Valentinius. Believing in the God of creation and of prevenient grace, they embraced whatever pagan insights they could harmonize with divine revelation. Thus we find a unique openness to classical Greek thought in the first (and in many ways the *only*) "Christian school" of the Early Church, established toward the end of the second century in Alexandria. Here St. Clement of Alexandria found a place to think and teach and write works such as *Christ the Educator*, setting forth a Christian worldview which encompassed all that's true, whether rooted in Scripture or creation or pagan philosophy.

Following Clement came Origen, clearly one of the greatest of all Christian theologians. Origen first sought simply to study Scripture. Yet his scholarly renown attracted men who were widely read in Greek philosophy, so he felt compelled "to examine the doctrines of the schools and see what the philosophers had said concerning the truth" (qtd. in Murray 153).

And so he did. He and his students explored both Alexandria's Museum (the world's greatest library) and the sacred scriptures. They stalked and snared eternal truth in both the wisdom of Hellenism and the doctrines of the Church. They sought to reconcile finite truths with infinite Truth, to establish a creative synthesis wherein all truth was discerned as God's Truth. Thus he established a *didaskaleion*, a school which followed the typical "Hellenic disciplines" of the day. He asserted the worth of the ancient Greek *paideia* and its humanistic studies; but he insisted it needed the soul-nurturing truth of Christ added to its mind-expanding curriculum.

According to one of his most gifted students, Gregory of Neocaesarea (Gregory "Thaumaturgus"—the "wonder-worker"), "Nothing was forbidden us, nothing hidden from us, nothing inaccessible to us." They studied everything! Yet this was only part of the process; there was the teacher's presence, the teacher's mentoring. Origen himself, Gregory says, "went on with us, . . . directing us, pointing out to us all that was true and useful, putting aside all that was false" (qtd. in Murray 157-158).

The liberal arts, the learning of the Greeks, was to be studied—but never dispassionately, never without a Christian commitment, never without prayer. Indeed, Origen said, "the most necessary thing for the understanding of divine matters is prayer" (qtd. in Murray 157-158). And one ought study nothing without carefully subjecting non-Christian truth-claims to the deeper authority of God's Word. With St. Ambrose, who later insisted that "the Word of God permeates every creature in the constitution of the world" (232), Origen discerned the underlying unity of all Truth, the *Word of God*—"the Holy Word, the loveliest thing there is"(qtd. in Murray 160).

There is, I think, a profound pattern evident in Origen's Alexandrian *didaskaleion*, where Christ was worshipped as *logos*, the *truth* who reconciles all humanly-discerned truths. The Alexandrines, and the Cappadocians who shaped Eastern Orthodoxy, established an educational strategy—what I will call *education as reconciliation*—as a creatively viable Christian approach to the liberal arts. Rather than separate from, or accommodate to, the secular society, *education as reconciliation* seeks to honestly dialogue with truth-seekers everywhere, trying to clear away misunderstandings, to dig out deeply buried commonalities, to establish *shalom* through listening and discussion.

Interestingly enough, this ancient pattern finds a certain confirmation in the thought of a more modern theologian, John Wesley, who deeply admired the Ancient Church Fathers (and especially some spokesmen for Eastern Orthodoxy). So there is, I think, within the Wesleyan tradition a healthy context for a reconciling strategy of education which enables educators to sustain a solidly biblical faith while staying in touch with the ever-shifting tides of secular learning. As John's brother Charles declared in one of his hymns: "Unite the pair so long disjoined, / Knowledge and vital piety: / Learning and holiness combined, / And truth and love, let all men see / In these whom up to thee we give, / Thine, wholly thine, to die and live" (Wesley, "Hymns," *Works*, Oxford ed. 7:644).

The Wesleyan Quadrilateral

A contemporary Wesleyan endeavor to synthesize knowledge and vital piety may clearly be envisioned in terms of the "Wesleyan Quadrilateral"—Scripture, Tradition, Reason, Experience. Since 1960, when Albert C. Outler coined the term, the "quadrilateral" has served as a useful paradigm with which to conceptualize "Wesleyan" theology.

The "quadrilateral," in some ways, is an ungainly label for an ungainly geometric pattern: a four-sided figure of unequal sides. Beyond its visual imagery, however helpful or distracting, the Wesleyan Quadrilateral's real import is its insistence on interlocking *synthesis*. No single authority, no monistic mode of thinking, no singular doctrinal system, no magisterial theologian will suffice. Truth, to Wesleyans, is knit together and sustained by mixing, combining, reconciling, a variety of themes and thinkers. The Anglican stance, the *via media*, provides Wesley a strategy for formulating a Christian philosophy of education which has marked parallels with that of Origen's approach in ancient Alexandria.

Scripture

Like Origen, John Wesley fundamentally styled himself a *biblical* thinker and preacher. Scripture clearly served as the steel-girdered superstructure for all he said and did. Martin Luther's call for *sola scriptura* routinely re-echoed in Wesley's works. He revered Scripture as "the inviolable Word" of God, filled with "words 'of the Spirit of God'" ("Seek," 4:220 and "Circumcision," 1:402, *Works*, Bicentennial ed). In a 1739 letter he said, "I allow no other rule, whether of faith or practice, than the Holy Scriptures" (*Letters* 1:285). Fifty years later, in his *Explanatory Notes Upon The New Testament*, he urged his followers to "keep close to the Bible. Be not wise above what is written. Enjoin nothing that the Bible does not clearly enjoin. Forbid nothing that it does not clearly forbid" (2 Tim. 3:16, 794).

As a churchman, as a busy evangelist and discipleship group leader, Wesley mainly related Scripture to salvation issues. He wanted, above all, to chart the highway to heaven. Yet educators of the Wesleyan persuasion ought to carefully heed Wesley's call to constantly consider God's written Word. If education is to be authentically Christian it must be fundamentally biblical—Scripture ought to shine as its morning and evening stars! A biblical perspective, a knowledge of the Bible's message, must encompass and provide a compass for the educational journey.

Here Wesley and Origen concur. For all his vast erudition, Origen remained, throughout his life, absorbed in biblical study and interpretation. Ultimately, Gregory of Neocaesarea remembered Origen's *didaskaleion* elicited a profound "piety"—a love of truths rooted in the Truth disclosed increasingly to those seeking to synthesize all truths with a commitment to "the Holy Word, the loveliest thing there is" (qtd. in Murray 155).

Granted that Scripture provides the *essential* ingredient for Christian education, one might, as did Tertullian, restrict one's inquiries to its contents. One might, to preserve the *Christian* essence of education, develop Bible schools or Bible colleges, to follow a particularistic rather than an ecumenical educational path. Such might seem to be the rigorous logic of following the Protestant principle of *sola scriptura*—or John Wesley's frequent assertion: *homo unius libri*—"I am a man of one book."

Yet neither Origen nor Wesley limited their studies to the Bible alone. To rightly grasp biblical truth, they thought, demands a truly catholic, synthesizing mind, for one must reconcile and integrate all truths with the God of Truth. Wesley, securely rooted in the Anglican approach so ably carved out by Richard Hooker and others, embraced the integrative, "catholic," *via media* of his church, which he judged "nearer the scriptural plan than any other" (Thorsen 128). Thus he freely borrowed from various sources—church Fathers; medieval mystics; Eastern Orthodox, Roman Catholic, Reformed and Puritan theologians. While Scripture is the *sole* authority, it must ever be interpreted out of a broader context. Scripture alone cannot explain itself, and Wesley "was not content to use the principle of *sola scriptura* in a way that excluded other sources of religious authority" (Thorsen 135). Throughout his life he interpreted *sola* as mainly rather than solely.

But today we wonder: given the tides of secularism, can Wesley's "catholic spirit" find expression in colleges committed to an authoritative Scripture? Can, in fact, "knowledge and vital piety" enjoy conjugal bliss? If so, how? Clearly one giant step is necessary to establish such; making Scripture the *primary* text, cited and relied on in general education classes, and reconciling all other forms of knowledge with its illuminating principles.

Tradition

Tradition, especially in the United States, often lacks strong advocates. Consequently, historians discern only minimal resemblances between historic Christianity and its American offspring. To many Americans, inherited traditions restrict freedom and threaten the "democratic way of life." Yet ironically, as G.K. Chesterton wisely wrote: "Tradition may be defined as an extension of the franchise. Tradition means giving votes to the most obscure of all classes, our ancestors" (48).

Persons cannot function without memory. What we think and do grows out of an awareness of our past. Deeper than mere details concerning what we have done and suffered, we need the *meaning* which comes from a sense of ordering, of purposeful development. Memory provides the incubator for our creative imagination, the context for coherent thought, the rote-mastery of vital skills.

Similarly, societies without shared histories cannot long endure. Without a common linkage to the past which provides an umbilical bond, societies dissolve into the churning chaos of individual preferences. And deprived of a meaningful past, a commonality with ancestors and their achievements and values, societies fail to provide any *raison d'etre.*

John Wesley's traditionalism focused mainly on "the *religion of the primitive church,* of the whole church in the purest ages" ("Laying," *Works* Bicentennial 586). Even more distant in time, he valued the ancient, pre-biblical religion of mankind, a "heart-religion" singularly marked by the love of God.

This notion reached back as far as Eusebius, who, in his *Ecclesiastical History,* declared that though Christians were in a sense "new" to the world, "nevertheless our life and our conduct, with our doctrines of religion, have not been lately invented by us, but from the first creation of man, so to speak, have been established by the natural understanding of divinely favored men of old" (87).

This "old religion" developed into and continually suffused the religion of the patriarchs and of the Bible, the religion of the primitive Church, the religion of the Church of England and its Methodist reformers. Reading Scripture within the context of this broad tradition enables one to more clearly discern its meaning. Wesley continually sought to recover a patristic perspective. He revered the ancient Church Fathers, the Ecumenical Creeds, and the formative works of prominent Anglicans. He seemed content with the essential orthodoxy defined by Vincent of Lerins: "that faith which has been believed everywhere, always, by all" (132).

Discerning the essentials, evident within the orthodox Christian tradition, freed Wesley from fretting unduly with incidentals. He allowed for communities of faith, such as his Methodist societies, to set certain standards, positions not mandated in Scripture; but he refused to make them points of division. In fact, he said, Methodists "require no unity in opinions, or in modes of worship, but barely that they 'fear God and work righteousness'" ("Prophets," *Works,* Bicentennial 83-84). This "catholic spirit," suffused with "universal love," enabled him to remain friends with men like George Whitefield, though they heatedly disputed certain theological issues.

Yet not all opinions, not all ethical views, could be tolerated or accepted. Some issues were clear. Some doctrines rightly delineate the "Gospel" in its fullness. These major themes could be best discerned within the context of the Christian tradition, which often helps in "the explication of a doctrine that is not sufficiently explained, or for a confirmation of a doctrine generally received" (Preface, *Works,* Jackson ed. 87).

The Wesleyan educator, like Origen, seeks to illuminate the everlasting Gospel of Jesus Christ by setting it within the ever-developing tradition of the Church. Just as Wesley's "Christian Library" set circulating books he judged worth reading for believers in his day, so too Wesleyan educators must explain the Gospel within the context of a "Christian library"—relevant readings, which make it intelligible and dynamic for each generation of students. A Christian college, in the Wesleyan mode, should focus much of its attention on those texts (e.g. Augustine's *Confessions*; Chaucer's *Canterbury Tales*; Dante's *Divine Comedy*; C.S. Lewis' *Mere Christianity*) which best reveal truth about God and His creation, about human nature and destiny.

One of the primary justifications for education is simply the preservation, through the study of the past, of those traditional stories and teachings which have wisely guided our ancestors. So a Christian college, in the Origenist-Wesleyan tradition, certainly emphasizes history of all sorts in general education. An education should give students a sense of where they have come from, of who they are as the "now" generation.

Amidst much talk of pluralism, of "multiculturalism," sometimes laced with strident anti-Western rhetoric, Christian educators may well consider their commitment to the Christian tradition. Could it be that Christian colleges, like Benedictine monasteries in the Middle Ages, should assume the role of *preserving* the classics of the Western tradition?

In short: for educators, history, in the fullest sense of the word, especially including and emphasizing the history of Western Christian culture, highlights an essential side of the Wesleyan Quadrilateral: Tradition.

Reason

Wesley revered reason's religious role. In one of his letters, he wrote: "It is a fundamental principle with us [Methodists] that to renounce reason is to renounce religion, that religion and reason go hand in hand, and that all irrational religion is false religion" (*Letters*, 5:364). Committed to the notion that human beings were created in the image of God, an image defaced but not destroyed by Adam's fall, Wesley insisted that the ability to reason is one of the prime ingredients of personhood.

He stressed that the "image of God" still resides in man. While he fully appreciated the corrupting reality of sin's ravages on the race, Wesley retained a robust confidence in reason's integrity. The principles of logical thought, right reasoning, enable Christians to properly interpret Scripture within Tradition's context. As St. Augustine said, "the laws of valid reasoning may be learnt in the schools, outside the pale of the Church. But the truth of propositions must be inquired into in the sacred books of the Church" (31).

Though some Protestants, notably Luther, claimed to despise reason and logic, Wesley shared an Anglican confidence in the edifying worth of clear thinking. In its more Arminian advocates such as Wesley, Anglicanism insisted that Adam's fall thoroughly corrupted man's *heart*, but not his head. Unlike many modern philosophers locked into an iron-celled subjectivism, Wesley shared the ancient notion that "*veritas est adaequatio intellectus et rei*" (truth is the equating of the mind and matter).

Given this common sense assumption that the external world is real and that we can adequately understand it, we may confidently seek and claim to know what is true. Thus humans can, in fact, reason their way God-ward. Though the human heart bends toward evil, the mind functions freely and tends toward truth.

Wesley's confidence in reason, rather similar in some ways to the "moderate realism" of St. Thomas Aquinas, allowed him to embrace Aristotle's logic as well as selected aspects of John Locke's empiricism (though Wesley usually trusted what he called "experimentalism"). Born with the capacity to reason, we develop it through observation, associations, proper intellectual disciplines, and syllogistic logic.

While recognizing its limits, educators committed to *education as reconciliation* must emphasize the dignity of reason and seek to cultivate its attributes within students. Given the allure of existential subjectivism (with its purely internal truth-tests) and irrationalism (with its celebration of immediacy and power), men and women of "reason" must raise the standard of Right Reason on the jousting fields of academia!

Experience

Wesleyan theology, with its focus on *love*, has always had a strongly relational texture. While Wesley's concern for Scripture, Tradition, and Reason have many counterparts in the Christian world, his concern for Experience is considered by many "one of his greatest contributions to the development of Christian theology" (Thorsen 201). Though he always insisted it be bounded by strict scriptural and reasonable parameters, he highly valued religious experience.

Just as we know empirically through the senses which enable us to encounter and understand the physical world, so we know experientially as our "spiritual senses," our heart awarenesses, assure us that we have encountered and understood the spiritual world. While we know this subjectively, the knowledge itself is not *purely* subjective, for it is knowledge derived from an objectively real supernatural world. As Thorsen says, "Perceiving—literally feeling—God's presence is a powerful epistemological guarantee for the truth of Christian belief" (209). As Wesley expressed it, those who are spiritually alive have both "the *hearing* ear and the *seeing* eye . . . a new class of senses" which discern "'the *evidence* of things not seen'" ("Appeal," *Works*, Oxford ed. 6:188).

It's somewhat like aesthetic knowledge. The sights and sounds of artistic works provide the visible symbols which grant us, experientially, access to the realms of beauty. Hans-Georg Gadamer, a contemporary philosopher, has thoughtfully discussed the epistemological truthfulness, the *knowable* reality of art. In a profound way, Gadamer argues, "the being of representation is superior to the being of the material represented, the Achilles of Homer more than the original Achilles" (87). For great art does not simply *copy* something: "it is not merely a second version, a copy, but a recognition of its essence" (103).

What Gadamer says for aesthetic experience Wesley, in a sense, believed true for religious experience. One does in fact enter into and really *know* God; one does in fact know *truth*, through illuminating, transforming experiences. Wesley himself had a "heart-warming" experience at Aldersgate which secured his faith and proved the turning point in his ministry.

Rooted in a "theology of love" (cf. Wynkoop), Wesleyans should stress the role of affections, the knowledge of the "heart," in the learning process. In the past, as Parker Palmer suggests, either curiosity or the desire to control have prompted the quest for knowledge. Yet, he says, "another kind of knowledge is available to us,"—a knowledge rooted "not in curiosity or control but in compassion, or love" which aims at "reconciling the world to itself" (7-8).

Following this approach, one seeks "truth" rather than collected data or speculative theories. Such truth, Palmer says, develops in deeply personal relationships. Just as Wesley encouraged his followers to open themselves to the particularized workings of God's Spirit in their hearts, so Wesleyan educators should encourage their students to open themselves to a Creator and His creation—realities truly "other" than themselves.

Such learning takes place by silently listening, reverently wondering at the mysterious world of being, and *praying*. Primary to Origen's *didaskaleion*, central to the Christian tradition Wesley espoused, is prayer. Palmer says: "In prayer we acknowledge the spiritual bonds that tie us and our world together" (31). The knowledge which comes from prayer "becomes a knowledge that draws us into a faithful relationship with all of life. In prayer we find the ultimate space in which to practice obedience to truth, the space created by that Spirit who keeps troth with us all" (Palmer 125). It is a knowledge grounded in personal experience, a knowledge which develops through participation in a relationship, a heart-based particular knowledge which confirms the truth of Scripture, Tradition, and Reason.

Conclusion

While John Wesley (schooled at Oxford and hardly concerned with "liberal arts colleges" as we understand them) cannot be conscripted to provide a model for Wesleyan educators, I think his theology has educational applications. Envisioned along the lines of the "Quadrilateral," sustained by the synthesizing "catholic" spirit he incarnated, Wesley's theology could help his heirs to think through and implement viable educational programs sustained by a commitment to *education as reconciliation.*

CHAPTER EIGHTEEN

REFLECTIONS ON A LIFE

Bruce Paul

My father had a deep appreciation for the complexity of the human personality. Much of his interest in psychology was rooted in the understanding that we change. That which drives us today may not be that which drives us tomorrow. The Christian, he believed, had access to a power that could make personal evolution dynamic. Through the healing power of God's Holy Spirit we can grow to become that which God intended us to be and thus escape the destructive cycles of sin that trap far too many in our society. As old patterns of sin are broken down, new patterns, rich in color emerge and give life to us and others.

As I look back at my father's life I see many colorful patterns that emerged from his personality and how they contributed to the brilliant tapestry which was his life. My vision is limited, however, and there is much of his life, his thoughts and dreams which lie beyond my personal horizon. Thus, there is a certain futility in trying to sum up such a life in a few short words.

The desire to do so is, however, understandable. When someone we love dies we want to take something of them with us, perhaps some motto which will help us better understand them and the impact they made on our life. Such mottos, always fall short and can be misleading. To create one would be especially unfair to my father who at the time of his death was still growing. New adventures had just begun. New roles for him were just taking shape. His life, like all our lives, escapes an easy summary and is best understood by those who helped him live it, whether students, colleagues, family or friends. Even then our view of him is partial and incomplete.

While I will always be envious of those who viewed him from different vantage points, I treasure the view I had of him as his son. When I try to sum up his intellectual thought world I cannot get past the man who taught me to walk, to laugh, and to love. What of that view can I share that will have meaning for you?

Countless images flood my mind when I reflect back on his life. Images so unimportant to others, so priceless to me. Did you know he did yard work wearing dress slacks and sneakers? That he used to perspire when he ate spaghetti? That he built an electric guitar when he was in high school? That he made popcorn for us on Sunday nights? That his voice cracked when he got emotional?

Did you know—that he didn't enter a church until he was eighteen? That he helped us bury our pets in the backyard? That his favorite treat as a boy was a Mexican Hat sundae? That he could only swim using the side stroke? That he cried at my wedding? That he wanted to be a Mountie? That he hugged you with his eyes?

This is trivia, however. Perhaps the following insights will have more meaning for you.

Dad believed in the unlimited potential of everyone in my family. Not the potential to be all that we desired; rather, he believed that we had the unlimited potential to be all that God wanted us to be. After all, Dad would argue, this is the only potential worth fulfilling.

Dad was a great believer in God-given gifts. He relished the opportunity to ferret them out. Most often when he saw evidence for such a gift, regardless of how meager that evidence was, he would nudge us to pursue that area a little more. None of us were exempt from his probing eye, even Mom. Needless to say we often disagreed with his perceived vision for us, but more often than not he was on the right track.

Since his death I have heard several people outside the family recount similar tales. Many have, in fact, remarked that he seemed to have an uncanny ability to help individuals discover gifts and talents that had previously remained hidden, even from that individual. He was always pushing people to stretch beyond their limited view of themselves. Those who heeded his advice often discovered secret treasure stores within and Dad came out looking like a genius. Time and time again I was surprised by the people he expected great things from when all I could see was mediocrity. Time and time again his vision proved true.

There were, to be sure, disappointments—people who Dad had either misjudged or who failed to catch a vision for their lives. However, more often than not Dad's faith in others was rewarded. Those with limiting histories began to see an unlimited future. Those who had previously been fixated on what they could not do began to see their unique gifts. He helped us develop a future orientation. We became excited about tomorrow.

Some have suggested that this ability to discern others' gifts was Dad's unique God-given gift. Was it a gift? Perhaps, but if so it was only the fruit of a superior gift, the gift of love. He listened to people, be they friends, family or students as if he had a personal stake in what they were sharing. He had the ability to remember little details, to remember something you did well or a clever comment made years ago. More importantly he listened so as to hear what moved you and what gave you meaning.

Dad was, however, a discerning listener. As both a professional and as a parent he had to listen to many disjointed conversations. He had to sift through arguments or complaints piled on by us out of fear, frustration or stubbornness. He took it all in but was able to disregard that which was not germane and, with the accuracy of a laser beam, zero in on the real issue at hand. This, of course, made him frustrating to debate with.

Although conflict was not something Dad enjoyed, it was not something he ran away from either. A few nights after his death a group of his family and friends gathered to share both their grief and their thoughts about him. Searching for something meaningful to share I came up with: "I always knew where I stood with Dad. I always knew what would please him and what would make him angry." Some of his friends rolled their eyes and one said: "I wish you'd told me."

The truth is that Dad was just as human as any of us and had his good moods and bad. However, his anger, at its most pure, was most often directed at those Christian individuals or institutions which refused to embrace their Christ-won freedom. It was directed at those who seemed intent on reviving that which had died, that which had failed and that which debases.

Dad believed that in Christ we are empowered to reclaim that which God has always intended for us. No longer are we limited to the stagnant waters of our past. We are now set free to drink deeply from the pool of life. Unfortunately, too many of us linger at foul waters even after drinking from a living water.

Dad was a good psychologist and understood the need for healing and the need for process in spiritual growth. He understood that some personal histories made destructive life patterns difficult to give up. He also knew that some embraced those patterns willingly and were not interested in growth. He understood the power of sin.

As both a parent to his children and as a mentor to others Dad was forced into a difficult balancing act. He wanted to affirm and love us at whatever stage of life we were in, all the while pushing us to new growth and confronting us when he saw evidence that our growth had slowed or reversed.

Perhaps this is why Dad valued the concept of Christian community so highly. It is within community that we can lift each other up, bear each others' burdens and provide the modeling needed for those struggling with life-stage issues and struggling with their faith. If we are to live out what it means to be the body of Christ then we must live, work and function as part of a community. How can we be part of the body of Christ if we are cut off from one another?

It is no mere coincidence then that so much of his life was devoted to community-building efforts. From his years as pastor of the Blue Hill Community Church, to his founding of the Beechwood Community Center, to his various leadership roles at Eastern Nazarene College, he was obsessed with the promise of community. Only in community can we draw on the unique gifts of each to the betterment of all. Only in community can we most fully be what God intends for us.

While the Christian community was a source of great joy and excitement for my father, it was also often a source of great frustration and anguish. He found that many Christian communities and institutions had a surprising tendency to return to worldly models despite their records of failure and destruction. Too often he found that when we were called to lift each other up, we lifted ourselves instead. Too often when we were called to bear each others' burdens, we validated our inaction by pointing to our own needs and our own scars.

He was, in many ways, a prophet. He would point to the good being done by non-Christian individuals and communities and ask "Can't we do better?"

He took God's promises seriously and dared us to dream dreams. He pushed us and even shamed us by his work ethic. He labored hard, not out of guilt or out of selfish ambition but out of responsibility. For him work was a form of Christian respiration, breathing back out for others that which God had breathed into him. Work was a form of worship.

Reverend Russ Metcalfe mentioned that when he went into my father's office shortly after his death he found a hand-scribbled note from a text my father was working on. If we insist on finding some motto by which to remember him this serves as good as any. It read: "Not sold out to the world; sold out to mission!"

While this statement reads as a fitting epitaph for my father, it was meant for us. It is, essentially, a paraphrase of Romans 12:2: "Do not be conformed to this world, but be transformed by the renewing of your minds" (NRSV). It too was written by a Christian trying to call his community into the fullness of what God had intended for them.

I am struck by an image of my father sitting at his desk, late in the day of what would be his last day at work, trying one more time to get his message across. What new way can he word the simple call to live beyond self for the good of others? What fresh approach can he take to help others abandon the failed models of the world and embrace the one given us by Christ?

"Not sold out to the world, sold out to mission!" It is as much a plea as it is a rallying cry and it breaks my heart if I think about it too much.

I am, however, struck by another, more encouraging image from my youth. I see my dad, dressed in his black preaching robe walking to the back door of the sanctuary, preparing to send us out with words of benediction. They were words he not only treasured, but words he lived out. They were the words that gave him hope both in us and in himself regardless of the failings and disappointments of the past. They are words of promise and point us to the bright light of tomorrow.

He is ready now. He stretches out his arm over us and proclaims in boldness:

> Now to him who by the power at work within us is able to accomplish abundantly far more than all we can ask or imagine, to him be glory in the church and in Christ Jesus to all generations, forever and ever. Amen
> (Ephesians 3:20-21 NRSV).

BIBLIOGRAPHY

* In the *Festschrift* several essayists have referred to Cecil Paul's address "The People Called Nazarenes: Getting There," presented February 21, 1989 to the Nazarene Leadership Conference. Each reference to this address is denoted with an asterisk.

Chapter 1: The Nazarene College President as Servant Leader

Benezet, Louis T., Joseph Katz, and Frances W. Magnusson. *Style and Substance: Leadership and the College Presidency.* Washington: American Council on Educ., 1981.

Bemis, Warren. *Why Leaders Can't Lead.* San Francisco: Jossey, 1989.

DePree, Max. *Leadership Is An Art.* East Lansing: Michigan State UP, 1987.

Fisker, James L. *The Board and the President.* New York: Macmillan, 1991.

—. *Power of the Presidency.* New York: Macmillan, 1984.

Greenleaf, Robert K. *Servant Leadership.* New York: Paulist P, 1977.

Habecker, Eugene B. *The Other Side of Leadership.* Wheaton: Victor, 1987.

Hersey, Paul. *The Situational Leader.* New York: Warren, 1985.

McKenna, David L. *Power to Follow, Grace to Lead.* Dallas: Word, 1989.

Mulder, Carl T. "Biblical Leadership in Christian Organizations." *Faculty Dialogue* 13 Winter 1990.

Palmer, Parker J. *Leading From Within.* Indianapolis: Indiana Office For Campus Ministries, 1990.

Stoke, Harold W. *The American College President.* New York: Harper, 1959.

Torrance, Thomas F. "Service in Jesus Christ." *Theological Foundations For Ministry.* Ed. Ray S. Anderson. Grand Rapids: Eerdmans, 1979.

Weber, E. P., "The Genius of a Christian College's Distinctiveness With Suggestions For Implementation." *Faculty Dialogue* 4 Fall 1985.

Chapter 3: What Makes a College "Nazarene"?

Bangs, Carl. *Phineas F. Bresee: His Life in Methodism, The Holiness Movement, and the Church of the Nazarene.* Kansas City: Beacon Hill P, 1995.

Bassett, Paul. "The Theological Identity of the North American Holiness Movement: Its Understanding of the Nature and Role of the Bible." *The Variety of American Evangelicalism.* Ed. Donald W. Dayton and Robert K. Johnston. Downers Grove: InterVarsity P, 1991.

Dunn, Samuel L. and Joseph Nielson. "The Theology and Practice of Wesleyan Higher Education." *Faculty Dialogue* 7 (1986-87): 71-82.

Dussel, Enrique. *A History of the Church in Latin America.* Trans. Alan Neely. Grand Rapids: Eerdmans, 1981.

Fichte, Johann G. *Science of Knowledge.* Trans. Peter Heath and John Lachs. Cambridge: Cambridge UP, 1982.

Flew, Antony and Alasdair Macintyre, eds. *New Essays in Philosophical Theology.* London: SCM P, 1953.

Geertz, Clifford. *The Interpretation of Cultures: Selected Essays.* New York: Basic, 1975.

Heron, Alasdair. *A Century of Protestant Theology.* Philadelphia: Westminster P, 1980.

Holmes, Arthur. *Contours of a World View.* Grand Rapids: Eerdmans, 1983.

——. *The Idea of a Christian College.* Rev. ed. Grand Rapids: Eerdmans, 1987.

Laird, Rebecca. "Distinctly Us." *Herald of Holiness* Aug. 1995: 11.

Leclerc, Ivor. *Whitehead's Metaphysics: An Introductory Exposition.* New York: Macmillan, 1958.

Leith, John, ed. *Creeds of the Churches.* 3rd ed. Atlanta: John Knox P, 1982.

Locke, John. *An Essay Concerning Human Understanding.* Ed. Peter H. Nidditch. Oxford: Clarendon P, 1975.

Maddox, Randy. *Responsible Grace: John Wesley's Practical Theology.* Nashville: Kingswood, 1994.

Manual: Church of the Nazarene 1993-97. Kansas City, MO: Nazarene, n.d.

McGrath, Alister. *Understanding Doctrine: Its Relevance and Purpose for Today.* Grand Rapids: Zondervan, 1990.

Metz, Donald. *Some Crucial Issues in the Church of the Nazarene.* Olathe: Pioneer P, 1993.

Moltmann, Jurgen. *Theology of Hope: On the Ground and the Implications of a Christian Eschatology.* Trans. James W. Leitch. New York: Harper, 1967.

Outler, Albert C. *The Wesleyan Theological Heritage: Essays of Albert C. Outler.* Ed. Thomas C. Oden and Leicester R. Longden. Grand Rapids: Zondervan, 1991.

Pechter, Edward. *What is Shakespeare?* Ithaca: Cornell UP, 1995.

Robinson, Richard. *Plato's Earlier Dialectic.* 2nd ed. New York: Oxford UP, 1964.

Ritchey, Russell E. "History as a Bearer of Denominational Identity: Methodism as a Case Study." Rpt. in *Perspectives on American Methodism: Interpretative Essays.* Ed. Russell E. Ritchey et al. Nashville: Kingswood, 1993.

Smith, Timothy. *Called unto Holiness: The Story of the Nazarenes.* Kansas City: Nazarene, 1962.

Thornton, Martin. *English Spirituality.* Cambridge, MA: Cowley, 1986.

Wall, John N. "Anglican Spirituality: A Historical Introduction." *Spiritual Traditions for the Contemporary Church.* Ed. Robin Maas and Gabriel O'Donnell. Nashville: Abingdon, 1990.

Wesley, John. "Thoughts on Methodism." *The Works of John Wesley.* Vol. 13. Grand Rapids: Zondervan, n.d.

Whitehead, Alfred North. *Modes of Thought.* New York: Free P, 1968.

—. *Process and Reality: An Essay in Cosmology.* Corrected ed. David Ray Griffin and Donald Sherburne. New York: Free P, 1978.

—. *Science and Philosophy.* Paterson: Littlefield, 1964.

Wuthnow, Robert. *Christianity in the 21st Century.* New York: Oxford UP, 1993.

Chapter 4: The College-Church Partnership: Past

DeJong, Arthur J. *Reclaiming a Mission, New Direction for the Church-Related College.* Grand Rapids, MI: Eerdmans, 1990.

Education Commission Report. Early draft. Church of the Nazarene. 1964

Catalog. Eastern Nazarene College. Quincy, MA.

Personal letters (2) to the author.

Mann, E.S. "The Church and the College as Partners." Address. Education Commission. Church of the Nazarene, 1973.

Catalog. Olivet Nazarene College. Kankakee, IL.

Patlillo, Jr., Manning M. and Donald M. Mackenzie. *Eight Hundred Colleges Face the Future:* A Preliminary Report of the Danforth Commission on Church Colleges and Universities. St. Louis, MO: Danforth Foundation, 1965.

Catalog. Point Loma Nazarene College. San Diego: 1996

Wicke, Myron F. *The Church Related College.* Washington: Center for Applied Research and Education, 1964.

Chapter 5: The College-Church Partnership: Present and Future

Christian Scholar. ENC. Summer 1990.

Christian Scholar. ENC. Summer 1993.

Nielson, John M. "Challenges to Nazarene Higher Education." Unpublished paper. Distributed to ENC Board of Trustees and pastors of Education Region. Church of the Nazarene, 1987.

Sanner, A. Elwood. "Toward A Philosophy of Christian Education for Nazarene Colleges." Unpublished paper. Department of Education and the Ministry. Northwest Nazarene College, Nampa, ID. November 11, 1969

Wiley, H. Orton. "Education." *Herald of Holiness* 14 Jan. 1920.

Chapter 6: Non-traditional Education and the Nazarene College: Issues of Mission-Fit, Distinctiveness, and Survival

Aslanian, Carol. "The Admission Strategist." *The College Board.* Spring, 1993:

Bowling, John. [article] *The Olivetian.* Olivet Nazarene College. Kankakee, IL: December, 1994.

Catalog(s) from Nazarene Colleges and Universities, 1995.

Dehne, George. "A Look at the Future of the Private College." Self-published manuscript of 1993 address given to a group of college presidents in Annapolis, MD. 1994.

Dunn, Samuel L. and Myron M. Miller. "From the Industrial to the Virtual University: An Analysis of the 21st Century University." Unpublished Manuscript, 1995.

Dunn, Samuel L. "Looking into the Future: Cutting Edge Trends in Higher Education." Address given at the Christian Adult Higher Education Conference, Indianapolis, 18 July 1995.

Dunn, Samuel L. and Joseph Nielson. "The Theology and Practice of Wesleyan Higher Education," *Faculty Dialogue* Fall-Winter 1986-87, 71-82.

Hill, Kent R. Address to the Eastern Nazarene College Board of Trustees, 16 Oct. 1995.

Hubbard, Robert. "Proposal to the Faculty for Design, Development, and Implementation of a Degree Completion Program." Unpublished Document, 1988.

Metz, Donald. *MidAmerica Nazarene College: The Pioneer Years, 1966-1981.* Kansas City, MO: Nazarene, 1991.

MHR Unpublished Document, Southern Nazarene University, 1985.

Paul, Cecil R. Address to the Eastern Nazarene College Board of Trustees, Oct. 1991.

Proposal for a Bachelor of Administration Degree to the Ohio Board of Regents, Mount Vernon Nazarene College, 1992.

Wolf, Earl C., ed. *The Best of Bertha Munro*. Kansas City: Beacon Hill P, 1987.

Chapter 7: The Symbolic Value of Place

Bruns, Gerald C. *Hermeneutics Ancient and Modern*. New Haven: Yale UP, 1992.

Cameron, James R. *Eastern Nazarene College: The First Fifty Years 1900-1950*. Kansas City, MO: Nazarene, 1968.

Carver, Frank. *My Three Johns*. Unpublished book.

Cohn, Robert L. *The Shape of Sacred Space: Four Biblical Studies*. Chico, CA: Scholars P, 1981.

Cohen, Anthony P. *The Symbolic Construction of Community*. London and New York: Routledge, 1989.

Coming of Age: Mount Vernon Nazarene College 1968-1993. MVNC, 1994.

Dudney, Bennett. *E*N*B*C Miracle in Busingen*. Kansas City, MO: Nazarene, 1980.

Eliade, Mircea. *The Sacred and the Profane: The Nature of Religion*. Trans. Willard R. Trask. New York: Harcourt, 1959.

Grusczynski, Mary Lauriana. *Belief in a Catholic College: Madonna College as a Catholic College*. Rept. Livonia, MI: Madonna College, June 1985.

Hatch, Nathan. O with Michael S. Hamilton, "Taking the Measure of the Evangelical Resurgence, 1942-1992." *Reckoning with the Past: Historical Essays on American Evangelicalism*. Ed. D.G. Hart. Institute for the Study of American Evangelicals. Grand Rapids: Baker 1995: 395-412.

Hauerwas, Stanley and William H. Willimon, *Resident Aliens: Life in the Christian Colony*. Nashville: Abingdon P, 1989.

Kirkemo, Ronald B. *For Zion's Sake: A History of Pasadena/Point Loma College*. San Diego: Point Loma P, 1992.

Lane, Belden. "Landscape and Spirituality: A Tension Between Place and Placelessness in Christian Thought," *The Way*. Spring 1992: 4-13.

——. *Landscapes of the Sacred: Geography and Narrative in American Spirituality*. Isaac Hecker Studies in Religion and American Culture, Ed. John A. Coleman. New York: Paulist P, 1988.

Marsden, George. *The Soul of the American University*. Oxford: Oxford UP, 1994.

McClain, Carl S. *I Remember My Fifty-Seven Years at Olivet Nazarene College*. Kansas City, MO: Pedestal P, 1983.

Metz, Donald S. *MidAmerica Nazarene College: The Pioneer Years 1966-1991*. Kansas City, MO: Nazarene, 1991.

McGinn, Lisa Graham. "Evangelical Protestant Colleges and Secularization: An Analysis of Superficial Versus Core Value Change." *Research on Christian Higher Education.* Ed. Ronald Burwell 2 (1995): 93-106.

Noll, Mark A. *The Scandal of the Evangelical Mind.* Grand Rapids: Eerdmans, 1994.

Nord, Warren A. *Religion & American Education: Rethinking a National Dilemma.* Chapel Hill: U of North Carolina P, 1995.

Point Loma Nazarene College. *1985 Institutional Self-Study, Western Association of Schools and Colleges,* Chap. 2: "Institutional Purposes, Planning, and Effectiveness."

Price, Ross E. "H. Orton Wiley: Servant and Savant of the Sage-Brush College." Lecture. Northwest Nazarene College, Nampa, ID. Founder's Day 29 Sept. 1967.

Riley, John E. *From Sagebrush to Ivy: The Story of Northwest Nazarene College . . . 1913-1988.* Nampa, ID: Pacific P, 1988.

Robbins, Helen McMichael. Letter to Frank C. Sutherland. Library Archives, Northwest Nazarene College, Nampa, ID. 6 Dec. 1960.

Smith, Timothy L. *Called Unto Holiness—The Story of the Nazarenes: The Formative Years.* Kansas City, MO: Nazarene, 1962.

—. *Nazarenes and the Wesleyan Mission: Can We Learn From Our History?* Kansas City, MO: Beacon Hill P, 1979.

Smith-Rosenberg, Carroll. "Women and Religious Revivals: Anti-Ritualism, Liminality, and the Emergence of the American Bourgeoisie." *The Evangelical Tradition in America.* Ed. Leonard I. Sweet. Macon, GA: Mercer UP, 1984: 199-231.

Thomson, C.E. *The Story of Canadian Nazarene College.* Red Deer, Alta: Canadian Nazarene College P, n.d.

Thomson, Dorothy J. *Vine of His Planting: History of Canadian Nazarene College.* Edmonton, Alta: Commercial Printers, 1960.

Vaughan, Ruth. *Fools Have No Miracles: The Story of the Bethany Nazarene College "Miracle Offering."* Prtd. for BNC. Kansas City, MO: Nazarene, 1971.

Wynkoop, Mildred Bangs. *The Trevecca Story: 75 Years of Christian Service.* Nashville: Trevecca P, 1976.

Chapter 8: Thinking About Economics and Ethics as a Wesleyan

Beversluis, Eric H. "A Critique of Ronald Nash on Economic Justice and the State." *Economic Justice and the State: A Debate Between Ronald H. Nash and Eric H. Beversluis.* Christian College Coalition Study Guides. Ed. John A. Bernbaum. Grand Rapids: Baker, 1986.

Building Economic Justice: The Bishops' Pastoral Letter and Tools for Action. U. S. Catholic Conference. 1987.

Bibliography

Diehl, William E. "The Guided-Market System." *Wealth & Poverty: Four Christian Views of Economics.* Ed. Robert G. Clouse. Downers Grove, IL: InterVarsity P, 1984.

Gathered for Life: Official Report [of the] VI Assembly [of the] World Council of Churches. Ed. David Gill. Geneva: World Council of Churches and Grand Rapids: Eerdmans, 1983.

Gish, Art. "Decentralist Economics." *Wealth & Poverty: Four Christian Views of Economics.* Ed. Robert G. Clouse. Downers Grove, IL: InterVarsity P, 1984.

Graham, W. Fred, et al. *Reforming Economics: Calvinist Studies on Methods and Institutions.* Ed. John P. Tiemstra. Vol. 48 of *Toronto Studies in Theology.* Lewiston, NY: Mellen P, 1990.

Griffiths, Brian. *The Creation of Wealth.* London: Hodder and Stoughton, 1984.

Halteman, Jim. *Market Capitalism and Christianity.* Grand Rapids: Baker, 1988.

Hay, Donald A. *Economics Today: A Christian Critique.* Leicester: Apollos, 1989.

Haywood, C. Robert. "Was John Wesley a Political Economist?" *Church History* 33 (1964): 314-321.

Hynson, Leon O. "Implications of Wesley's Ethical and Political Thought." *Wesleyan Theology Today: A Bicentennial Theological Consultation.* Ed. Theodore Runyon. Nashville: Kingswood, 1985.

———. *To Reform the Nation: Theological Foundations of Wesley's Ethics.* Grand Rapids: Francis Asbury P, 1984.

Jennings, Jr., Theodore W. *Good News for the Poor: John Wesley's Evangelical Economics.* Nashville: Abingdon P, 1990.

Justice in the Marketplace: Collected Statements of the Vatican and the United States Catholic Bishops on Economic Policy, 1891-1984. Ed. David M. Byers. Washington: U. S. Catholic Conference, 1985.

Logan, James C. "Toward a Wesleyan Social Ethic." *Wesleyan Theology Today: A Bicentennial Theological Consultation.* Ed. Theodore Runyon. Nashville: Kingswood, 1985.

Madron, Thomas W. "John Wesley on Economics." *Sanctification and Liberation: Liberation Theologies in the Light of the Wesleyan Tradition.* Ed. Theodore Runyon. Nashville: Abingdon, 1981.

Nash, Ronald H. "The Economics of Justice: A Conservative's View." *Economic Justice and the State: A Debate Between Ronald H. Nash and Eric H. Beversluis.* Christian College Coalition Study Guides. Ed. John A. Bernbaum. Grand Rapids: Baker, 1986.

North, Gary. "Free Market Capitalism." *Wealth & Poverty: Four Christian Views of Economics.* Ed. Robert G. Clouse. Downers Grove, IL: InterVarsity P, 1984.

Runyon, Theodore. Introduction. *Sanctification and Liberation: Liberation Theologies in Light of the Wesleyan Tradition.* Ed. Runyon. Nashville: Abingdon P, 1981.

Schilling, S. Paul. *Methodism and Society in Theological Perspectives*. Vol. 3 of *Methodism and Society*. New York: Abingdon P, 1960.

Wogaman, J. Philip. "The Wesleyan Tradition and the Social Changes of the Next Century." *Wesleyan Theology Today: A Bicentennial Theological Consultation*. Ed. Theodore Runyon. 1985. Nashville: Kingswood, 1987.

Chapter 9: From "Barely" to "Fully" Personal: On the Therapeutic Action of Prevenient Grace *Within* the Personality

Allen, Joseph J. *Inner Way: Toward a Rebirth of Eastern Christian Spiritual Direction*. Grand Rapids: Eerdmans, 1994.

Becker, E. *The Denial of Death*. New York: Free P, 1973.

Brightman, Edgar S. *The Spiritual Life*. New York: Abingdon, 1979.

Browning, Don S. *Religious Thought and the Modern Psychologies: A Critical Conversation in the Theology of Culture*. Philadelphia: Fortress P, 1989.

Chessick, Richard D. *The Technique and Practice of Intensive Psychotherapy*. New York: Aronson, 1983.

Erikson, Erik H. *Childhood and Society*. New York: Norton, 1950.

—. *Insight and Responsibility*. New York: Norton, 1964.

—. *The Life Cycle Completed*. New York: Norton, 1962.

Greenberg, Jay, and Stephen Mitchell, *Object Relations in Psychoanalytic Theory*. Cambridge: Harvard UP, 1983.

Holmes, Urban T. *What is Anglicanism?* Harrisburg, PA: Morehouse, 1982.

Jaspers, Karl *Philosophy*. Trans. E. B. Ashton. Vol. 3. Chicago: U of Chicago P, 1971.

Johnson, Stephen M. *Characterological Transformation: The Hard Work Miracle*. New York: Norton, 1985.

Jones, James W. *Contemporary Psychoanalysis and Religion: Transference and Transcendence*. New Haven: Yale UP, 1991.

Leech, Kenneth *Soul Friend*. San Francisco: Harper, 1977.

Loewald, Hans "On the therapeutic action of psychoanalysis." *Papers in Psychoanalysis*. New Haven: Yale UP, 1980. 221-56.

Lossky, Vladimir *The Mystical Theology of the Eastern Church*. Crestwood, NY: St. Vladimir's Seminary P, 1976.

Maddox, Randy L. *Responsible Grace: John Wesley's Practical Theology*. Nashville: Kingswood, 1994.

McAdams, Dan P., Ed. de St. Aubin, and Regina L. Logan. "Generativity among young, midlife, and older adults." *Psychology and Aging*. 8 (1993):221-30.

Meissner, William W. *Psychoanalysis and Religious Experience.* New Haven: Yale UP, 1984.

Ogden, Thomas H. *The Matrix of the Mind: Object Relations and the Psychoanalytic Dialogue.* Northvale, NJ: Aronson, 1990.

Outler, Albert C. "Pastoral Care in the Wesleyan Spirit." *Perkins Journal* Fall 1971: 4-11.

Roth, Sheldon *Psychotherapy: The Art of Wooing Nature.* Northvale, NJ: Aronson, 1987.

Settlage, Calvin F. "Psychoanalytic observations on adult development in life and in the therapeutic relationship." *Psychoanalysis and Contemporary Thought,* 15:349-74.

Weisman, Avery D. *The Existential Core of Psychoanalysis.* Boston: Little, 1965.

Whitehead, Evelyn E. and James D. Whitehead. *Christian Life Patterns.* Garden City: Doubleday, 1979.

Wiley, H. Orton *Christian Theology* Vol. 2. Kansas City: Beacon Hill P, 1952.

Winnicott, Donald W. *The Maturational Processes and the Facilitating Environment.* London: Hogarth, 1965.

Wittgenstein, Ludwig *Philosophical Investigations.* Trans. G. E. M. Anscombe. New York: Macmillan, 1953.

Wynkoop, Mildred Bangs *A Theology of Love.* Kansas City: Beacon Hill P, 1972.

Chapter 10: Ecumenism in Nazarene Higher Education

Catalog. Northwest Nazarene College. Nampa, ID.

Manual: Church of the Nazarene 1993-97. Kansas City, MO: Nazarene, n.d.

Nicholson, Roy S. "John Wesley and Ecumenicity." *Wesleyan Theological Journal* 2 (1967): 66-81.

Redford, M. E. *The Rise of the Church of the Nazarene.* 1948. Kansas City,MO: Beacon Hill P, 1974.

Wesley, John. *The Works of John Wesley.* Ed. Thomas Jackson. London: 1872. Computer software. Wesley Ctr. for App. Th. Nampa, ID: 1995.

Chapter 11: The Nazarene Mind: Sunlight and Scandal

Haas, Jr. John W. "Eighteenth Century Evangelical Responses to Science: John Wesley's Enduring Legacy." *Science and Christian Belief.* Oct. 1994: 83-102.

Maddox, Randy L. *Responsible Grace: John Wesley's Practical Theology.* Nashville: Kingswood, 1994.

Noll, Mark. *The Scandal of the Evangelical Mind.* Grand Rapids: Eerdmans, 1994.

Numbers, Ronald *The Creationists: The Evolution of Scientific Creationism.* New York: 1992.

Thorsen, Donald A. D. "The Future of Biblical Studies in the Wesleyan Tradition: A Theological Perspective." *Wesleyan Theological Journal* Fall, 1995: 182-202.

Wiley, H. Orton *Christian Theology*. Kansas City, MO: Beacon Hill P, 1940.

Chapter 12: Excellence in Education: Parrot or Learner

Berger, Peter. *Invitation to Sociology*. New York: Anchor, 1963.

Blamires, Harry. *The Christian Mind*. 1963. Ann Arbor, MI: Servant, 1978.

Coleman, James S. *The Adolescent Society*. New York: Free P, 1961.

Colson, Chuck with Ellen S. Vaughn. *Against The Night: Living in the New Dark Ages*. Ann Arbor, MI: Servant, 1989.

Cuzzort, R. P. and E. W. King. *Humanity and Modern Social Thought*. 2nd ed. Hinsdale, IL: Dryden P, 1976.

Giamatti, A. Bartlett. *A Free and Ordered Space: The Real World of the University*. New York: Norton, 1988.

Holmes, Arthur F. *The Idea of a Christian College*. Grand Rapids, MI: Eerdmans, 1975

Rosovsky, Henry. *The University: An Owner's Manual*. New York: Norton, 1990.

Chapter 13: Prophet and Priest: Pioneer and Preserver in Partnership

Arnold, Charles H. *Near the Edge of Battle: A Short History of the Divinity School and the "Chicago School of Theology" 1866-1966*. Chicago: Divinity School Assn., U of Chicago. 1966

Cloete, G. D. and D.J. Smit, eds. *A Moment of Truth: The Confession of the Dutch Reformed Mission Church 1982*. Grand Rapids: Eerdmans, 1984.

Ellul, Jacques. *In Season, Out of Season: An Introduction to the Thought of Jacques Ellul*. San Francisco: Harper, 1982.

Fowl, Stephen E. and L. Gregory Jones. *Reading in Communion: Scripture and Ethics in Christian Life*. Grand Rapids: Eerdmans, 1991.

Kirkemo, Ronald B. *For Zion's Sake: A History of Pasadena/Point Loma College*. San Diego: Point Loma P, 1992.

Maddox, Randy L. *Responsible Grace: John Wesley's Practical Theology*. Nashville: Kingswood, 1994.

Marty, Martin E. "Creative Misuses of Jacques Ellul." *Jacques Ellul: Interpretive Essays*. Eds. C. G. Christians and J. M. van Hook. Urbana: U of IL, 1981.

—. "The Modes of Being, Doing, Teaching and Discovering: The Contexts of Theological Schools and Religious Departments." AAR Annual Meeting. Philadelphia, 19 Nov. 1995.

—. "The Protestant for this summer." *National Catholic Reporter* July 1970.

McCarter, Jr., P. Kyle. *I Samuel: A New Translation with Introduction and Notes & Commentary.* Vol. 8 in *The Anchor Bible.* Garden City, NY: Doubleday, 1985.

Peden, Creighton. *The Chicago School: Voices in Liberal Religious Thought.* Bristol, IN: Wyndham Hall P, 1987.

Plessis, John du. *Andrew Murray: His Life and Work.* Cape Town: 1918.

Robinson, John A. T. *The Roots of a Radical.* New York: Crossroad, 1981.

Schneidau, Herbert N. *Sacred Discontent: The Bible and Western Tradition.* Berkeley: U of CA P, 1976.

Sternberg, Meir. *The Poetics of Biblical Narrative: Ideological Literature and the Drama of Reading.* Bloomington: IN U P, 1985.

Tracy, David. *The Analogical Imagination: Christian Theology and the Culture of Pluralism.* New York: Crossroad, 1989.

Whitelaw, David P. "Comparative Patterns of Church Historiography: North America and Southern Africa." Wesleyan Theological Society. Nampa, ID, 4 Nov. 1995. To be published in *Wesleyan Theological Journal.*

—. "A Crisis of Credibility: Contemporary Dialogue with Colenso and du Plessis." *Journal of Theology for Southern Africa* 60 (1987):12-27.

—. "Heading Towards a Post-Apartheid Society." *Perspectives on Kairos.* Eds. J. W. Hofmeyr, J. H. H. du Toit, and C. J. J. Froneman. Cape Town: Lux Verbi, 1987.

Wilkes, Paul. "The Hands that Shape our Soul." *Atlantic Monthly* Dec. 1990: 59-78.

Verryn, Trevor D. *Outside the Camp: A Study of Religious Authority and Conversion.* D Th. Pretoria: UNISA, 1980.

Young, Edward J. *My Servants the Prophets.* 1952. Grand Rapids: Eerdmans, 1961.

Chapter 14: A Trinitarian Paradigm of Theosis: A Context for the Emergence of a Wesleyan Notion of Christ Transfiguring Culture

Allchin, A. M. *Participation in God: A Forgotten Strand in Anglican Tradition.* Wilton, CT: Morehouse-Barlow, 1988.

Aquinas, Thomas. *Aquinas on Nature and Grace.* Philadelphia: Westminster P, 1954. 137-292.

—. *Summa Contra Gentiles.* Notre Dame: U of Notre Dame P, 1975.

Augustine. "On the Holy Trinity." Bks. 6-8 in *The Nicene and Post Nicene Fathers.*

Berkhof, Hendrikus. *Christian Faith: An Introduction to the Study of the Faith.* Grand Rapids, MI: Eerdmans, 1979.

Burns, J. Patout. "The Economy of Salvation: Two Patristic Traditions." *ThSt.* 37 (1967): 598-619.

Gunton, Colin. "Augustine, The Trinity and the Theological Crisis of the West." *Scottish Journal of Theology* Vol. 43

Harakas, Stanley S. "The Integrity of Creation and Ethics." *St. Vladimir's Theological Quarterly* 32. 1 (1988): 27-42.

Johnson, William, ed. *The Cloud Of Unknowing*. New York: Image.

Langford, Thomas A. *Practical Divinity: Theology in the Wesleyan Tradition*. Nashville: Abingdon P, 1983.

Lossky, Vladimir. *The Mystical Theology of the Eastern Church*. Crestwood, NY: St. Vladimir's Seminary P, 1976.

Luther, Martin. "Lectures on Galatians." Vol 26. in *Luther's Works*. St. Louis: Concordia, 1964.

McKenna, Stephan. Introduction. *Saint Augustine, The Trinity*. Washington: Catholic U of America P, 1963.

The Methodist Hymnbook. London: Methodist, 1933.

Meyendorff, John. *Byzantine Theology: Historical Trends and Doctrinal Themes*. New York: Fordham UP, 1979.

Nellas, Panayiotis. *Deification in Christ*. Crestwood, NY: St. Vladimir's Seminary P, 1987.

Niebuhr, H. Richard. *Christ and Culture*. New York: Harper, 1951.

Oberman, Heiko. *The Dawn of the Reformation*. Edinburgh: T. and T. Clark Ltd., 1986.

—. *Forerunners of the Reformation*. Philadelphia: Fortress P, 1966.

—. *The Harvest of Medieval Theology*. Durham: Labyrinth P, 1983.

Outler, Albert C., ed. *The Bicentennial Edition of the Works of John Wesley*. Nashville: Abington P, 1985.

—, ed. *John Wesley*. New York: Oxford UP, 1978.

—. "The Place of Wesley in the Christian Tradition." *The Place of Wesley in the Christian Tradition*. Ed. Kenneth E. Rowe. Metuchen, NJ: Scarecrow, 1976.

—. *Theology in the Wesleyan Spirit*. Nashville: Discipleship Resources, 1975.

Pelikan, Jaroslav. *The Vindication of Tradition*. New Haven, CT: Yale UP, 1984.

Roberts, Alexander and Donaldson, James. *The Ante-Nicene Fathers*. Vol. 1. Grand Rapids, MI: Eerdmans, 1979.

Schaff, Philip. and Henry Wace,.eds. *A Select Library of Nicene and Post-Nicene Fathers of the Christian Church*. 2nd ser. Grand Rapids, MI: Eerdmans, 1978.

Wesley, John. *Explanatory Notes Upon the New Testament*. Vol. 2. Grand Rapids, MI: Baker, 1981.

—. *The Letters of the Rev. John Wesley, A.M.* Ed. John Telford. London: Epworth P, 1960.

—. *The Works of John Wesley*. 3rd ed. Kansas City, MO: Beacon Hill P, 1978.

Zizioulas, John D. *Being as Communion*. Crestwood, NY: St. Vladimir's Seminary P, 1985.

Chapter 15: Gifts From a Visionary: Continuing the Wesleyan Tradition of the Development of All Persons

Alsdurf, James and Phyllis Alsdurf. *Battered Into Submission: The Tragedy of Wife Abuse in the Christian Home*. Downers Grove, IL: InterVarsity P, 1989.

Chilcote, Paul Wesley. *John Wesley and the Women Preachers of Early Methodism*. ATLA Monograph Ser. 25 (1991). Metuchen, N.J.: American Theological Lib. Assn. and the Scarecrow P.

Cowles, C.S. *A Woman's Place? Leadership in the Church?* Kansas City, MO: Beacon Hill P, 1993.

Dayton, Donald W. *Discovering An Evangelical Heritage*. New York: Harper, 1976.

Frankl, Viktor E. *Man's Search For Meaning*. New York: Pocket, 1959.

Hassey, Jeanette. *No Time For Silence: Evangelical Women in Public Ministry Around the Turn of the Century*. Grand Rapids, MI: Academie, 1986.

Heggen, Carolyn Holderread. *Sexual Abuse in Christian Homes and Churches*. Scottdale, PA: Herald, 1983.

Moltmann, Jurgen. *The Passion For Life: A Messianic Lifestyle*. Philadelphia: Fortress, 1978.

Neal, Cynthia J. and Michael W. Mangis. "Unwanted Sexual Experiences Among Christian College Women: Saying No on the Inside." *Journal of Psychology and Theology* 23 (1995):171-179.

Paul, C. and J. Lanham. *Choices: In Pursuit of Wholeness*. Kansas City, MO: Beacon Hill, 1982.

Telford, John, ed. *The Letters of John Wesley*. Std. ed. Vol. 8. London: Epworth P, 1931.

Chapter 16: Retracing the Vision: The Imaginative Mind in a Nazarene College

Bloom, Allan. *The Closing of the American Mind*. New York: Simon, 1987.

Chesterton, Gilbert K. *Orthodoxy*. New York: Lane, 1908.

Koestler, Arthur. *The Act of Creation*. New York: Macmillan, 1964.

L'Engle, Madeleine. *Walking on Water: Reflections on Faith and Art*. Wheaton, IL: Shaw, 1980.

Miller, Calvin. "Preaching in the Vulgate." *Leadership* 4.2 (Spring 1983): 12-21.

Munro, Bertha. *The Years Teach: Remembrances to Bless*. Kansas City, IL: Beacon Hill, 1970.

Peterson, Eugene H. *Reversed Thunder: The Revelation of John and the Praying Imagination.* San Francisco: Harper, 1988.

Towns, Elmer. "The College That Faith Built." *Christian Life* (June 1974): 70-71.

Wiersbe, Warren W. "Imagination: The Preacher's Neglected Ally." *Leadership* 4.2 (Spring 1983): 22-27.

Chapter 17: Education as Reconciliation

Ambrose. *Hexameron, Paradise, and Cain and Abel.* Trans. John J. Savage. New York: The Fathers of the Church, Inc. 1961.

Augustine. *Christian Instruction (De doctrina Christiana).* Trans. John J. Gavigan. Washington: The Catholic U of America P, 1966.

Chesterton, G.K. *Orthodoxy.* Garden City, NY: Image Books, 1959.

Eusebius. *Ecclesiastical History.* Trans. Arthur Cushman McGiffert. Ed. Philip Schaff. Vol 1. in *Nicene and Post-Nicene Fathers of the Christian Church.* Grand Rapids: Eerdmans, 1986.

Gadamer, Hans-Georg. *Truth and Method.* New York: Sheed and Ward, 1975.

Marrou, Henri. *Histoire de l'education dans la antiquitie.* sixieme edition, revue et augmentie. Paris: Editions du Seuil, 1965.

Murray, John Courtney. "The Christian Idea of Education." *The Christian Idea of Education.* Ed. Edmund Fuller. New Haven: Yale UP, 1957.

Outler, Albert C., ed. *John Wesley.* New York: Oxford UP, 1980.

Palmer, Parker. *To Know as We Are Known: A Spirituality of Education.* San Francisco: Harper, 1983.

Thorsen, Donald A.D. *The Wesleyan Quadrilateral: Scripture, Tradition, Reason and Experience as a Model of Evangelical Theology.* Grand Rapids: Zondervan, 1991.

Vincent of Lerins. *A Commonitory.* Vol. 11 in *Nicene and Post-Nicene Fathers of the Church.* Ed. Philip Schaff. 2nd ser. Grand Rapids: Eerdmans, 1986.

Wesley, John. *Explanatory Notes Upon the New Testament.* London: Epworth P, 1976.

—. *The Letters of John Wesley.* Ed. John Telford. London: Epworth P, 1931.

—. *The Works of John Wesley.* Ed. Thomas Jackson. London 1929-31. Grand Rapids: Baker, 1978.

—. *The Works of John Wesley.* Bicentennial ed. Nashville: Abingdon P, 1984.

—. *The Works of John Wesley.* New York: Oxford UP, in process.